Child Protection Systems in the United Kingdom

by the same author

Constructive Work with Offenders
Edited by Kevin Gorman, Marilyn Gregory, Michelle Hayles and Nigel Parton
ISBN 978 1 84310 345 5

Constructing Clienthood in Social Work and Human Services
Interaction, Identities and Practices
Edited by Chris Hall, Kirsi Juhila, Nigel Parton and Tarja Pösö
ISBN 978 1 84310 073 7

of related interest

Safeguarding Children Across Services
Messages from Research
Carolyn Davies and Harriet Ward
ISBN 978 1 84905 124 8
Safeguarding Children Across Services series

Caring for Abused and Neglected Children
Making the Right Decisions for Reunification or Long-Term Care
Jim Wade, Nina Biehal, Nicola Farrelly and Ian Sinclair
ISBN 978 1 84905 207 8
Safeguarding Children Across Services series

Recognizing and Helping the Neglected Child
Evidence-Based Practice for Assessment and Intervention
Brigid Daniel, Julie Taylor and Jane Scott
Foreword by Enid Hendry
ISBN 978 1 84905 093 7
Safeguarding Children Across Services series

Social Work Reclaimed
Innovative Frameworks for Child and Family Social Work Practice
Steve Goodman and Isabelle Trowler
ISBN 978 1 84905 202 3

Good Practice in Safeguarding Children
Working Effectively in Child Protection
Edited by Liz Hughes and Hilary Owen
ISBN 978 1 84310 945 7
Good Practice in Health, Social Care and Criminal Justice series

Improving Outcomes for Children and Families
Finding and Using International Evidence
Edited by Anthony N. Maluccio, Cinzia Canali, Tiziano Vecchiato,
Anita Lightburn, Jane Aldgate and Wendy Rose
Foreword by James K. Whittaker
ISBN 978 1 84905 819 3
Child Welfare Outcomes series

Child Protection Systems in the United Kingdom

A Comparative Analysis

Anne Stafford,
Nigel Parton,
Sharon Vincent and
Connie Smith

Jessica Kingsley *Publishers*
London and Philadelphia

Contains public sector information licensed under the Open Government Licence v1.0
Table 3.1 on p.44 from Gilbert 1997 is reproduced with permission from Oxford
University Press
Table 3.3 on p.53 from Gilbert, Parton and Skivenes 2011b is reproduced with
permission from Oxford University Press

First published in 2012
by Jessica Kingsley Publishers
116 Pentonville Road
London N1 9JB, UK
and
400 Market Street, Suite 400
Philadelphia, PA 19106, USA

www.jkp.com

Library of Congress Cataloging in Publication Data
A CIP catalog record for this book is available from the Library of Congress

British Library Cataloguing in Publication Data
A CIP catalogue record for this book is available from the British Library

ISBN 978 1 84905 067 8
eISBN 978 0 85700 254 9

Printed and bound in Great Britain

Contents

Acknowledgements

A number of people have helped us in the production of this book; we have benefited greatly from the information they provided, from their comments and suggestions. We wish to record our thanks to all of the staff who worked in the Centre for Learning in Child Protection during the writing of our book; it is the result of our collective work. Thanks in particular to Debi Fry for writing various key sections. We are grateful to Andrew Mott from Scottish Government for keeping us abreast of developments in Scotland in relation to Chapter 9. We thank the NSPCC for funding our work, and Phillip Noyes, the NSPCC Director of Strategy and Development, in particular, for his ongoing support. We also acknowledge the contribution of our institutions: the Moray House School of Education at the University of Edinburgh and the University of Huddersfield.

Chapter 1

Introduction
About this Book

1.1 PART 1 INTRODUCTION AND CONTEXT

The University of Edinburgh/National Society for the Prevention of Cruelty to Children (NSPCC) Centre for UK-wide Learning in Child Protection (the Centre) was set up in 2007 to oversee developments in child protection across the UK. This book distils and synthesises much of the work and thinking that has occurred in the Centre in its first few years of existence.

A major reason the Centre was set up was in recognition that one consequence of devolution in the UK might be to open up new opportunities for child protection systems and processes to diverge from each other; for the devolved parts of the UK to seek new and more local solutions to long standing child protection problems. Our detailed remit is to track child protection developments across the UK, analyse and comment on the way systems have shifted and changed in response to devolution – and other drivers for change, and to feed new insights and knowledge into the child protection policy decision making process in the UK. From a situation in 2007 where there was relatively scant detailed comparative research available on the similarities and differences between child protection systems in different parts of the UK, a new body of work has been built as a result of the work of the Centre. These findings have been pulled together for this book. In effect, the story of the development of the Centre is the story of the development of this book.

In Chapter 2 we begin by setting out some of the factors which have driven change in child protection systems across the UK. These are convoluted and intertwined. For the purposes of this book we have tried to untangle those which seem to us to have played a key role in driving recent system change.

The chapter looks first at the policy making process itself as a driver of policy change. We examine the policy making process at three levels:

the macro level which includes global forces such as the recession; the micro level, where even one individual can be responsible for major policy shifts (we use the example of the role of Tony Blair in taking the UK into the Iraq war). Third, we examine the meso level where a country's institutions and networks can be so important in setting the direction of change for individual countries, for example in mediating macro-level change.

We also analyse the relatively unique role the media has played in shaping child protection policy across the UK. We track this from the reporting of the Maria Colwell case in England in 1974, through the reporting of the Cleveland sex abuse scandal in England and the Orkney case in Scotland in the 1980s. We discuss changes in the reporting of child abuse and child death cases over time, and changes to the media itself, particularly in relation to the tabloid press and growth of new technology, all of which have led to the current intense media scrutiny of those caught up in high profile cases.

In Chapter 3 and as part of our quest to understand the unfolding story of child protection across the UK in the context of devolution, we begin by stepping back from our own system to view it from the widest possible perspective. This chapter attempts to set our understanding of child protection in the UK within an understanding of child protection systems internationally. Over the past 15 years there has been a growing literature comparing child protection systems throughout the world. We discuss how research interest in conducting international comparative studies grew out of perceived problems with the systems of the UK which were seen to be inadequately protecting children and failing to deal with burgeoning levels of referrals. This was an explicit search for what other countries may do better than ourselves, and it had an explicit objective of finding ways to improve the way children are protected across the UK.

In Chapter 4 we discuss the purpose of the Centre's role in describing and understanding developments in child protection across the UK. We note that while this is a worthwhile exercise in its own right, our work needs to extend to ensuring that the information and knowledge we generate about the different systems of the UK is widely shared and ultimately able to contribute to the process of creating better quality child protection systems throughout the UK. Thus at the heart of the work of the Centre and of this book are the twin concepts of 'learning' and 'comparing'; here we set the scene for the book by describing the conceptual and methodological challenges involved in conducting this kind of comparative research. In addition, we look at the impact devolution has had in shaping policy across the UK. We argue that it is impossible to understand developments in child protection across the UK without some insight into the process of devolution and its role in shaping and driving child protection.

1.2 PART 2 CHILD PROTECTION PROCESSES AND STRUCTURES

Having looked at UK child protection systems from the wide vantage point of systems across the world, and discussed some of the meso-level factors which have driven change in the systems of the UK, we then apply our case study, intra-country comparative approach to key aspects of child protection systems in each part of the UK. We compare and contrast the main features that make up child protection systems across the UK. Once again our purpose is to hold a mirror to each of the systems to better understand the one we are operating in, and to better understand the whole. Essentially, we present a snapshot of child protection systems across the UK at March 2011. The past ten years of child protection in the UK has been a time of fast-moving reform and unprecedented change: a snapshot is difficult to capture! As we try, we are also aware that major change lies ahead in the form of the Munro Review of Child Protection in England; the effect of the financial crisis and pressure on local authorities' ability to deliver effective services; the significant changes in UK politics where, for the first time, we have a different complexion of government in each part of the UK. The scale of change likely to result is difficult to read from our current vantage point.

In Chapter 5 we examine the broad legislative and policy frameworks underpinning child protection systems across the UK. Each part of the UK has its own separate overarching framework document setting out its own vision for how children should be cared for and protected.

In Chapter 6 we shift from comparing wider structures, mechanisms and processes for managing child protection, to zoom in even closer to examine arrangements to protect individual children who may be at risk of child abuse and neglect. We examine the different processes and mechanisms that exist across the UK to respond to referrals and investigate concerns. We compare emergency protection measures across the UK and look at arrangements for information sharing for the registration of children at risk of abuse.

Chapter 7 examines the frameworks for assessing children's needs, including their child protection needs. Currently, each part of the UK is at a different stage in the development and introduction of national comprehensive assessment tools or frameworks for assessing the needs of children including those who may be in need of protection and we look at this in detail.

In Chapter 8, we look at the most serious end of the child abuse continuum, and arrangements that exist to review cases where a child has died as a result of child abuse and neglect. While processes exist for this throughout the UK, they are at different stages of development; once again we look at this in detail.

Throughout this book we have compared and contrasted aspects of child protection as they directly relate to protecting children. In Chapter 9 we examine arrangements and mechanisms across the UK for keeping children safe from adults who may pose a risk to them. This includes: consideration of arrangements for the management of violent and sexual offenders, systems for 'vetting' individuals and checking their suitability to work with children and 'barring' systems which ban those already deemed to be a risk to children. We track the rise of these systems and compare and contrast them across the UK. Again, in this fast moving area of policy, we set out arrangements as they currently stand and provide pointers to likely future developments.

Part 1

Introduction and Context

The book sets out to understand child protection systems across the UK by providing both a broad and a deep perspective. Part 1 of the book is concerned with the wide picture. We begin by unravelling the complex and interrelated factors driving change and reform of child protection in the UK; we look further afield to gauge how our systems in the UK compare with other systems across the world; and we highlight the usefulness of comparing one system against another to provide new knowledge and understanding.

Chapter 2

Context and Drivers of Policy Change in Child Protection across the UK

2.1 INTRODUCTION

In this chapter we set the scene for the book by looking at some of the major factors which have driven change in child protection systems across the UK. These are convoluted and intertwined and we have attempted to unravel those which seem to us to have played a key role in driving recent system change including the policy making process itself and the role of the media.

2.2 THE POLICY MAKING PROCESS

The main focus of this section is on how the prime contexts and drivers of policy change in child protection have played out across the four parts of the UK. The focus will be upon the policy analysis of change over recent years and we will draw, in particular, on the analytic framework developed by Hudson and Lowe (2009), for whom:

> Policy analysis has emerged primarily as a sub-field of political science that tries to understand and build up knowledge of the whole process of public policy beginning from the big picture of the global economy, through the complex issues of which policies are chosen for inclusion on the political agenda (and which are excluded), who designs them, and how, finally, they are delivered. (Hudson and Lowe 2009, p.5)

Hudson and Lowe draw attention to three 'layers' of the policy process: the Macro, Meso and Micro levels. While each layer has a rather different focus they argue that all three need to be taken into account if we are to understand and analyse policy change in any particular area.

Macro-level analysis is concerned with the broad issues that shape the wider context in which policy is made and needs to take into account some of the major historical, economic and social changes that have an impact on the way problems are identified and responded to. Hudson and Lowe argue that, over the last 30 years, the impact of globalisation is central, together with changes in the economy, the nature of power and technology.

Micro-level analysis operates at the opposite end of the continuum to macro-level analysis. Here the focus is the impact and significance of particular decisions by individuals such as politicians or civil servants and those who are responsible for applying and delivering certain policies. The focus is the detail of day-to-day policy decisions and their possible impact.

Meso-level analysis comes between macro and micro and, for Hudson and Lowe, plays the key role in bridging the macro and the micro levels of analysis. Meso-level institutions and networks are crucial as they filter the macro changes and therefore have a major influence in the way problems and policy responses are framed, and thereby constrain the nature and range of decisions that are seen to be available to key decision makers. Hudson and Lowe suggest that such middle-range approaches are sensitive to the cultural and historical factors that underlie and inform the differences between different countries. It is particularly at the meso level that the importance of more recent changes in governance arrangements – including that of devolution – can be seen to impact on policy development. It is also at this level that the significance of the media – a central issue in understanding changes in child protection policies – becomes most evident. Increasingly the media has been seen as playing a key role in informing and influencing the priority and content of social policies.

a. Macro-level analysis
Globalisation and its implications
There is now considerable agreement that from the early 1970s we have witnessed major change in the organisation of production, markets and exchange across the world (Giddens 1990; Held and McGrew 2000; Hutton and Giddens 2001). There has been: tremendous growth in the spread and power of transnational companies; increases in economic integration and inter-dependence; and a huge transformation in the range and speed of communication – all of which has been associated with the central significance and impact of globalisation.

More specifically, globalisation entails a transformation of social institutions, and the growing importance and strength of economic organisations, such as banks, corporations and the broad financial sectors, which are international in their reach. Through international agencies, such as the International Monetary Fund, the World Bank, and the World Trade Organisations, the programmes for the new world order have promoted forms of collective life based on competition in global markets, at the expense of forms based on traditions, political authority, informal organisation or communal sharing (Jordan 2006). The changes have impacted on individual identities, affiliations and the way we live our lives (Bauman 1998). The period has witnessed the rapid emergence of new technologies, new social processes, new economic forces and alignments and new political processes and structures. There is a greater inter-connectedness; a speeding up of time and places have been brought closer together.

Manuel Castells (2000a, 2000b) has called the emergent capitalist formation a new economy, which, he argues, has three fundamental features:

- It is *global*, in the sense that its core strategic activities have the capacity to work on a planetary scale in real or chosen time, particularly in relation to financial markets, communication media, skilled labour, many production firms and, increasingly, goods and services.

- It is *informational*, in that the capacity to generate knowledge and to process and manage information determines the productivity, competitiveness and efficiency of all kinds of economic units, regions and countries.

- It is *networked*, for at the heart of the connectivity of the global economy and the flexibility of informational production, there is a new form of organisation – the *networked enterprise* – made up of a variety of alliances for the purpose of particular projects.

In the process the role and nature of the nation state has undergone a major transformation. For while globalisation does not mean the end of nation states, they have been required to redefine their role and purpose in the face of these new challenges. Increasingly the unified nation state has loosened its structures and adopted new organisational forms and new ways of working in order to keep up with and respond to change. Globalisation is partly about greater speed, not just in the movement of information, services and currencies around the world, but also in how ideas and policies can be moved from place to place and adapted to local conditions. As a consequence, the British state has restructured from a centralised unitary national system based on the traditional Westminster model of government to a form of governance that is looser, more devolved and characterised by overlapping and increasingly detached policy networks. We will discuss this development in more detail when we look at the meso-level of analysis later.

The individualisation of social and cultural life

As Eric Hobsbawm (1994) has argued, the other major process of social change along with globalisation since the early 1970s has been that of individualisation. The grip of tradition, community, church and family has reduced in a culture that has increasingly stressed individual rights and freedoms. The growth in individualisation has been closely associated with consumerism, where the individual is encouraged/required to construct an identity through active choices in the market, and success and fulfilment are associated with consumption and the display of a variety of material signs and artifacts.

Such developments have been closely interrelated with changes in the organisation and meaning of 'family' life, the institution of marriage and the gendered balance of work. Not only do women make up an increasing proportion of the employed labour force but the facts of family change have become increasingly evident. In one generation the number of first marriages in Britain more than halved from 390,000 in 1975 to 175,000 in 1997, while re-marriages made up two-thirds of the total. The number of divorces more than doubled between 1961 and 1997 when the total was 175,000, only slightly less than the number of first marriages (Office of National Statistics (ONS) 1998). The proportion of children born outside marriage quadrupled and by the end of the 1980s fewer than 50 per cent of 18–24 year-olds thought it necessary to marry before having children (Kiernan and Estaugh 1993). Two-thirds of first partnerships in the early 1990s were cohabitations, compared to one-third 20 years earlier, and 22 per cent of children were born into cohabiting unions, compared to two per cent 20 years earlier (Ermisch and Francesconi 1999).

What becomes apparent is that the major changes in the economy and the labour market were paralleled by changes in the domestic sphere in that relationships, like work, were becoming increasingly fragile and impermanent. The idea of lifelong marriage as the only sanctioned framework for sexual partnerships and parenthood had become increasingly outmoded by the end of the twentieth century.

Drawing on simultaneous follow-up surveys tracking the lives of three large, representative cohort studies born in 1946, 1958 and 1970, Ferri, Bynner and Wadsworth (2003) provide a picture which strikingly demonstrates the increasing diversity and fluidity of family life in Britain. Partnership breakdown was a more frequent experience of successive cohorts, as was lone parenthood – predominantly involving mothers raising children on their own. However, the breakdown of one relationship did not appear to be a deterrent to repartnering, and another increasingly common feature of family life in the younger cohorts was 'social parenting', in which children were being raised in homes in which one adult, usually the father figure, was not their biological parent.

Ferri *et al.* (2003) argue that a major factor which underlies such trends in family life and personal relationships 'is the extent to which they are rooted in the changing position of women' (2003, p.302). Increased participation in paid work has provided women with opportunities for avoiding or leaving relationships with men or carrying out relationships differently than before. In addition, the development of more sophisticated and effective contraception and new forms of genetic manipulation have given women much greater control over the timing and frequency of child-rearing. As a result of these various developments the model of the 'normal' nuclear family, based on the institution of marriage and premised on the male breadwinner model, increasingly seemed outmoded in the last quarter of the twentieth century.

Social anxiety and increased concerns about childhood

The various and overlapping changes related to globalisation and individualisation can be seen to have had a considerable impact on the nature of social relationships. Whereas previously tradition (past-oriented belief and practice) acted as a means of connecting the present to our expectations of the future, and the community acted as a spatially and socially bounded place which provided a familiar milieu for its members, increasingly this no longer seemed to be the case.

Anthony Giddens (1990, 1991) has contended that we now inhabit a world where personal relationships of friendship or sexual intimacy act as the key means of stabilising social ties, instead of kinship, whilst abstract expert systems act as the means of stabilising relations across indefinite spans of time and space. At the same time our sense of certainty becomes weakened and an absolute sense of one's normality becomes disorientated by the growing relativism of values. Individualisation, with its emphasis on existential choice and self-creation, can contribute to a heightened sense of insecurity and a view of contemporary society as, essentially, a 'risk society' (Beck 1992), where increasingly the normative basis of society has become concerns with safety and the utopia has become negative and defensive – preventing the worst and protecting from harm.

A number of commentators have gone further and argued that the focus for many of these anxieties has become the child. For example, Buckingham (2000) has argued that while:

> the figure of the child has always been the focus of adult fears and fantasies…in recent years, debates about childhood have become invested with a growing sense of anxiety and panic. Traditional certainties about the meaning and status of childhood have been steadily eroded and undermined. (p.3)

Many of the issues related to risk and uncertainty can be seen to coalesce more generally around the figure of the child and childhood. In many respects the child–parent relationship has become the most fundamental and 'natural' of contemporary relationships. The trust that was previously anticipated from marriage and the family is now focused more on the child. Rather than being secondary to that of marriage, the parent–child relationship has increasingly taken on a primary significance.

The loss of traditional families embedded within secure communities and the growth of individualisation create a context in which there is greater adult investment in children in what seems a more uncertain and less safe world. Thus what happens to children increasingly seems to symbolise the key benchmark for the kind of society we have become and a primary focus for the aspirations, projections and longings on the part of adults, together with adult investments for the future. Both individual children and the institution of childhood therefore become potentially key sites for trying to bring about a better world both now and in the future. However, how and whether these issues become the subject of public policy depends on how they are understood, explained and made the subject of intervention. This is dependent upon political and governmental processes at the meso level – which we look at in the next section.

b. Meso-level analysis

Hudson and Lowe (2009) identify four broad areas which need to be considered at the meso level of policy analysis: the changing nature of governance; policy networks; institutions; and policy transfer. We discuss these in turn.

The changing nature of governance

Hudson and Lowe argue that while globalisation has created new complexities and challenges it has not meant the end of the nation state – in fact, far from it. Rather, globalisation has had the effect of loosening certain state structures and led to the development of new organisational forms and new ways of working. Globalisation does not lead to a simple convergence amongst different nation states, nor does it mean there is a straightforward takeover of the state by financial institutions and multi-national corporations. Rather, it means that nations respond to these new global pressures from their own diverse historical, cultural and political contexts. At the same time new layers of governance and new forms of politics have been established. Increasingly, political science has used the idea of governance rather than government to capture the different layers and tiers of organisations involved in the process of governing. This has meant being alert to the changing boundaries between the public, the private and voluntary sectors (Rhodes 1996, 1997).

Hudson and Lowe (2009) argue that the most useful and succinct explanation of the new governance arrangements is that Britain is now best conceptualised as a 'competition state' (Cerny and Evans 1999; Evans and Cerny 2003). They argue that in the post-war period social policy was a relatively autonomous, domestic field, unimpeded by wider economic concerns. In many respects the state acted as a restraint on the power of the free market and, guided by Keynesian demand management, had a strong redistributive purpose. However, the recent changes have undermined these conditions so that we have seen the emergence of the 'competition state' where the primary purpose of government is upon providing the conditions for economic success in the global market and uses all the tools it has available, including social policy, to that end. As a result the centralised Westminster model, based on the idea of the unitary, top-down, nation state has not been seen as adequate to the tasks. These have therefore been broken down and reconfigured to create a more business-like and entrepreneurial style of government. The adoption of New Public Management techniques has been central to this, together with a decisive shift of power away from the central apparatus. Devolution has been a key part of this process and something we look at in greater detail in Chapter 4. The key point we wish to underline here is that globalisation has underpinned and accelerated the break-up of Britain as a unitary state into a much more fragmented and differentiated polity and devolution has been an important element of this.

This is not to say that the centre does not still aim to exert control. In many respects the processes of fragmentation and differentiation require an emphasis on even greater performance measurement, monitoring and regulation from the centre if it wishes its policies to be implemented locally. However, how this is carried out in the different parts of the UK may be quite different and the spaces available for policy and practice variation, potentially, increase. Political and constitutional reform as instruments of political modernisation loosen the ties between the political executive and other parts of the nation state and can have unpredictable results, providing for a range of diverse locations for policy development and political decision making.

Policy networks

Because the centre, in the more fragmented polity, faces increased challenges, new linkages are required to manage the system and develop and implement policy. In this context Hudson and Lowe (2009) suggest that the role of 'policy networks' takes on a greater significance. Following Rhodes (1988, 1990) they suggest there are five distinct types of policy network: policy community; professional network; intergovernmental network; producer network; and issue network. While the nature and impact of the different networks will vary according to the policy sector being studied, Rhodes suggests that the types of network can be located along a continuum, with the most integrated and closed 'policy community' at the one end, and the more open and less stable 'issue network' at the other.

While this approach to 'policy networks' has been subject to considerable subsequent debate and revision it is agreed that policy networks have an important impact on the pace and direction of policy change. Policy networks are central to understanding how the nature of changes at the macro level are mediated, resisted and understood and the way political institutions and practices adapt.

Hudson and Lowe are in no doubt that 'something has changed over the last 20 years in terms of the delivery of social policies and that interorganisational networks have become increasingly important in the delivery of policy' (2009, p.167). As society has become more complex and policy problems become more seemingly intractable we have witnessed not just 'new governance' arrangements but also the increased significance of new networks which attempt to influence the way policy problems are framed and responded to. At the same time the state plays a key role in the creation, management and general configuration of a number of such policy networks.

Institutions

Research (for example Castles 1998, 2001; Hall and Taylor 1996) has investigated the role of political institutions in filtering change so that when faced with similar pressures – such as globalisation – states respond in distinctive and sometimes divergent ways that reflect their different histories and political cultures. Here the focus is upon the role of institutions in the policy process. Hudson and Lowe (2009) argue that an examination of institutions provides a key focus for understanding social and political life and for understanding the differences between countries even when they appear to be faced with similar challenges. The approach demonstrates that while macro-level forces have an important impact on social and economic conditions and contexts – politics still matters.

The focus on institutions does not only underline the fact that politics matters but also that history matters, for the past has a strong impact on the present and provides a key framework within which policy change is attempted. Institutions can be difficult to remove or reform, for they persist and develop over time which tends to ensure that change can rarely be quick and without cost.

Thelan and Steinmo (1992) demonstrate that a focus on institutions illuminates how political struggles are mediated by the institutional setting in which they take place. Not only are the histories and configuration of political institutions in the four UK nations different, but the nature of development has taken a new turn since devolution. Examples of some of the elements of the institutional dimensions which are relevant to influencing the policy process include: the election rules and voting systems; party structures and systems; the relationship between the different branches of government; the structures and organisation of key interest groups; and the structure, funding and delivery systems of different welfare agencies. In encouraging an approach which emphasises how the institutions in different political cultures play a key influence upon current policies in sometimes obscure and unusual ways, it also means that seemingly common institutions might produce different outcomes in different places.

Policy transfer

The fourth key area for meso-level policy analysis identified by Hudson and Lowe is policy transfer, for in a period of increased globalisation there is clear evidence of policy transfer between different countries and different sectors in the area of policy development. Dolowitz and Marsh (1996) define policy transfer as:

the process in which knowledge about policies, administrative arrangements, institutions etc. in one time and/or place is used in the development of policies, administrative arrangements and institutions in another time and/or place. (p.344)

The term 'policy transfer' is a generic term and can include a range of different reasons for and conceptions of the process by which ideas, institutions or programmes from one time or place might be used in another. These include (Stone 1999): policy 'bandwagoning', policy emulation, policy harmonisation, systematically pinching ideas, policy penetration, external inducements, direct coercive transfer, policy diffusion, policy convergence and cross-national policy learning.

Clearly a whole range of people, groups and processes can be involved and the term 'policy transfer' covers a wide range of possibilities. Hudson and Lowe (2009) suggest three key questions that need to be considered in order to be as clear and specific as possible. What is being transferred and how complete is the transfer? What are the barriers to transfer and how successful is it? Where does the transferred policy originate from? In recognising the difficulties in addressing these questions and that explanations of policy change based on policy transfer may over-simplify what is involved, Hudson and Lowe argue that we need to locate policy transfer in a broader framework that also acknowledges the importance of other factors in bringing about policy change. It is important that the processes and drivers of policy exchange are located alongside and in interaction with the changing governance arrangements and the policy networks and political institutions we discussed earlier. Together they provide important bridges at the meso level of analysis for understanding the links between micro-decisions and broad macro-level changes.

c. Micro-level analysis

Recent years have witnessed a growing interest in how policies impact at the point of implementation. In part this is in recognition that front-line practitioners play a key role in how clients, patients, service users and others experience policies, and whether policies are 'successful'. The primary concern of micro-level analysis is to consider what happens to policy at the point when it is finally delivered. It is a recognition that what we mean by policy cannot simply be read from the official policy documents and the formal statements about the aims, intentions and planned outcomes of policy change – much of which is top-down and over-rationalistic. On the ground, policy has as many unintended outcomes as intended outcomes and is much messier than the impression given by most 'official' policy documents.

The work of Charles Lindblom is particularly important here. He argued that policy could not be understood as a series of packaged stages but was essentially a process of gradual change and accretion and was best characterised as 'the science of muddling through' (Lindblom 1959). He developed the idea that front-line practitioners could be helpfully conceptualised as 'street-level bureaucrats' (Lindblom 1979). Practitioners tried to do their best in difficult circumstances and used the discretion available to them to develop a wide range of informal rules and practices in order to get the job done with the resources and tools available to them. Thereby they had a vital direct impact upon the implementation of policy. There are now many research studies available which demonstrate how this works in practice, including in different child welfare and child protection settings (see, for example, Peckover, White and Hall 2009). Such micro-level analysis will not be a major focus for our work here.

There is, however, another dimension to micro-level policy analysis which will be of much greater significance to our analysis. This is the recognition that certain actors can play a key role in influencing decisions at the policy development stage. Hudson and Lowe (2009) give the example of Tony Blair in his role as prime minister of the British government and in particular the decision to take Britain to war in Iraq in 2003. This was a decision for the British government and not one for the devolved administrations. They ask the question whether the same decision would have been taken if Gordon Brown or Charles Kennedy (leader of the Liberal Democrat party) had been prime minister at the time. Clearly we will never know, but it does demonstrate that certain individuals can have a major influence upon policy. While clearly the influence of the macro level was important (for example Britain's relationship with the US) and there was clearly considerable activity at the meso level (for example in terms of a range of networks and interest groups), the decisions of certain individuals cannot be dismissed. Who takes decisions, on what basis, etc. are important issues to consider when trying to analyse policy development and change.

2.3 THE ROLE OF THE MEDIA

In this section we analyse the relatively unique role the media has played in shaping child protection policy across the UK, arguing that it is not possible to understand child protection system change without understanding the role of the media as one of the major drivers. In this section we track the role the media has played in contributing to the shaping of child protection in the UK since the reporting of the Maria Colwell case in England in 1974, through the reporting of the Cleveland sex abuse scandal in England and the Orkney case in Scotland in the 1980s. We discuss changes in the reporting of child abuse and child death cases over time, the changing role of the media, the tabloid press in particular and of new technology leading to the current intense media scrutiny of those caught up in high profile cases.

We will argue that one of the major drivers of policy change in child protection across the UK has been the media but that its impact and influence varies somewhat over time and in different places. There can be little doubt that one of the major factors that has ensured that child abuse has become an issue of major public and political concern is the way it has been taken up and portrayed by different parts of the media. It has similarly had an important impact on the direction and content of policy and practice. Media reporting of the public inquiry into the tragic death of Maria Colwell (Secretary of State 1974) in 1973/4 had the effect of making the issue of child abuse a matter of major public concern for the first time in the modern era and at the same time highlighted the activities of a range of health and welfare professionals, particularly social workers, and subjecting them to intense critical scrutiny (Parton 1985). We cannot overestimate the impact that the case had on both policy and professional practice across the UK. In England and Wales a new system of child abuse management was inaugurated with the publication of a Department of Health and Social Security (DHSS) circular (DHSS 1974) following Maria's death. There followed a series of very high profile public inquiries, usually where children died, throughout the 1970s, 1980s and 1990s and on each occasion the issues and criticisms were subjected to intense media coverage, often having a direct impact on policy including the introduction of new legislation and procedural guidance. For example, a major political driver behind the passage of the 1989 Children Act in England and Wales was the need for the government to be seen to be responding to the Cleveland child abuse scandal in the north-east of England (Secretary of State 1988; and see Parton 1991 for a detailed analysis). Similarly, the events in Cleveland and in Orkney in the late 1980s together brought change along the same lines to Scotland. In many respects we can see such developments as being dependent on changes at a macro level of analysis and also as being a key issue to take into account at the meso level.

At the macro level one of the major changes of the last 50 years has been the rapid development of and changes in the media itself. While mass circulation newspapers had been established during the nineteenth century, it was not until the development of broadcast radio in the 1920s and 1930s, and the spread of television in the post-war period, that the 'mass media' established itself as a central institution of modern life. In the UK the television viewing audience grew from nothing to virtually universal coverage in less than a generation (Thompson 1990, 1996) and as television's viewing figures increased, its share of advertising revenue and its growing impact upon popular tastes forced newspapers to compete more and more on television's terms. The consequence was a greater concentration in newspaper ownership, the advent of the tabloid newspaper and a growing tendency towards a general 'dumbing down' in quality, together with an imperceptible merging of news and entertainment (Franklin 1997).

Consumption patterns and lifestyles that were once confined to the rich and famous were increasingly projected as available to everyone, while issues and problems which were previously localised were thrust into the living rooms of the whole population, as with child abuse from 1973 onwards. The visibility of events and individuals ceased to depend on a shared locale and direct experience, and came instead to depend on the media which was reporting things faster and from all over the world. Television news conveyed a sense of immediacy and intimacy and increasingly emphasised the personalities involved and the emotive aspects of events (Thompson 1990).

Claire Wardle (2006) has compared broadsheet and tabloid newspaper coverage of 12 similar child murder cases in the US and UK over three decades: the 1930s, the 1960s and the 1990s. Combining quantitative and qualitative analyses she established that by the 1990s coverage had become increasingly focused on the personal and societal elements of the story, with a new emphasis on the victims' families and how the crimes impacted on the wider community. The coverage was increasingly raw and emotional and the sexual elements of the cases were highlighted wherever possible.

Thomas Mathiesen (1997) has argued that the pervasiveness of the penetration of the media into our 'lived realities' has produced a 'viewer society'. He develops the concept of 'synopticism', or the social phenomenon of the many viewing the activities of the few, facilitated by the media, as being a fundamental aspect of contemporary society. So, for example, the families and professionals involved in high profile child abuse cases are subject to intense attention from the media. Their private and public lives receive considerable scrutiny. As a result the many view the few.

These major macro-level developments have clearly impacted at the meso level. To an overwhelming extent people receive their information on the basis of which they form their political opinions and structure their behaviour, through the media – particularly via television and radio and increasingly through internet sites. As a consequence, the media has become the primary space of politics so that the presentation of policy has become at least as significant as the substantive policy content. As a result the facility with which policy options lend themselves to media presentation has become a crucial ingredient in policy making (Franklin 1994). Representations of politics and policy in the media need to convey simple messages, where the simplest message is an image and the most individualised in age is a person. Stories of sex, crime and scandal take centre stage as mechanisms for both grabbing the attention of the reader/viewer and communicating the key boundaries of what constitutes good and bad behaviour. As Anne Hills commented 30 years ago:

> Child abuse makes for good copy. There is the trial which involves hundreds of column inches devoted to details of the child's grisly end. This allows for both public conscience and appetite for horror to be satisfied at the same time. Then there is the ritual purification: the inquiry into what went wrong and the execution of the guilty parties – the social workers. (Hills 1980, p.19)

Thus while such changes have helped to create a greater level of transparency and accountability, they have also had the effect of changing the boundaries between the public and the private and thereby opened up the possibility that something which may previously have been seen as a private issue could become a public problem and thereby the subject of public policy intervention. However, not only does the media have the power to transform the private into the public, it also has the power – at the same time – to undermine trust, reputation and legitimacy in the process. This has been a key tension in public policy in relation to child protection across the UK over the last 40 years.

Not surprisingly at the meso level of analysis issues around public relations, image and news management now play a key role. These issues have been well illustrated during the period of the New Labour government at Westminster from 1997 to 2010. As a number of commentators have demonstrated (Fairclough 2000; Franklin 2003) New Labour gave a very high priority to news management and its relationship with the media. As a consequence, there seemed to be a continual tension between short-termism – where the government attempted to respond to 'public opinion' – and its longer term 'modernisation' project of reforming public services. As a consequence, New Labour often did not seem confident in the face of high profile 'bad news' stories and wanted to be seen as decisive, authoritative and 'tough'. Nowhere has this tension been more evident than with its policies in relation to child protection in England, particularly in relation to its response to the tragic death of 'Baby Peter'. It is important to remember, however, that the media is simply one of the influences upon policy. Not only are there different types of media, it also operates at a number of levels – local, regional, national – and in a number of forms: print, radio, television and internet. The way it impacts on and is responded to will vary at different times and in different national and cultural contexts.

2.4 CONCLUSION

In this chapter we have focused on the factors that seem to us to have been most influential in driving reform of child protection across the UK. These are multi-layered, convoluted and difficult to unravel. We used the framework for policy analysis developed by Hudson and Lowe (2009) who tried to build understanding of the policy making world at three levels: the macro level, the micro level and the meso level. We suggested that at the macro level, globalisation had loosened certain state structures leading to new organisational forms and ways of working. One effect of this has been to underpin and accelerate the break-up of Britain as a unitary state into a fragmented and differentiated polity, with devolution central to this. We were interested in how global forces, in the context of devolution, are taken up at the meso level, mediated by local networks and institutions, which then impact on child protection in each part of the UK. At micro level, we claim that policy cannot be read from official documents: so we have tried to understand how policy impacts at the point of implementation; at how policy is mediated and translated by practitioners.

We have also argued that it is not possible to understand reform of child protection in the UK without an understanding of the unique role the UK media plays in reporting high profile child death and child abuse cases. We concluded that the media has been and remains one of the main drivers of system change and the effect of this has increased greatly over the past 15 years.

Chapter 3

Child Protection across the UK in an International Context

3.1 INTRODUCTION

In this chapter, as part of our quest to understand the unfolding story of child protection across the UK in the context of devolution, we begin by stepping back from our own system to view it from the widest possible perspective. This chapter attempts to set our understanding of child protection in the UK in the context of child protection systems in an international context.

Over the past 15 years there has been a growing literature comparing child protection systems throughout the world. The interest in conducting international comparative studies in this area grew out of perceived problems with the systems of the UK to adequately protect children and to deal with burgeoning numbers of referrals into the system. This kind of research was an explicit search for what other countries may do better than ourselves with the clear objective of finding ways to improve the way children are protected across the UK.

The major purpose of this chapter is to summarise and critically review this literature so that we are in a better position to assess developments across the UK and thereby identify the nature and direction of any change over time.

What will become evident is that, first, this literature is based almost exclusively on comparisons of child protection systems in North America, Scandinavia and northern Europe, together with analyses of systems in Australia and New Zealand. Second, and central to these comparisons, much of the literature identifies two broad approaches or orientations in the systems designed to protect children: one we will call a child protection orientation and the other a family service orientation. The former is seen as reflecting systems in North America, the UK and Australia, and the latter is seen as much more evident in northern Europe and Scandinavia. Both orientations have been subject to critique and further more recent development.

Third, much of the research and writing is subject to both analytic and normative influences, for while there has been a clear attempt to identify different approaches and orientations in order to try and compare systems and services in different countries, most writers are fairly clear which approach they feel is most appropriate. More particularly it is apparent that the primary driver for engaging in such research has been the view that systems and services in certain countries were no longer carrying out the tasks expected of them and were, in some respects, failing. As a result researchers and policy makers looked elsewhere to see if other countries did things differently (and better) such that this might inform how to reform the system 'at home'. It is no coincidence that the first serious interest in comparing child protection systems took place in the 1990s, the period when policy makers in a number of countries were feeling the need to try and reform their child protection systems.

3.2 THE GROWING CRISIS IN CHILD PROTECTION

In many respects the interest in comparing child protection systems was prompted by increasing concerns about the operation of child protection systems in particular countries – those located in the English-speaking industrialised countries of North America, the UK and Oceania, all of which had very much adopted the approach originally developed in the US in the 1960s in response to the (re)discovery of child abuse in the form of the 'battered child syndrome'.

It was Henry Kempe *et al.*'s identification of the 'battered child syndrome' (Kempe *et al.* 1962) which catapulted the issue of child abuse onto professional, public and political agendas, initially in the US (Nelson 1984) and subsequently in the UK (Parton 1985) and Australia (Scott and Swain 2002). Both the article and the approach were to have an enormous influence on the way child abuse was conceptualised and responded to in those countries for many years to come.

There was an immediate impact in the US. In 1963 the Children's Bureau issued a model reporting law whereby certain health and welfare professionals would be required, or mandated, to report cases of actual and suspected child abuse to designated public authorities, and all 50 US states adopted such a law by 1967 (Hutchison 1993). This was followed by the first national child protection legislation, the Child Abuse and Prevention and Treatment Act (CAPTA) in 1974, which, among other things, required states to have such mandatory reporting laws in place. Most Australian states introduced mandatory reporting from the late 1970s onwards (Ainsworth 2002). While mandatory reporting legislation was particularly associated with the growing emerging problems with the child protection systems in the US and Australia, the UK never had such legislation even though it also began to experience similar problems. It seemed the underlying problems were more fundamental than whether there was mandatory reporting and seemed to emanate from a number of key assumptions which underpinned the systems from the outset. As Gary Melton (2005) argued it seems the original designers of modern child protection systems made two interconnected and fundamental errors, and both could be seen to emanate from assumptions which underpinned the notion of 'the battered child syndrome'; both the *scope* and the *complexity* of the problem of child abuse were underestimated:

> The assumption early in the history of the modern child protection system was that the problem of child maltreatment was reducible to 'syndromes' – in effect, that abusive and neglecting parents were either very sick or very evil and that they could thus be appropriately characterized as 'those people' who were fundamentally different from ourselves... Although such cases do occur, they are relatively rare. Most cases involve neglect...further, searches for distinctive behavioural syndromes have proven elusive. (Melton 2005, p.11)

This original failure to recognise both the scope and complexity of the problem was exacerbated by the subsequent broadening of the concept of child abuse. While the notion of 'the battered child syndrome' proved the dominant underlying metaphor for many years, the category of child abuse was also subject to various 'mouldings' (Hacking 1988, 1991, 1992) and 'diagnostic inflation' (Dingwall 1989, p.29), so that by the late 1980s it included emotional abuse, neglect and sexual abuse as well as physical abuse and was no longer focused only on babies and young children but included young people up to the age of 18.

Having established the new systems to protect children in the mid 1960s, the next 30 years witnessed a huge increase in the number of children being reported in the US from 9,563 (0.1/100,000 children) in 1984, to 3,126,000 (47.0/100,000 children) in 1996 (Lonne *et al.* 2009, p.26). However, while the proportion of reported cases which were 'substantiated' as child abuse was over 60 per cent in the 1970s, the figure had dropped to well below 40 per cent by the early 1990s.

Similar trends were evident in Canada (Swift 1997; Trocme, Tam and McPhee 1995) and were even more marked in Australia. While the way statistics were collated varied between Australian states, the rate of growth of child abuse reports was even greater than in the US. For example, in the state of Victoria reports of child abuse and neglect increased more than 5,000 per cent between 1977/8 and 1993/4 from 517 to 26,622 (Parton, Thorpe and Wattam 1997, p.3).

In England there were no comparable statistics. The only statistics available which cover the last quarter of the twentieth century relate to the numbers of children on the child protection 'register' (see Chapter 6). A child's name was placed on the register where, following an investigation and a multidisciplinary case conference, it was felt that they had been and/or continued to be at risk of suffering abuse or neglect and were to be subject to a 'child protection plan'. The numbers of children on child protection registers in England quadrupled between 1978 and 1991 from 11,844 to 45,300.

By the mid 1990s there were a number of authoritative reports which were arguing that child protection systems in the US, England and Australia were, at best, out of balance, or, at worst, in crisis and in need of reform. For example, the US Advisory Board on Child Abuse and Neglect (US ABCAN) (1990) commented that:

> The most serious shortcomings of the nation's system of intervention on behalf of children is that it depends on reporting and response processes that has punitive connotations and requires massive resources dedicated to the investigation of allegations. State and County child welfare programs have not been designed to get immediate help to families based on voluntary requests for assistance. As a result, it has become far easier to pick up the telephone to report one's neighbour for child abuse than it is for that neighbour to pick up the telephone and receive help before that happens. (US ABCAN 1990, p.80)

And three years later:

> The result of the current design of the child protection system is that investigation often seems to occur for its own sake, without any realistic hope of meaningful treatment to prevent the recurrence of maltreatment or to ameliorate its effects, even if the report of suspected maltreatment is validated. (US ABCAN 1993, pp.10–11)

Increasingly, it seemed in the US, Australia and Canada that the child protection systems had developed wide 'nets' in which were caught a whole variety of concerns about children and that certain sections of the population, particularly the poor, single parent households and certain minority ethnic groups were at much greater risk of being caught in the nets than others (Thorpe 1994; Waldfogel 1998).

While a similar 'crisis' was developing in England, the process whereby this emerged and the context in which it happened was somewhat different. Like the US, Canada and Australia, a major driver of policy change was a series of high profile tragic deaths of children at the hands of their parents or immediate carers and where health and welfare professionals had failed to share information and intervene appropriately. Invariably subsequent public inquiries into the cases argued that the tragedies had been predictable and preventable and that the professionals, particularly social workers, were in some ways culpable. Between the publication of the public inquiry into the death of Maria Colwell in 1973 (Secretary of State 1974) and 1985 there were 30 inquiries into the deaths of children as a result of abuse (Corby, Doig and Roberts 1998).

The intense public and media interest reached a new peak in the mid 1980s following three high profile public inquiries into the deaths of children in three London boroughs (London Borough of Brent 1985; London Borough of Greenwich 1987; London Borough of Lambeth 1987). However, while central government was in the process of revising official guidance to take account of these most recent public inquiries, a rather different child abuse scandal exploded into the media and introduced a public and political debate of a rather different order.

The Cleveland 'affair' broke in the summer of 1987 and was focused on the activities of two paediatricians and social workers in a hospital in Middlesbrough in the north-east of England. During a period of a few weeks, over 100 children were removed from their families to an emergency place of safety (the hospital) on the basis of what was seen by the media (Franklin 1989) and two local members of Parliament (Bell 1988) as questionable diagnoses of sexual abuse. A public inquiry was established by the Secretary of State for Social Services which reported the following year (Secretary of State 1988). Not only was this the first scandal and public inquiry into possible over reaction by professionals, it was also the first on sexual abuse, and the first where medical science, as well as social work, was put under close scrutiny (Ashenden 1996, 2004; Parton 1991). Unlike most developments up until this point, which had very much carried the imprint of thinking in the US, developments in Cleveland were a very English affair and had a history and impact, both across the UK and abroad, of their own (Hacking 1991, 1992).

It is in this context that we need to understand the Children Act 1989. While the Act was not a simple reaction to the child abuse inquiries, it was very much concerned with trying to (re)construct a better balance, not just between the rights and responsibilities of individuals and agencies, but between the need to protect children and the need to enable parents to challenge intervention by the state into the upbringing of their children (Parton 1991, Chapter 6). It was, perhaps, the first attempt in the Anglophone world to carry out a serious appraisal of the impact of the child protection system(s) which had developed since the mid 1960s. It attempted to keep to a minimum the situations where social workers would rely upon a policing and investigatory approach dominated by a focus upon a narrowly defined forensic concern, and aimed to put in its place an emphasis, wherever possible, of providing help and support with the agreement of parents and children.

This attempt to 'refocus' children's services away from a narrow concern with child protection was reinforced a few years later by the publication of an Audit Commission report (1994) and the launch by the Department of Health of *Child Protection: Messages from Research* (Department of Health 1995). Both documents argued that the 1989 Children Act had not been successful in trying to 'refocus' children's services away from a narrow forensic concern with child protection to an approach which also aimed to provide services to 'children in need' on a voluntary basis and before situations were of crisis proportions (Parton 1997).

Both the Audit Commission report and *Messages from Research* were considerably influenced by the study carried out by Gibbons, Conroy and Bell (1995). This research, based on eight local authorities in England and carried out over a 16-week period in 1992, identified all children referred for a new child protection investigation (1888 cases) and tracked their progress through the child protection system for up to 26 weeks via social work records and case conference minutes. What was seen as particularly significant was the way a series of *filters* and *funnels* operated. At the first level, 26 per cent of referrals were filtered out by social work staff at the duty stage after initial checks and without any direct contact with the child or family. At the second, the investigation itself, another 50 per cent were filtered out and never reached an initial case conference. Of the total, just 15 per cent were placed on the child protection register – just one in seven of every child who entered the child protection system.

Of the original allegations/referrals 49 per cent were 'not substantiated' and the investigation led to no further action in a high proportion (44 per cent of those investigated). There were no interventions to protect the child nor were any services provided. The study also found that over one third (36%) of the total referrals were headed by a lone parent, and in only 30 per cent of cases were both natural parents living in the same household, while 57 per cent lacked a wage earner and 54 per cent were dependent on state income support. It was the most vulnerable sections of the population who were the most likely to become the object of the child protection system. The commonest picture was of children not reaching the threshold for child protection proceedings but not getting any preventive help either. The research by Gibbons *et al.* (1995) was the first time there had been any sort of map of the child protection system and how it operated in England or the UK more generally. While different in detail, it clearly had many similarities to that in the US, Canada and Australia.

By the early/mid 1990s, therefore, evidence was emerging in all the Anglophone countries that there were significant problems with their child protection systems. Public inquiries, authoritative official reports and research were all pointing to significant challenges which needed to be addressed. The Harvard Executive Session on Child Protective Services was convened in 1994 to consider ways forward for the US. It was felt that there were five major problems with the US child protection system – and all could be seen to apply to the other Anglophone systems as well (Waldfogel 1998, 2008).

The first problem identified was *over-inclusion*, whereby some children and families who were low risk but were subjected to an unnecessary adversarial and forensic investigation. At the same time, and second, there was the problem of *under-inclusion*, where some children and families who should have been included in the child protection system were not. This may have been because they were missed and not reported, or because families asked for voluntary assistance at an earlier stage of difficulty but did not meet the threshold for inclusion. The third problem, which both reflected and arose from the first two, was *capacity*. The number of reports had increased so dramatically over the previous 30 years that the number of children and families involved far exceeded the capacity of the system to serve them.

The fourth problem was what Waldfogel called *service delivery*, for even if children and families did manage to cross the threshold for inclusion, many did not receive the right sort of service, or, in many cases, any service at all. The fifth problem was to do with *service orientation*. For, in being so concerned to investigate cases of child abuse there was a failure to engage with children and families and try to address their particular needs. Such an approach was not only stigmatising and antagonistic to those it confronted, it also acted to discourage others – both families and professionals – from approaching the service when they may need help and support. It seemed that the child protection system was failing on numerous fronts and Waldfogel and her colleagues argued that what was needed was a 'paradigm shift'. It is in this context of increased concerns about child protection systems that researchers and policy makers in the US, Canada, the UK and Australia began to look elsewhere to see if other countries approached these issues differently and whether they had any more success in the process.

3.3 COMPARING CHILD PROTECTION SYSTEMS

It is not by coincidence then that the beginnings of research comparing child protection systems was to be found in the UK and the US. We will look at each in turn.

The driver in the UK was quite specific and very much focused on the increasing problems in England and Wales. This was made very clear at the beginning of the first book published comparing child protection systems by Andrew Cooper and his colleagues, which compared the child protection systems in England and France:

> This book is concerned with the *crisis* in the child protection system of England and Wales and how it might be overcome. The implementation of the Children Act 1989 notwithstanding, child protection social work in England and Wales is characterised by high professional anxiety, political ambiguity and a feeling of 'stuckness'. This is a product of the confusing and contradictory relationship which has come to exist between the law, the citizen, social work and the state in England. It is underpinned by the profound ambivalence of governance to social intervention in families. Child protection social work in England has been *bureaucratised*, *legalised* and *systematised*. Meanwhile, social workers have been pilloried in the press and castigated by government. Yet, as far as we can tell, vulnerable children are no safer and the log-jam of unallocated child protection cases is undiminished. (Cooper *et al.* 1995, p.viii, emphasis added)

The research compared the child protection systems in England and France and built on comparative work which had been carried out at Brunel University in London for a few years (Cooper 1992a, 1992b; Cooper *et al.* 1992). The researchers talked with child protection workers in both countries and studied the respective histories and operation of their child protection systems. All those involved – researchers, practitioners and managers – recognised that being faced by a country which did things differently provided for an ongoing process of critical reflection and insights into how things might be done differently. Cooper *et al.* argued that all were provided with opportunities for identifying different ways of looking at familiar dilemmas and with stimulating creative ideas for developing and changing both policy and day-to-day practice.

However, as the above quotation demonstrates, Cooper *et al.* were not simply engaged with an analytic exercise as the drivers were strongly normative and were centrally concerned with trying to improve child protection in England. Not only did the research help sharpen the researchers' ideas about what was wrong with the English child protection system but they were also provided with ideas about how things might be improved. They became very aware that there were major cultural differences between the two countries and that this could be seen to permeate all areas of law, policy and practice. In particular, while the French system seemed to be infused with both an *optimism* and *trust* of both families and social workers' abilities to look after children, this was not the case in England where *pessimism* and *distrust* seemed to dominate. As the title suggested, the main purpose of the book was to encourage a 'positive' approach to child protection in England by looking at how things operated in France.

In this respect the project aims chimed very neatly with the refocusing debate in England prompted by the Audit Commission report *Seen But Not Heard* (1994) and *Child Protection: Messages From Research* (DH 1995). This link became even more evident with the publication of a further study by the same research team two years later (Hetherington *et al.* 1997), where the Foreword was written by Rupert Hughes CBE, who until recently had been assistant secretary at the Department of Health and had been one of the key architects of the Children Act 1989 as well as the prime commissioner of the research which informed *Child Protection: Messages from Research*.

This was an ambitious book. Not only were the researchers reporting on a much bigger study in that this time they had compared child protection systems from eight countries – the Belgium Flemish community, the Belgium Francophone community, France, Germany, Italy, the Netherlands, England and Scotland – but their political and policy aims were even more ambitious and explicit. The focus was what they called 'a particular and important moment in the history of child care and protection work in England and Wales' (Hetherington *et al.* 1997, p.4). For the book was written 'first and foremost' as a contribution to the process of change, particularly in relation to 'the continuing struggle to implement the radical vision of the Children Act 1989' (p.4) and 'the importance of recovering an ability to think new, creative and even dangerous thoughts in pursuit of change and reinvigoration in child protection work' (pp.4–5). In examining seven other European child protection systems, Hetherington *et al.* (1997) argued that they were holding up:

> seven mirrors to the English system, and each time seen new things reflected back. These may be ways of thinking, doing, organising, conceptualising, valorising, or processing. The space which has now opened up to think about change in England is both bounded and free. (p.111)

It was quite clear that the main purpose for engaging in comparative research and analysis was to contribute to bringing about change in England.

The aim of the research was twofold: to learn about the child protection system in the 'other country' in terms of how it worked for those directly involved in operating it; and, second, to elicit the views of social workers in one country about the practice and system of another. The researchers wanted to work with practitioners in order to gain their understanding of how their own system worked, and also to get their reflections on alternative ways of working as demonstrated in another country. Therefore, in each country the researchers identified a small group of social workers who met for two 'seminars' to help the practitioners understand the system of child protection compared to that in England. In England the researchers found a new group of social workers to work with for each system studied – seven in total; six from West London and one from Humberside.

In the first seminar the social workers were each given a case outline and asked to give written answers to questions. The case was divided into four stages, describing escalating difficulties in the family. The questions were designed to discover what the social workers would do, why they would do it, what the legal constraints and possibilities might be, and what the theoretical and conceptual basis of their thinking was. Having written down their answers the social workers then engaged in a discussion of the case and what plan they might have at the end, which was video recorded.

In the second seminar the purpose was to discover the participants' reactions to the responses of the social workers from the other country and the discussion they had. They were given a brief description of the child protection system in question, shown the video recording, and asked for their reactions.

While a number of important similarities were noted in the systems, there were also important differences, particularly between England and to a lesser extent Scotland and the other countries, especially in relation to the roles, authority and responsibilities of social workers and the overall cultural context in which the work took place.

Some years later the core members of the research team brought their findings and ideas together to outline a set of principles and a framework for reforming the child protection system in England (Cooper, Hetherington and Katz 2003). They commented that their comparative research had demonstrated that the morale of English social workers, compared with their colleagues in other countries, was particularly low and they felt unsupported by the child protection system. From the lessons they had learned from studying other European systems, Cooper *et al.* (2003) argued that the reform of the child protection system in England should be based on the principles of *trust, authority* and *negotiation,* all of which they argued were currently lacking. There needed to be:

- The legitimation of professionals within the system who carried sufficient *authority* to intervene in families where there was abuse, within a framework where legal compulsion was ultimately possible.

- The development of *confidential spaces* where the different parties could explore their complex dilemmas within defined and mutually understood boundaries of confidentiality. These would involve multidisciplinary teams of competent, trained professionals who were able to act authoritatively and provided with regular supervision. The limits of confidentiality would be clearly stated but the process of *negotiation* would be central.

- There would be a principle that no more compulsion should be used than was necessary to achieve the primary objectives of the intervention.

Compared to the situation in the other European countries the English system was characterised as one of increased managerialism and a culture of defensive accountability where accountability had been reduced to checking whether procedures had been followed and where there was a pervasive anxiety about things going wrong; all of which undermined the broad aims of the Children Act 1989.

At the same time as Cooper *et al.* were carrying out their research, another project was being carried out, based in the US, and led by Neil Gilbert (1997). While the policy and practice concerns driving the research were rather different and the methodology adopted was much more focused on policy analysis, the research very much complemented that by Cooper *et al. Combating Child Abuse: International Perspectives and Trends* (Gilbert 1997) was prompted primarily by the rapid increase in reports of child maltreatment in the US and the considerable strains on its child welfare systems between 1980 and 1993. While similar trends could be identified in other countries it seemed that it was in the US where the trends were the most extreme and conspicuous and it had witnessed a vigorous debate about how best to organise responses and services. Academic researchers were recruited to analyse the child protection systems in nine North American and northern European countries. An analytic framework was developed for analysing each country in terms of:

- What are the criteria which define child maltreatment?

- Who is responsible for reporting suspected cases of child maltreatment?

- What are the processes for enquiring into these reports?

- How are the allegations of maltreatment substantiated, and what is the state's response?

- What are the patterns and make-up of out-of-home placements?

The researchers looked at differences in response as well as common problems and emerging policy responses. It was thought that a major reason for the upsurge in reports in the US and the subsequent strains in the system arose, at least in part, from the mandatory reporting system and the vague definitions of child abuse evident. Comparing the US system with systems elsewhere would provide one way of testing out these assumptions. The nine countries included in the study were: Belgium, Canada, Denmark, England, Finland, Germany, the Netherlands, Sweden and the US. After producing the draft case studies for each country, the researchers met to review, clarify and compare the findings from each country.

The key finding was that there were important variations between the countries concerning the extent to which systems emphasised a *child protection* or *family service* orientation, and these did not depend on whether there was a mandatory reporting system in place. The two orientations were distinguished along a number of dimensions as shown in Table 3.1.

TABLE 3.1 CHARACTERISTICS OF CHILD PROTECTION AND FAMILY SERVICE ORIENTATIONS

	Child protection	**Family service**
Problem frame	individualist/moralistic	social/psychological
Preliminary intervention	legalistic/investigatory	therapeutic/needs assessment
State/parent relationship	adversarial	partnership
Out-of-home placement	involuntary	voluntary

Source: Gilbert 1997, p.233

Four dimensions for distinguishing the two orientations were outlined. First, and perhaps the most significant, was the way the problem of child abuse was framed. In some systems abuse was conceived as an act which demanded the protection of children from harm by 'degenerative relatives'; whereas in other systems abuse was conceived as a problem of family conflict or dysfunction which arose from social and psychological difficulties but which responded to help and support.

Second, and depending on how child abuse was framed, the response operated either as a mechanism for investigating deviance in a highly legalistic way, or as a service response responding to a family's needs much more therapeutically and where the initial focus was the assessment of need. As a result, third, the child welfare professionals functioned either in the child protection orientation, a highly adversarial way or in the family service orientation, in a spirit of partnership – particularly with parents. Finally while there seemed to be a high rate of voluntary arrangements with parents in making out-of-home placements with the family service orientation, in the child protection orientation the majority of out-of-home placements was compelled through the coercive powers of the state, usually in the form of court orders. However, the use of mandatory reporting laws did not appear to be linked to either the child protection or family service orientations. The analysis suggested, therefore, that it was possible to group the countries into three broad categories:

1. *Child Protection*: United States, Canada, England

2. *Family Service – Mandatory Reporting*: Denmark, Sweden, Finland

3. *Family Service – Non-Mandatory Reporting*: Belgium, the Netherlands, Germany.

What the research suggested was that there did seem to be important differences in the way Anglo-American child welfare services were organised and the way they responded to concerns about child abuse, when compared to northern European and Nordic countries. However, there did not seem to be clear links between placement rates and the orientation of reporting systems. The US, with a child protection orientation, and Denmark, with a family service orientation, had the highest out-of-home placement rates in 1992/93, while the lowest placement rates were in family service oriented Netherlands and child protection oriented England. The researchers argued that while the details of different programmes and policies were important, the way different systems operated were also influenced by wider cultural and societal conditions.

There is no doubt that the book edited by Neil Gilbert (1997) was published at an important time and coincided with a number of policy makers and politicians, internationally, looking at other countries to see if they could learn any lessons about how to organise their own child protection systems. There was a particular interest in comparing European approaches to those adopted in Anglo-American countries and the distinction between the *child protection* and *family service orientations* (sometimes in a slightly revised way) was often adopted from this point as, perhaps, the key way to represent and distinguish between different approaches. The two orientations seemed to provide something of a benchmark for discussions and analyses in both research and various government reports.

A good example can be found in the *Report of the Child Protection Audit and Review* for the Scottish Executive (2002), which was established following the publication of the Hammond review into the death of Kennedy McFarlane in Dumfries and Galloway (Hammond 2001). The report aimed to: 'promote the reduction of abuse or neglect of children who experience abuse or neglect' (Scottish Executive 2002, p.2) in Scotland. To aid the work of the review a seminar was organised to look at international perspectives on child protection, and a number of international speakers were invited. The aim was to locate the Scottish system in a comparative context in order to examine alternative approaches and critically examine the Scottish situation in the light of the differences and similarities that emerged. A report on the seminar was included as an appendix to the main report and its findings had many similarities to those in *Combating Child Abuse*. A table included in the appendix (Table 3.2) is particularly instructive:

TABLE 3.2 DIFFERENCES BETWEEN UK/NORTH AMERICAN AND CONTINENTAL WEST EUROPEAN SYSTEMS

Broad type of system	UK/North American	Continental West European
Countries covered at the seminar	Australia, Canada, Scotland, England	Belgium, Sweden, France, Germany
Type of welfare state	tendency to residual and selective provision	tendency to comprehension and universal provision
Place of child protection services	separated from family support services	embedded within and normalised by broad child welfare or public health services
Type of child protection system	legal, bureaucratic, investigative, adversarial	voluntary, flexible, solution-focused, collaborative
Orientation to children and families	emphasis on individual children's rights. Professionals' primary responsibility for child's welfare	emphasis on family unit. Professionals usually work with the family as a whole
Basis of the service	investigating risk in order to formulate child safety plan	supportive or therapeutic responses to meeting needs or resolving problems
Coverage	resources are concentrated on families where risks of (re)abuse are immediate and high	resources are available to more families at an earlier stage

Source: Scottish Executive 2002

While often implicit it is quite clear that many researchers and writers who have developed and used the distinction between the *child protection* and *family service orientations* outlined in *Combating Child Abuse* (Gilbert 1997) (see also Bromfield and Holzer 2007), where the former is particularly associated with the UK and North America and the latter with Continental west and north Europe, have a clear preference for the latter. This was clear in the title of the first book from Andrew Cooper and his colleagues (Cooper *et al.* 1995) called *Positive Child Protection: A View from Abroad.*

This was even more evident in the work emanating from the Faculty of Social Work at Wilfrid Laurier University, Canada, which studied international comparisons. The main publications were *Towards Positive Systems of Child and Family Welfare: International Comparisons of Child Protection, Family Service, and Community Caring Systems* (Freymond and Cameron 2006) and *Moving Towards Positive Systems of Child and Family Welfare: Current Issues and Future Directions* (Cameron, Coady and Adams 2007). As the titles suggest, the work builds on that by Andrew Cooper and Rachael Hetherington. It quite explicitly argued that the research aimed to critique and move beyond the 'Anglo-American Child Protection Paradigm' (Cameron *et al.* 2007).

However, rather than just two models or systems it is argued that there were three generic systems of child and family welfare which could be identified in 'developed relatively affluent' countries: child protection, family service and community caring. While the first two – child protection and family service – were very similar to those found in Gilbert (1997) and the Scottish Office Report (Hill, Stafford and Lister-Green 2002), the third was rather different.

With *child protection systems*:

> The state is a regulator of social and moral arrangements, with an emphasis on individual rights and responsibilities. There is a clear division between private and public domains that protects the privacy of the family. The primary focus of child protection is to protect children from harm in their own homes. Child protection service providers increasingly rely on adversarial judicial systems to confer authority on their work…the child protection mandate is conferred on a stand-alone authority with minimal formal involvement by other service sectors or the broader community. (Freymond and Cameron 2006, p.6)

England, Canada and the United States were the main examples.

In contrast, with *Family Service Systems*:

> The state supports child and family welfare systems that reflect communal ideals about children, family, and community. Principles of social solidarity and, in some settings, of subsidiarity (local responsibility) are emphasised. Fostering the proper care of children is seen as a shared responsibility. Providing support for parent-child relationships and the care of children are seen as primary focuses. Demonstrating risks of harming children is not a necessary precursor for families or children to receive assistance. Some child and family welfare services are not separate from services to the general population. Legal systems are inquisitorial, and mediating dialogues with specialized judges and mandated officials are common in many settings. Ideally, there is an emphasis on reaching consensual agreements with families. (Freymond and Cameron 2006, p.5)

France, the Netherlands and Sweden were seen as good examples of this approach.

The third system takes its inspiration from many aboriginal communities around the world and was called *Community Care Systems* by Freymond and Cameron. Here:

> Ties to extended family, community, place, history, and spirit are considered integral to healthy individual identities: ideally, community caring relies on consultations with parents, extended family, and the local community about the protection and care of children. Because of the devastating effects on Indigenous Peoples of colonialism, residential care, and child protection systems, a strong connection is made between caring for children and fostering a healing process for whole communities. A strong value is given to keeping children within their families, and communities. Respect for traditional Aboriginal values and procedures is integral to community care processes. (Freymond and Cameron 2006, p.6)

First Nation communities in Canada and the experiences of the Maori in Aotearoa/New Zealand were seen as good examples. While these systems were constructed as ideal types for the analytic purpose of comparing different countries' systems, the authors made it quite clear that their preference was for *Family Service Systems* rather than *Child Protection Systems* and that *Community Care Systems* should be supported wherever appropriate.

One of the few people who has argued consistently against the overall preference of researchers for the family service orientation is

Keith Pringle. While critical of the child protection orientation (Harder and Pringle 1997), he has raised a number of major concerns about the ability of the family services, or family support, approach to protect children, particularly in relation to child sexual abuse. In a critical overview of different responses to child sexual abuse across different European countries (Pringle 1998), he argued there was evidence that many western and northern European family service oriented systems recognised and responded to child sexual abuse far less effectively than the more child protection oriented English approach in the 1990s.

Part of his explanation was that there was a strong reliance on family systems thinking in western and northern European countries in a way which was not so evident in England. As a consequence, there was a failure to appreciate or address the power dynamics related to issues of gender and other social divisions which he argues underpin sexual abuse and other forms of child abuse (Pringle 2005). He connected this greater adherence to family systems thinking to more general difficulties arising from broader cultural and social patterns. He suggested there was a connection between the family service orientations and the more solidaristic/collectivist discourses and traditions that tended to permeate the social institutions in western and northern European countries – compared to the far more individualistic ethos evident in England, and, by implication, the US and Canada (Pringle 1998; Pringle and Harder 1999). At the same time he suggested that the dynamics of the solidaristic discourses in France and Germany, for example, were different to those in the Nordic countries.

He argued that Nordic welfare systems were primarily concerned with addressing problems associated with poverty and work, including those associated with the home, for example day care provision, and parental leave. They were much less concerned with addressing dimensions of marginalisation associated with 'bodily integrity or citizenship' (Pringle 2005; 2010). Included in the latter concept were forms of exclusion associated with, for example, violence to women, violence to children, ageism (in relation to younger as well as older age), racism, heterosexism/homophobia, disablism. While perhaps dealing poorly with problems related to poverty and the labour market, Pringle therefore argues that when it comes to issues like racism, disablism, and gendered violence – all of which are key to child sexual abuse and child abuse more generally – that England can be seen to perform better than the Nordic and other western European countries (Pringle 2010).

These arguments clearly provide an important counterweight to what have almost become the dominant perspectives and assumptions which have underpinned much comparative child protection and child welfare research since 1995. What the arguments do not do, however, is detract from the outline analytic framework and orientations which have developed during this period, particularly in terms of the differentiation between the *child protection* and *family service orientations*. The argument is much more about what the orientations overlook and, in particular, how positive we should be about the orientations in practice and their implications for the children, young people, men and women who are affected by them. It does seem, however, that there is a considerable agreement about the validity and usefulness of using these two orientations as broad frameworks for comparing different child protection systems.

3.4 UPDATING CHILD PROTECTION ORIENTATIONS

More recently, there has been an attempt to update the comparative research originally reported in *Combating Child Abuse* (Gilbert 1997) and this time comparing the same ten countries – Belgium, Canada, Denmark, England, Finland, Germany, the Netherlands, Sweden, the United States and Norway. The overall conclusion (Gilbert, Parton and Skivenes 2011a) is that while the two original orientations, child protection and family service, were still relevant they needed to be revised in the light of the developments in the various countries during the intervening 15 years up to 2008/9.

The findings suggested that approaches to protecting children from abuse had become much more complex than those operating in the early/mid 1990s. Countries previously identified with the child protection orientation, for example England and the US, had taken on some of the elements of the family service orientation. At the same time there was also evidence that those countries which had previously operated according to a clear family service orientation had made efforts to respond to increasing concerns about harm to children. This seemed to be the case in all the Nordic countries, with the possible exception of Sweden, and all the north European countries studied.

In addition to the various attempts to strike a new set of balances between the *child protection* and *family service orientations*, Gilbert, Parton and Skivenes also felt it was possible to discern the emergence of a new approach which they called a *child-focused orientation* (Gilbert, Parton and Skivenes 2011b). This orientation concentrates its focus on the child as an individual with an independent relation to the state. It is not restricted to narrow concerns about harm and abuse; rather the object of concern is the child's overall development and well-being. The programs aim to go beyond protecting children from risk to promoting children's welfare. In this context, concerns about harm and abuse become relevant as just one set of factors that might affect a child's development and well-being. If for any reason there is concern about a child's development, the state seeks to intervene early to offer support or more authoritative intervention if this is required. With a child-focused orientation, the state takes on a growing role for itself in terms of providing a wide range of early intervention and preventive services. The child-focused orientation often involves arrangements which are adjusted to meet children's needs, competencies and maturity by taking into account the views and wishes of the child.

While this emerging orientation can be seen to borrow elements from both the child protection and family service orientations, Gilbert *et al.* (2011b) suggest that it has a rather different character, which is shaped by two major and somewhat contrasting lines of influence. On the one hand it has been influenced by ideas, related to 'the social investment state', and on the other hand, it has been influenced by a growing priority allotted to the importance of processes of 'individualisation' as these apply to children and emphasises children's rights. However, these two lines of influence do not sit easily together and can lead to tensions, which signifies that the child-focused orientation can take different forms in different countries.

The idea of 'social investment' emerged in the 1990s as an ideal promoted by the Organisation for Economic Co-operation and Development (OECD) and the European Union (EU), among others. According to this view, investment in children takes on a strategic significance for a state keen to equip its citizens to respond and adapt to global economic change in order to enhance individual and national competitiveness. In this respect trying to ensure that all children maximise their developmental opportunities, educational attainment and overall health and well-being becomes a key priority for social and economic policy. This is a future-oriented approach, which considers childhood as a preparation for adulthood, so that investment in children in the present is designed to ensure that they will later develop into productive and law abiding adults. The state takes on this new and pre-emptive role primarily because the challenges are now seen as so great that 'the family' is no longer seen as adequate, on its own, for carrying out the tasks expected of it.

In contrast is the rationale for policies and practices that perceive children as individuals in the here and now, perceiving them as different but equally as valuable as adults. These policies are concerned with the quality of children's childhood, stating that it is a social justice issue to make sure that children are treated with respect and given a loving upbringing. This is the state aiming to promote a happy and caring childhood, securing children the same rights granted to others, and aiming to give children in the child welfare system the same opportunities as other children in society. Children are not seen so much as future workers, but as current citizens. This perspective reflected the fact that all the countries studied, with the exception of the US, had ratified the 1989 UN Convention of Children's Rights (CRC) and had made various attempts to apply it in legislation, policy and practice.

Overall, the *child-focused orientation* puts children's rights above parents' rights and emphasises parental obligations and responsibilities as carers. The child welfare systems provide services to promote children's needs and well-being, often with and via the parents and carers, but in return demands change and 'outcomes' for the child.

Gilbert *et al.* (2011b) have summarised the key elements of the three orientations as shown in Table 3.3.

They do not suggest that they form three distinct models – hence the preference for the term 'orientation'. The orientations can be seen to range along a continuum from a more laissez-faire neo-liberal approach which emphasises the night-watchman functions of government to the more social democratic approach which advances policies much more associated with defamilialisation. However, while some countries might emphasise one of the orientations more than the others, all of the countries studied contained elements of each. This suggests that rather than locate a country somewhere along the line of a continuum from child focus to family service to child protection, we might think of where a country sits within a three dimensional framework – closer to some planes than others. Gilbert *et al.* (2011b) also noted the volatile character of child protection, particularly in some countries where cases could receive huge and vociferous media and public debate. As a result, at any one time, a particular line of development towards a particular orientation might be interrupted or redirected altogether.

TABLE 3.3 ROLE OF THE STATE VIS-À-VIS CHILD AND FAMILY IN ORIENTATIONS TO CHILD MALTREATMENT: CHILD FOCUS, FAMILY SERVICE AND CHILD PROTECTION

	Child focus	Family service	Child protection
Driver for intervention	the individual child's needs in a present and future perspective/ societies need healthy and contributing citizens	the family unit needs assistance	parents being neglectful towards children (maltreatment)
Role of the state	paternalistic/ defamilialisation – state assumes parent role, but seeks to refamilialise child by foster home/kinship/ adoption	parental support – state seeks to strengthen family relations	sanctioning – state functions as 'night-watchman' to ensure child's safety
Problem frame	child's development and unequal outcomes for children	social/ psychological (family systems, poverty, inequality)	individual/ moralistic
Mode of intervention	early intervention and regulatory/need assessment	therapeutic/ needs assessment	legalistic/ investigative
Aim of intervention	promote well-being via social investment and/or equal opportunity	prevention/social bonding	protection/harm reduction
State–parent relationship	substitutive/ partnership	partnership	adversarial
Balance of rights	children's rights/ parental responsibility	parents' rights to family life mediated by professional social workers	children's/ parents' rights enforced with legal means

Source: Gilbert *et al.* 2011b

3.5 CONCLUSION

As part of our quest to understand the unfolding story of child protection across the UK, we stepped back from our own system to consider where it sits in relation to other systems world-wide. We reviewed international comparative research in this area conducted over the past 15 years. We highlighted that these studies emerged from a growing perception in the 1990s that systems in the countries of the US, the UK and Australia which all took similar approaches to the protection of children had become at best out of kilter and at worst were in 'crisis'. The growth in comparative studies was an explicit attempt to examine whether or not other systems were faring better and to learn from these systems to better enhance the protection of children in the UK.

Across these studies, two broad types of system were identified. The more investigative, narrowly procedurally focused systems of North America, the UK and Australia; and on the other hand, the systems of the Nordic countries and Continental Europe with their broader focus on family support, attempting to address child protection in the context of wider family services and support.

The studies identified that in the 1990s the Anglophone countries' systems seemed to be displaying the twin problems of over-identification of children at risk, and under-identification.

Information from these studies also highlighted that this 'crisis' in the systems of the Anglophone countries was not necessarily being replicated in other countries with other types of systems. Some studies identified that where the UK system seemed to be characterised by low morale and pessimism; in other countries there was optimism and trust, and public confidence in the system was high.

Since the 1990s, there has been further work to update our understanding of how child protection systems across the world have developed. Gilbert *et al.* (2011b) have suggested that while the two orientations still stand, the different systems seem to be moving closer towards each other. This is due in part to globalisation and to 'policy transfer'. Thus, those countries with a family support orientation seem to be taking more notice of the complexities of child sexual abuse and family violence; and the countries with a narrower child protection focus have moved in the direction of placing more emphasis on early intervention, prevention and family support.

In addition, Gilbert *et al.* (2011b) have identified a third orientation – 'the child focussed orientation'. Here all of the systems studied had developed in ways where children themselves, rather than families, were becoming the main focus of state intervention. The authors concluded that countries may no longer lie on a continuum line between a child protection orientation and a family service orientation; rather, they might now be better characterised as lying somewhere on a three dimensional framework, closer to some planes than others.

Stafford, Vincent and Parton (2010) have argued that in 2002, while the Scottish system with its welfare-based Children's Hearing System was more hybrid, all the systems in the UK could be seen to sit firmly within the child protection orientation. During the 2000s it seems that all of the countries of the UK began to develop in ways which were closer to the systems of Continental and northern Europe (Stafford and Vincent 2008). However, as we shall see, when we look at the changes in each particular nation, the picture is more complex and there have been considerable efforts to develop in ways which are very consistent with the *child focused orientation*. As we look in later chapters at the detail of how the story of child protection across the UK has unfolded, we will see that such changes have not been linear or smooth, rather, the process has been disrupted in the context of high profile child abuse scandals, the economic downturn and changes in national governments and the policy making process itself.

Chapter 4

Learning by Comparing
Some Conceptual and Methodological Issues in Conducting Comparative Research

4.1 INTRODUCTION

As we move away from our international comparison, and before we begin our detailed analysis of child protection systems across the UK, in this chapter we set out some of the conceptual and methodological challenges of conducting this kind of work. We begin by discussing the interest of the University of Edinburgh/NSPCC Centre for UK-wide Learning in Child Protection (the Centre) in describing and understanding developments in child protection across the UK, and why we think this is important. We have identified how at the heart of the book and of the Centre's work are the twin concepts of 'comparing' and 'learning'; and the belief that making comparison between one thing and another is an important way of learning.

A major reason for the establishment of the Centre was a recognition that one consequence of the process of devolution, formally introduced in 1999, was that we could begin to identify a number of differences as well as similarities in the nature and operation of child protection systems in the four nations of the United Kingdom. More particularly, not only do such developments have implications for policy and practice, but, as the title of the Centre makes explicit, they also open up new opportunities for learning. At the core of this book and at the core of our work is the assumption that making comparisons between one thing and another is an important way of learning and that therefore comparing child protection systems across the UK nations will increase our understanding and thereby open up new possibilities for acting and thinking in the future.

However, what do we mean by comparison and what do we mean by learning? What might the relationships be between comparing and learning? What sorts of approaches have been developed for comparing welfare services in different countries and contexts? How have these been developed and applied in the more specific areas of child welfare and child protection? What are some of the more specific characteristics of the process of devolution which we need to take into account in order to compare child protection systems in the UK? These are the central questions we will address in this chapter.

The chapter consists of five sections. First, we consider what we mean by comparison and why and how this has been considered in relation to public policy. Second, we consider the idea of learning, particularly in the context of public policy. We will demonstrate how the processes of comparing and learning are intimately interrelated. Third, we will outline a discussion by Rachael Hetherington (2006a) of learning from her consideration of differences in a range of child welfare systems that she has studied. Fourth, we discuss a different methodological approach to comparing social policies. Finally, we consider the issue of comparison in the more specific and unique context of devolution across the UK, and the implications and significance this might have for locating such work in the wider comparative child welfare literature derived from comparing nation states.

4.2 COMPARISON AND PUBLIC POLICY

In considering what is meant by comparison, Richard Freeman (2008) draws attention to the work of the nineteenth-century philosopher and psychologist James Sully, who defined comparison as:

> that act of the mind by which it concentrates attention on two mental contents in such a way as to ascertain their relation of similarity or dissimilarity. By a mental content is meant either a presentation or a representation. (Sully 1885, p.490, quoted in Freeman 2008, p.505)

Freeman suggests that such a definition has a number of implications. First, it emphasises that comparison is a *volitional* process, in which the mind actively relates to and makes sense of at least two objects. Second, it suggests that our assessments of similarity and difference are informed by what we take to be normal, and difference is very much related to how far we estimate its relationship to some customary standard, which is collectively determined. Third, in defining 'a mental content' in terms of 'either a presentation or a representation', Scully argues that comparison takes place not between things themselves, but between impressions and appreciations of them, mediated by the way they are presented to us. From this Freeman develops his own definition of comparison as:

> an active process, socially shaped and informed, which constructs relationships of similarity and difference between things, or more precisely representations of things. It is more active than assimilative, it is more than interpretation, and might be better described as translation. For it takes place somewhere between two objects, themselves less than fully defined. It is an unstable, mediating process, in which objects become defined in relation to each other, in that process of being compared. In this sense, comparison is generative rather than reflective, a mode of production as much as of regulation. (Freeman 2008, p.505)

In this sense we are all engaged in a variety of comparisons as part of our day-to-day life, and the processes of comparison make up a key element of what it is to be human. Processes of comparison are central to making decisions and judgements in nearly all areas of social life. In this respect carrying out comparisons, far from being a distant, abstract, rational, analytic process, is embedded in all areas of policy making and day-to-day professional practice. Policy makers and practitioners are continually required to engage in a series of comparisons of a contingent and restricted range of alternatives, in order to make decisions and 'get the work done' (Lindblom 1959). Processes of comparison are therefore everyday, ordinary and often quite mundane; they are taken for granted and often go unnoticed. Making comparisons is a central element to wherever decisions and judgements are needed.

However, the last 40 years have witnessed an enormous growth in interest in developing much more formalised systems for comparison in all areas of public policy and social welfare, such that they have come to characterise and shape the services and professionals they have come to represent. In particular, the systems of audit (Power 1997) and performance management (Newman 2001) are heavily reliant on the construction of league tables and other targets and tools which look to improve quality by comparing outcomes of different agencies such as schools, hospitals and, increasingly, children's services (Tilbury 2004). Comparing organisations and agencies by various formal means of performance assessment has become one of the principal mechanisms of governance in most areas of public policy in the UK and elsewhere in the twenty-first century.

More generally the period has also witnessed a growing interest amongst academic researchers in carrying out cross-national comparisons of a wide range of health and welfare services (for example Esping-Anderson 1990, 1999) and amongst a number of high profile international agencies. In relation to child welfare and child protection, both the Organisation for Economic Co-operation and Development (OECD) and the United Nations Children's Fund (UNICEF) have produced important cross-national comparisons (Bradshaw, Hoelscher and Richardson 2007; UNICEF 2003, 2007).

Essentially there are seen to be two prime purposes for carrying out such cross-national studies. The first is primarily *evaluative*; that is to consider by comparing different approaches, what kinds of services, systems and policies seem the most effective in meeting certain specified needs or addressing particular problems. The second purpose is primarily *explanatory*. Here the focus is trying to work out why different services, systems and policies – and the social, economic and political structures and processes in which they are located – appear to work in the way that they do.

More particularly it is claimed that *policy analysis* is improved by comparative cross-national research in three ways (Klein and Marmor 2007). One is to help define more clearly what is on the policy agenda in any one country by reference to quite similar or quite different formulations elsewhere. The more similar the problems or policy responses, the more likely one can portray the particular formulations in any one country. The more dissimilar, the more striking the contrast with what one might 'take for granted' in the policy response in any one country. In the process we are provided with perspectives which may help provide explanatory insight and an ability to draw out lessons and implications.

Second, cross-national enquiry can be drawn upon to consider the adequacy of nation-specific accounts. Such approaches provide something of a defence against 'explanatory provincialism'. For example, in order to consider how decisive (as opposed to simply present) a feature or characteristic is in explaining a particular development or outcome, it is helpful to look at other countries where similar developments or outcomes are evident but where there is no evidence of a similarly decisive feature or characteristic – or look for a country where there is a similar configuration of features or characteristics but no comparable outcomes or developments.

Third, comparing cross-national experiences can also be used in a quasi-experimental way to test out what sorts of policies and practices have been tried in other places and with what success, and trying to identify some of the organisational elements and contextual factors that have contributed to that success (or not).

However, we should not underestimate the challenges in carrying out such work. For even identifying comparable problems which require attention, let alone identifying the policies and practices which have been developed to respond to them, is rarely straightforward. For example, a recent study which attempted to compare child protection systems in ten western European and North American countries (Gilbert *et al.* 2011a) found that there was considerable variation in the definition and understanding of the terms 'child protection' and 'child abuse and neglect' in the different countries. The same words often did not mean the same things, while different words may denote similar phenomena.

We have argued that the two key elements, which are claimed for the importance of comparison in the context of research based policy analysis, are its contribution to aiding both evaluation and explanation. However, as Richard Freeman argues (2009) there is a third function to comparison; one that may come prior to both of them and which, formally, receives very little attention:

> Because it seems more ordinary, more ubiquitous, it often passes unnoticed. *This is comparison as a form of explanation, of self as much as others.* Researchers figure out who they are and what they do by reference to others, by association with them, and in distinction from them. (Freeman 2009, p.207, emphasis added)

He refers to the medical sociologist Philip Strong's discussion in *The Ceremonial Order of the Clinic* (2001) where he describes that it was only when he observed clinical encounters in the United States that he understood how those in the UK 'really worked'. Similarly one of us (Nigel Parton) vividly remembers that it was when he visited a number of offices in the Western Australian state child welfare department in the mid 1990s that he felt he began to understand the nature and implications of the debate which was then going on in England about attempts to 'refocus' the balance between child protection and family support (Parton 1997; Parton *et al.* 1997).

Such processes of exploration by comparison, of course, do not apply only to researchers, they apply to all of us. In the context of public policy they apply to any policy maker, politician or practitioner who finds themselves in a 'new' comparable context. Working comparatively opens up a whole variety of possibilities and requirements for exploration, reflection and seeing the world.

The main claim for the importance of carrying out cross-national comparisons, then, is that they offer new perspectives on problems and often require 'factual' adjustments to national descriptions and explanations. However, perhaps the most important, but often very implicit, contribution of making comparisons is that it provides a key element to learning. Much of our learning both over time and between places turns on comparison. There is an intimate relationship between comparison and learning and, increasingly, making cross-national comparisons is an important part of this, particularly in terms of policy analysis and policy development. Before looking more specifically at approaches to comparative policy analysis, it is important, therefore, to think about what we mean by learning.

4.3 LEARNING AND PUBLIC POLICY

In another article about how policy makers and practitioners make sense of learning and 'come to know what they know', Richard Freeman (2007) argues that while learning is now deemed essential to both individual and institutional performance and is very much seen as a policy 'good', there is very little understanding of learning such that discussions rarely move beyond the rhetorical and usually rest on a series of implicit normative claims. Freeman draws on the work of Gregory Bateson (1972) who argues that learning denotes *change* of some kind and distinguishes *successive orders of such change.*

The first – Learning Zero – occurs when a given stimulus evokes the same given response on each occasion – a pattern which Bateson suggests should not be classified as learning at all. The simplest learning – Learning I – is evident when an organism begins to select between different responses to a given stimulus, on the basis of trial and error. It is a kind of learning from experience whereby conclusions about previous actions are incorporated in future ones. Learning II refers to the selection of a different category or set of responses and indicates a degree of 'learning about learning', so that we increasingly understand the potential of learning and can draw on this to change our actions and ways of thinking.

Freeman suggests that the logic of Bateson's argument is that we can identify a Learning III which would indicate a degree of reflexivity about learning itself, and entails the organism learning to learn differently or 'learning about learning to learn'. It thus becomes important to reflect on the different processes and circumstances in which learning takes place and the ways that these are understood. It involves learning about theories of learning in order that the 'capacity for reflexivity' (Freeman 2007, p.478) in public policy making and professional practice can be enhanced.

In order to consider how Learning III might be further advanced in relation to learning in the field of public policy, Freeman outlines three broad approaches to learning in the policy-relevant field. These reflect the dominant analytic perspectives in contemporary social and political sciences more generally.

The first is *rationalist* and assumes that the relationship between a problem and policy may be formulated in terms of an explicit theory of cause and effect which will then be applicable to other similar instances of the problem. It privileges traditional scientific method over other ways of knowing, and is predicated on the assumption of the existence of universal reason. The approach tends to hold in conditions of relative stability, in which there is time for policy problems and goals to be well specified for research and evaluation to take place, and for solutions and interventions to be formulated. According to this approach, learning appears to be a process of establishing fact and disseminating information. The corollary is that failure can be attributed to a lack of information and/or the vagaries of implementation. It is very much the dominant approach to learning. However, it is interesting that though studies *for* learning are often conducted in this way, it is rarely reflected in studies *of* learning in practice. It seems that 'what is being achieved by spreading lessons is not very well understood by those involved in the processes of dissemination' (Wolman and Page 2002, p.498).

The second conception of learning identified by Freeman is *institutional* in approach and focuses primarily on the organisational structures, processes and cultures in which learning takes place. Here it is assumed that the nature and success of learning depends on the appropriateness to the institutional context and entails a process of adaptation of the new information and experiences to the local circumstances. Learning tends to be incremental and evolutionary. At the same time it is likely to fail or become very difficult to implement if the institutions and organisations have become too rigid and unable to change.

The third conception of learning discussed by Freeman is *constructionist*. It holds that problems and solutions are what we conceive and agree them to be and which we try to put into practice. Learning therefore becomes a collective and interactive *process*. The approach is concerned with trying to establish what people and organisations 'know what they know', how they come to know it and how this changes over time.

Where the rationalist assumes that knowledge and practice are quite separate, for the constructionist knowledge comes through practice. Here practice is not just concerned with what 'front-line' practitioners do and think but includes people across the organisation including managers, policy makers and researchers themselves. It assumes conditions of low stability, or rather assumes that stability is a function of the reproduction of consensus which is itself the result of a kind of learning. In this sense stability is *achieved*. Learning here can be seen to have failed where consensus cannot be achieved or where it is achieved uncritically. The approach requires high levels of reflexivity and can be seen to be very much related to Learning III which we discussed earlier.

While learning is often seen as important in contexts of uncertainty about what to do and the best ways of proceeding, the process of learning can itself lead to uncertainty. For if learning implies self-consciousness, learning about learning implies a changed understanding of self, an awareness of the contingency and mutability of what we know and what we are doing and also of who we are. The process and experience of learning can be as disorientating as it is potentially creative. As Freeman suggests, 'uncertainty can be either destructive or creative and generative' (2007, p.492). As anyone who has been involved in the teaching of mature and experienced students knows, it is common for them to say 'I no longer know what I thought I knew!'

What is important for our purposes is that in many ways learning can be seen to turn on comparison. As we saw in the previous section, the case for comparison in public policy rests primarily upon its ability to be a source of explanation as to why things happen in one place but not in others, and why they happen in different ways. In addition, it is claimed that comparison can serve as a means of evaluation – a way of judging policy and asking how it might be improved. However, in practice the lessons from comparative work are often difficult to draw and difficult to apply. The contexts in which policy is made, implemented and operationalised are complex, so that the relationship between policy cause and outcome is often unclear. Thus what we can learn from comparison is often far from straightforward.

However, much learning from comparison in public policy is derived from a rather different order of comparison. The learning is derived as much (if not more) from the *process* of comparison as it is from what is found out:

> For comparison is predicated on description and redescription, cognition and recognition, categorisation and classification, and understanding its implications is necessarily an *interpretive process*. To compare something with something else entails the logically prior recognition or assumption that they are comparable. It is to use the juxtaposition of things to make sense of them, both separately and together. (Freeman 2006, p.384, emphasis added)

Comparison entails the use and production of categories to describe different situations, something which we usually do in a 'taken for granted' way and rarely more than half consciously. It is for just this reason that carrying out cross-national comparison can be such a helpful vehicle for learning. It requires a more creative, slightly more abstract grammar and vocabulary than we might use when describing and discussing things we are familiar with. 'Comparison is realised in what might be described as a "third code", or a language of translation' (Freeman 2006, p.385). It requires us to make explicit what previously may have been taken for granted and described in often quite new ways so that it can be compared with something else. New and different words may need to be drawn on so that such a process of translation can take place. It is for just this reason that comparison can be so difficult and disorientating but also so creative and learning rich.

4.4 LEARNING FROM DIFFERENCE: COMPARING CHILD WELFARE AND CHILD PROTECTION SYSTEMS

These issues are well illustrated in the reflections of Rachael Hetherington, who has been involved in the comparison of child welfare and child protection systems for many years and has been involved in a number of studies (Cooper *et al.* 1995; Hetherington 1996; Hetherington *et al.* 2002; Hetherington *et al.* 1997; Hetherington and Piquardt 2001; Katz and Hetherington 2006). In the process she has reflected on a number of important methodological and conceptual issues, including the nature of learning that can be derived from comparative child welfare and protection research (Hetherington 2006).

She recognises that 'learning from difference is a complex process' (Hetherington 2006, p.27) but argues that the 'aim of using comparison and learning from difference is to identify possible improvements in child welfare systems' (p.32). Thus she sees the value primarily in normative and evaluative terms. Her discussion of how she sees the process of learning from difference very much follows some of the ideas we have outlined earlier. She argues that three elements are involved in the process of learning from difference in comparative research: description, comparison, and reflection.

First, in relation to *description* she suggests that the function of a child welfare system can be categorised under three headings: structures, professional ideology, and culture. While describing a child welfare system may start with an account of the formal structures it also needs to try and describe how it works on a day-to-day basis. This involves a complex interaction between various structures including the important element of resources. The professional ideology of the workers in terms of the theories, concepts and values of the professionals and the day-to-day technologies that they use very much influence how the structures are employed and used in practice. At the same time, the overall culture in which the system is located plays a key role in the way the system operates and the way it is experienced by the children, young people and adults – including parents and professionals – involved.

By culture she means the nexus of views, understandings, habits of mind, patterns of living, and use of language that are built up in a community, nation, or state by the shared history, experiences and social circumstances in which people live. The culture of a society is pervasive.

She was involved in comparing child welfare and protection systems in England with a number of countries in western and northern Europe and it became clear to her that differences between systems could not be explained by the structures of the systems or the professional ideology of the workers alone. The different cultures of both the systems and the social and political contexts in which they were located were key:

> Although culture, structures, and professional ideology all interact to shape the functioning of child welfare systems, their effects are not necessarily equally powerful. There is some evidence from the comparative studies that culture may be the most powerful factor (Hetherington 2006, p.43).

She argues that such a conclusion was thoroughly consistent with the policy analysis carried out by Neil Gilbert and his colleagues (Gilbert 1997) who also argued that the overall culture and values of a system may be the most powerful factor in determining the overall functioning of child welfare systems and the main differences.

Second, Hetherington emphasises a point that we have already made that a central problem in making *comparisons* is the difficulty of establishing whether two things that might appear the same are really the same, and whether two things that appear different are really different. There are problems of definition so that, for example, statistics may be compiled using quite different criteria. This is something which we always have to be sensitive to and connects with the third element which she sees as being key in the process of learning from comparative research – the importance of *reflection*.

She argues that such learning develops from self-questioning and requires the ability to be both reflective and critical. It is important to question and interrogate the material in such a way that we – as researcher, policy maker or practitioner – make our assumptions transparent so that they can be subject to change. Such an approach to learning from difference is very similar to the points made by Freeman which we discussed earlier.

4.5 COMPARATIVE SOCIAL POLICY: DIFFERING METHODOLOGICAL APPROACHES

The last 20 years have witnessed an enormous growth in research comparing different countries' child welfare (Cameron *et al.* 2007; Freymond and Cameron 2006; Khoo, Hyvönen and Nygren 2002; Pringle 1998; Thoburn 2007), child protection (Gilbert 1997; Gilbert *et al.* 2011a; Harder and Pringle 1997; Hill *et al.* 2002; May-Chahal and Herczog 2003) and family support (Canavan, Dolan and Pinkerton 2000; Hellinckx, Colton and Williams 1997; Katz and Pinkerton 2003; Miller and Warman 1996) systems and services.

This has arisen in part because of the growing interest in comparative studies in social and public policy more generally, to the point where it has become a sub-field of study in its own right (see, for example, Arts and Gelissen 2002; Clasen 1999; Jordan 2006; Kennett 2001; Yeates 2008) with a number of academic journals dedicated to the topic and where one author has claimed that 'the main tool for measurement in social policy and social welfare analysis is the comparative method' (Aspalter 2006, p.4).

A number of factors have fed into this growth in interest. Not least has been the growth of accessibility of communication, particularly by air travel and increasingly sophisticated systems of information communication technology (ICT). It also became evident from the mid

1970s that welfare systems were needing to find new ways of managing and responding to increased demand and need in a context of finite resources. But also, in a globalised world, relations between countries were becoming increasingly competitive so that it was important to try and improve social policies in order to try and get ahead economically. Essentially, global trends were creating both the requirements and the opportunities for international comparison and learning.

The situation in child protection and child welfare was no exception. Increasingly national systems were being found wanting (see Chapter 3 for a discussion), so that politicians, policy makers and researchers began to look elsewhere for ideas for reform and improvement.

While there are numerous studies which have been concerned with analysing and comparing the nature and development of different 'welfare regimes' (see Arts and Gelissen 2002 for a helpful overview), the majority are concerned with analysing particular services, or areas of policy such as social security, health or education, and many such studies try to identify measures and indicators that can be analysed across countries. Statistical data from large data sets are usually considered the most desirable. There are now a number of studies which have attempted to compare different societies' relative performance in relation to investing in policies for children (for example Gabel and Kamerman 2006) and in relation to the outcomes for the well-being of children (Bradshaw *et al.* 2007; UNICEF 2007) and which usually rely upon data from the OECD.

However, it is extremely difficult to obtain cross-national indicators or proxy outcome measures in relation to child protection because of the big differences in data definition, collection and reporting in different jurisdictions and we discuss this later in Chapter 6. Not only is such reliable data hard to find, there is also a limit to how much it can actually tell us. For comparative research requires detailed historical, legal and institutional knowledge about the countries being studied, together with an understanding of the interactions between the political systems, economic structures and wider social policies for the data to be understood. It is often argued that comparing different countries therefore cannot rely on quantitative data from large data sets alone (Mabbett and Bolderson 1999).

A cross-country case study approach where the researcher immerses themselves in each case, allowing issues and themes to emerge, is seen as more useful in generating rich data. A case study approach does not impose a standardised framework whereby only pre-selected items of data are accepted for inclusion in the analysis. It adopts a systematic but 'open' approach to gathering comparative material and encourages the researcher to tell a country-specific but complex 'story'. Data is often documentary and conversational in nature being derived from archives, site visits and face-to-face interviews, as well as a variety of official statistics and grey literature. The approach therefore generates some original material as well as relying on already existing information.

However, it can be difficult to obtain public documents and other forms of literature. As we have found in our own research, there is far more official and academic literature available in relation to England than for Scotland, Wales and Northern Ireland. In addition, it is important to remember that many documents are concerned with prescribed policy and practice, rather than actual policy and practice.

4.6 THE COMPARATIVE AND 'TRANSNATIONAL TWIST': THE MOVES TOWARDS DEVOLUTION

Most comparative social policy research has been concerned with comparing nation states because, as John Clarke (2005) has argued, social policy has traditionally understood and analysed welfare states as national phenomena. However, globalisation, regionalisation and Europeanisation are increasingly generating new types of multi-level governance and thereby disrupting the assumptions of a close fit between 'welfare states' and 'nation-states'. Rodriguez-Pose and Gill (2003) have argued, 'globalisation has been accompanied by an equally global tendency towards the devolution of authority and resources from nation-states to regions and localities' (p.333). While global processes can be seen to have changed the importance of the nation-state as the key unit and power-broker in economic and social policy, globalisation also seems to have had the effect of promoting a greater relevance to place, space and the transfer of power downwards to regions. This process, which involves the creation of new political entities and bodies at a subnational level and an increase in their content and power, is known as 'devolution' (Prud'homme 1995).

In trying to understand child protection across the UK, comparing similarities and differences in child protection in each of the constituent parts of the UK, we argue that understanding the process of devolution is key to understanding recent developments in child protection in the devolved parts of the UK. We set this out here as an important back-drop to our detailed comparative analysis of systems across the UK.

We begin by setting out the asymmetrical settlements that exist in the devolved parts of the UK, then move on to consider the role of England in devolution and reflect on the impact of devolution on policy in particular and child protection in general.

We look at the impact devolution has had in shaping policy across the UK arguing that it is impossible to understand developments in child protection across the UK without some insight into the process of devolution and its role in shaping and driving child protection. We examine in detail how policy change in the context of devolution is partly driven by political aims and objectives, introduced in part to demonstrate difference, to delineate one part of the UK from another, and to assert distinct national identities. While this is true for policy in general, it holds true for child protection as well.

Real policy difference in this context, we argue, can be tricky to unpick and in the case of devolution is partly a task of decoupling policy from its rhetoric. This is not simple. It justifies our case study approach which tries to understand policy change from a number of angles and to gain as deep an understanding as possible.

Devolution is a complex and diverse process and has itself taken on a variety of forms in different countries. Conceptualising and defining devolution is therefore far from straightforward. Donahue (1997) has characterised the process as being made up of three separate factors: legitimacy; the decentralisation of resources; and the decentralisation of authority. Any form of devolution implies some degree of subnational legitimacy and some form of decentralisation of authority and resources; consequently, any analysis of devolution needs, Donahue argues, to take these three factors into account when analysing the different types of devolution and the processes involved.

Until the late 1990s the UK could be seen to combine a political symmetry combined with administrative asymmetry. For while there was a highly centralised, but variable, *political system* there was an asymmetrical *territorial administration*, with the three territorial offices in Edinburgh, Cardiff and Belfast having distinctive and somewhat different administrative relations with London. In addition, there was a centralised and symmetrical *fiscal* system run by the Treasury in London.

Clearly it is not appropriate to assume that the history, structures and functions of nation states are the same. McEwen and Moreno (2005) have developed a typology of five national and constitutional structures in which welfare provision has taken shape. The examples in Table 4.1 are discussed in some detail in the different chapters in their book.

TABLE 4.1 A TYPOLOGY OF NATIONAL AND STATE STRUCTURES

	Union state	Unitary state	Decentralised/ federal state
Uni-national state		Denmark Finland France Norway Sweden	Germany (post-1949)
Pluri-national state	Spain (dated 1485) UK (dated 1707)	Belgium (1831) Italy (1870)	Canada Belgium (post-1994) Italy (post-1948) Spain (post-1978) UK (post-1999)

Source: Derived from McEwen and Moreno 2005, p.13

In *pluri-national states with union states*, state-wide institutions, parties, and policy networks often represent forces of integration which can contain territorial distinctiveness and ensure that its expression is channelled in apolitical ways. McEwen and Moreno suggest that the UK has been a good example of this. While politically centralised for much of its history, its pluri-national character has long been recognised in the institutions of civil society and public administration, which have included the Scottish and Welsh Offices, the Church and, in Scotland, the legal and educational systems. Distinctive national identities have also found expression in a range of cultural and sporting activities including separate football, rugby and other sporting teams (Brand 1978).

However, *pluri-national states with a decentralised structure* are characterised by a much more explicit division of sovereignty between different levels of the state. Where territorial units coincide with sub-state national, linguistic and cultural boundaries, their political significance is likely to be reinforced. Anthony Smith has argued that in multi-ethnic federations, where provincial and 'ethnic' boundaries coincide:

> The politics of nationalism is rarely far removed from the arena of federal politics, feeding into a set of grievances which in one form or another have the potential to mobilise individuals behind calls for the territorial redistribution of power, including independence. (Smith 1995, p.10)

Such developments have become increasingly evident in a number of countries, including Belgium, Italy and Spain – all of which have become decentralised/federal states in recent years.

The UK was the last of the large European states to adopt a programme of political decentralisation/devolution (Loughlin 2004, 2007). However, as we will discuss later, the period since 1999 has witnessed a period of potentially increased asymmetrical diversity in both the political and administrative frameworks and, to a much lesser extent, the fiscal areas. While there was always some difference between the four home nations, the twentieth-century welfare state encouraged uniformity and standardisation across the UK. Since the period of formal devolution began there is now a much greater potential increase to diversity. Thus while there has always been a degree of administrative diversity the establishment of the devolved elected assemblies/governments in Scotland, Wales and Northern Ireland has also increased the potential for a much greater political asymmetry.

What is important about these developments, for our purposes, is that debates and methodological approaches which have traditionally been associated with comparative analyses of nation states can be productively developed and applied at the level of devolved nations. The focus becomes the differences and tensions arising from devolved welfare services and governance, but in the context of a particular welfare state – the UK.

a. Comparing policy in a devolved UK: Nation-building and welfare

For some years the social policy literature has recognised the important role that welfare states have played in generating social solidarity across social, class and ethnic groups and contributing to the political legitimacy of the state amongst its citizens (Pierson 1994). Since the nineteenth-century systems of state welfare have played a significant role in shaping national identities and maintaining national unity. Welfare states have made a key contribution to 'nation-building' (McEwen 2001). It is not by coincidence that Germany in the 1880s was the first country to introduce compulsory social insurance – the clearest characteristic of modern welfare systems – at a key point in the establishment of the new German nation state (Flora and Heidenheimer 1981).

In the UK in the late nineteenth and early twentieth century, the welfare framework was constructed with very clear ideas about nation and nationality (Lewis 1998). However, it was with the development of the post-1945 Beveridgean welfare state that the assumption of the importance of a fit between state, welfare and nation was enshrined (Williams 1989). In this sense the establishment of the post-war *British* welfare state represented a clear 'nation-building' project (Eley and Suny 1996). The National Insurance Act 1946 in establishing a system of *national* assistance, and the National Health Service in attending to the *nation's* health, both made a considerable contribution to building a 'nation fit for heroes' and creating a sense of national unity and belongingness. Such developments conveyed a powerful symbol of the nature and importance of Britishness, reinforced a sense of national identity, solidarity and belonging, and provided a central element of what was distinctive about UK 'social citizenship' (Greer 2009).

At the same time, it is important to remember that the post-war welfare state was never as universal as many traditional histories have assumed (see, for example, Fraser 1984). As we discussed earlier, the UK is best understood as a *pluri-national state with union states.* One consequence is that Britishness means different things in different parts of the UK. While in England there might have been a tendency to conflate British citizenship with nationality, this has been much less so in Scotland and Wales where British citizenship was often contrasted with the national identities of Scottishness and Welshness (McCrone 2002) and the complexities in Northern Ireland. As we have seen, Scotland, Northern Ireland and, to a lesser extent, Wales have experienced considerable autonomy throughout the post-war period in relation to a range of welfare services. For example, while the education system in Scotland is part of a national British system it has remained distinctive and has retained its own identity throughout the period.

Thus while welfare has played a key role in nation-building, the way this takes place is clearly subject to variation and depends, in part, on what is meant by 'nation'. As Mooney and Williams have argued 'nation-building is rarely a one-off event or process, but requires remaking in the face of shifting contexts, such as devolution' (Mooney and Williams 2006, pp.614–615).

The period since devolution in 1999 has witnessed the emergence of a range of scholarship and research which has begun to engage in comparative policy analysis comparing developments in the four nations (Greer 2009; McEwen and Parry 2005; Mooney, Scott and Williams 2006; Mooney and Williams 2006; Mooney and Wright 2009; Williams and Mooney 2008). The newly established devolved governments have, in particular, emphasised their distinctiveness and distance from

Westminster via a range of social policy measures not only related to education and health but also in relation to social care services for adults:

> In both Wales and Scotland there is a new form of welfare nationalism in the making which conveys understandings and assumptions about 'the people' and 'the nation', about inclusions and exclusions, belongings and, of course, normative values about 'order' and normal behaviour...it also carries and mobilizes particular discourses around inequalities, differences and social divisions such as class and ethnicity. (Mooney and Williams 2006, p.616)

It seems that the opportunity for putting a particular national stamp on social policy is greater than ever in the context of devolved government, thus opening up new opportunities for comparative policy analysis and learning. It seems that social policy provides a key vehicle for nation-building for the newly devolved governments/assemblies. It has been suggested that developments since 1999 mean that the UK may provide a 'natural laboratory' for examining the effects of divergent policies where the contextual differences are relatively small or even stable (Raffe and Byrne 2005).

Such a development is of particular interest in the context of our focus upon child protection and child welfare more generally. Policies in relation to children have played a central role in attempts at nation-building since the late nineteenth century. As Harry Hendrick (2003) has argued during the course of the last quarter of the nineteenth century, child welfare moved from a concern with the rescue, reclamation and reform of children, mainly through philanthropic and Poor Law action, to seeing children as central to the interests and future of the British nation and therefore a central focus for welfare state attention. It is not surprising therefore if the newly devolved governments/assemblies see the interests and futures of their nations particularly associated with policies for children. How this is interpreted and operationalised in relation to child protection in the 'four nations' is the focus of this section of the book and indeed, the book itself.

This section sets out to provide some context for the consideration of comparative analysis of child protection policy in post devolution UK. The intention is to consider the factors affecting the scope for divergence of policy and policy learning between jurisdictions under devolution arrangements in the UK. These include the powers formally devolved, informal processes, and the context in which they must operate.

Earlier in this book we argued that it was the dissonance between the globalised market requirement for a competitive state and a centralised nation state that contributed to the devolution of power from the centre. Devolution in the late 1990s was not uniform for Scotland, Wales and Northern Ireland and has changed over time (Trench 2007). The nature of the institutions and powers devolved to Scotland, Wales and Northern Ireland differ: devolution remains asymmetric and changing in the UK.

In Wales and Scotland, the push for Parliamentary devolution was as we have argued above, at the same time the expression of national identity. In Northern Ireland, by contrast, the clear purpose of devolution was to 'build a sustainable peace' (Jeffrey, Lodge and Schmueck 2010). More recent pressure for devolution was concerned with the situation during part of the 1980s and 1990s within the UK where a government of one political party was able to govern and implement policy in jurisdictions where there were few or no MPs returned. This 'democratic deficit' meant that policies had been imposed by an English Government that did not meet the needs of populations in Scotland and Wales. If government from London was seen to have brought policy that did not match the needs of those in Scotland and Wales, the presumption was that devolution would bring policy agendas and solutions for local problems; that devolved areas would be able to implement their own tailored policy solutions to their specific economic, social and cultural circumstances. Devolution opened up the possibility of divergence along the policy/practice spectrum (from the meso level to the micro level and beyond).

Devolution it was presumed would enable local agenda setting; and the possibility of being able to frame issues differently, or develop different policy solutions for identical problems, or alternative policy for the same problems (Keating 2005). The aspiration was that the devolved areas would implement their own tailored policy solutions, more in tune with their own particular economic, social and cultural circumstances (McGarvey and Cairney 2008).

There have been a number of policy divergences. These have been high profile and widely reported and have included, free personal care for the elderly in Scotland; the setting up of the Older People's Commissioner in Wales; fully integrated health and social care in Northern Ireland; and the removal of prescription charges in all three devolved territories. As a whole, health policy has 'put the four systems on different trajectories' (Greer 2010). However, in general, there has been less policy divergence from England than was envisaged (McGarvey and Cairney 2008).

In this next section, we set out some of the dynamics that impact on policy in the context of devolution – both those which have driven change and are driving divergence, and those which are a barrier to it. First we set out the formal powers devolved to Scotland, Wales and Northern Ireland; in essence, the levers for divergence and difference in policy.

4.7 DEVOLVED POWERS IN THE UK

a. The Scottish Parliament and Scottish Executive

In Scotland, the Scottish Parliament (the legislature) has the power to scrutinise and pass primary legislation and hold the Scottish Government (the Executive) to account. The Scottish Government is able to devise and implement policy; propose primary and secondary legislation and allocate finance to the areas for which it has responsibility. The Scotland Act 1998 set out the policy areas, termed Reserved Matters, that would remain the sole authority of the UK Parliament and Government. In Scotland, Reserved Matters fall into four main categories. There are those that are concerned with the UK as 'a state' such as the Constitution, foreign affairs and defence. Second are those concerned with 'social citizenship', where UK parity was deemed to be important, reserved matters here include social security, equal opportunities and data protection (Trench 2007). Third are specific Reserved Matters such as macro-economic management, the regulation of financial institutions and professionals, energy policy, and areas of Home Affairs such as national security and immigration. Finally, some matters, such as abortion, are believed to be too controversial to be devolved, and remain with Westminster (Trench 2007).

Those remaining, the Devolved Matters, are those where the Scottish Parliament can legislate. All matters not specified as reserved are devolved. These are the main areas of social policy, and public services structures: health, economic development, education and training, culture, local government, housing, social work, police and fire services, most aspects of criminal and civil law and criminal justice, environment, agriculture, forestry and fishing, sport and public transport particular to Scotland. Framing it this way, it was argued, gave Scotland control over the broadest range of matters within the terms of the devolution settlement.

b. The Northern Ireland Assembly and Executive

The powers and structures devolved to Northern Ireland arise from its history, and have had the specific aim of bringing sustainable peace. The powers of the Northern Ireland Assembly (NIA) and Executive are prescribed by the Northern Ireland Act 1998 and the Northern Ireland (St Andrews Agreement) Act 2006. There are three formal categories of powers: Transferred Matters, Excepted Matters and Reserved Matters. Transferred Matters are devolved to the NIA. As in Scotland they cover the bulk of social policy and public institutions: health, social services and public safety, education, social development, enterprise, trade and investment, environment, including local government, culture, arts and leisure, employment, higher and further education, regional development, agriculture and rural development, finance and personnel, policing and justice (Leeke, Sear and Gay 2003). Social Security, child benefit and pensions are transferred to the NIA but there is provision for consultation and co-ordination between Northern Ireland and Britain regarding systems and parity but this does not necessarily remain the case.

Excepted matters are those which remain with the UK Government and Parliament retains sole authority. These include international relations, the Crown, elections, national taxation, national security and defence. Reserved matters remain presently with the UK Parliament, for example telecommunications, with the intention they should be passed to the NIA Assembly (Trench 2007).

The Northern Ireland Assembly met in July 1998 and powers devolved from the UK in late 1999. Only recently, however, has there been a period of consistent operation by the NIA and Executive. Political crises brought various suspensions of the Assembly with the longest one being from 2002 to 2007 when direct rule, as pre-devolution, was re-imposed on Northern Ireland. Only in recent years have the possibilities for policy development in Northern Ireland had the opportunity to unfold.

c. The National Assembly for Wales and the Welsh Assembly Government

There has been significant changes to the powers formally devolved to Wales since 1998. Under the Government of Wales Act 1998, the National Assembly for Wales (NAfW) was established with powers to initiate and pass secondary legislation. This was succeeded by the Government of Wales Act 2006 where the NAfW was granted further powers to devise and agree Assembly Measures (these have the same effect as primary legislation) in 20 policy fields. The introduction of a measure in a new policy area required the agreement of Westminster and the NAfW on a case-by-case basis (National Assembly for Wales 2007). Further changes are due as a consequence of a referendum about further powers in 2011. This will give the NAfW powers to pass laws on any subject in the 20 areas devolved without reference to the UK. The devolved areas relevant to child protection are social welfare, local government, health and health services and education (National Assembly for Wales Members' Research Service January 2011). Criminal justice and policing is not devolved.

Scotland, Wales and Northern Ireland now have substantial powers of governance over policy. Divisions between devolved and non-devolved powers are not clear and neat, however, and in practice, devolved policy often impacts on reserved matters and vice versa. Actual powers are not uniform, and devolution in the UK is asymmetric. These legal and technical aspects of devolution are elements of a more complex web that impact on policy.

d. England and the UK Parliament

We would argue that it is impossible to understand devolution in the UK and how this impacts on child protection policy without an understanding of the unique position occupied by England. England is the single largest territory, with the majority of the population and is responsible for the highest proportion of gross domestic product (GDP) (Jeffrey 2006). It is also alone in the UK in that it is without its own institutions for national governance; Westminster and Whitehall operate as the government and Parliament of England and of the UK, 'with Westminster and Whitehall combining and often confusing the territorial scales of their responsibilities' (Jeffrey *et al.* 2010, p.29). Government departments function as England departments where their field is equivalent to devolved responsibility, for example in relation to education, health and local government. Or they operate as UK Departments – for example the Department for Work and Pensions, the Foreign Office and the Ministry of Defence. Finally, there are those, most notably the Home Office, where functions can relate to England, to England and Wales or to the UK as a whole. There are also instances where there is apparently no UK central government for policy fields, for example in education (Keating 2010). In other cases England functions as a centre and has a dominant policy role to which the devolved areas are required to react.

This asymmetry of the UK and the continued role England plays impacts in particular ways on the development of policy. England continues to dominate much of the policy making, because of the UK market, the welfare state and security, and, as Jeffrey (2006) has argued, 'it is inevitable that decisions taken for the biggest part of those single areas will have impacts on the smaller parts' (p.4). The asymmetric nature of the devolved powers also militates against strong links between devolved administrations; relations tend to be from London, to Edinburgh, Cardiff and Belfast (Trench 2007). Concerns prior to devolution that the UK Government would try to exert undue pressure on the devolved administrations have not happened to any great extent in practice. Formally the UK/English Government has accepted that it has had, and continues to have, a stake in making devolution work (Birrell 2009). England seems to be more in the process of 'disengaging from devolution' than 'interfering' (Keating, Cairney and Hepburn forthcoming).

e. Opportunities and pressure for policy divergence and convergence

These formal devolved powers provide opportunities for policy divergence in the devolved areas. Public finance through the block grant system offers the possibility of budgetary freedom within the total amount allocated (Jeffrey 2006). In practice this has been used for changing the entitlement to services such as the removal of prescription charges in Scotland, Wales and Northern Ireland (Birrell 2010). In reality redistributing large proportions of the budget is not possible. Health and local government continue to command more than three quarters of the total. Policy spillover, where initiatives in areas of the UK are sought or assumed by the public to be available in another have caused devolved bodies to adopt similar policies (Jeffrey *et al.* 2010). Here, a favourable policy or funding announcement in one area of the UK is presumed to be the case elsewhere. This has been the case with the increase in health expenditure for England (Keating *et al.* forthcoming). More recently, the English Government's commitment to maintaining NHS funding has been met by the Scottish Government. Partly because of its size, England is more able to set the policy agenda from London; with the small jurisdictions in no position to compete regularly with the gravitational pull of major policy generated from England. The mainly London based media also provides a route for proposed policy to be carried to devolved areas, rather than from the devolved areas to London.

Notwithstanding the devolved powers, the policy making process itself contains many opportunities for divergence; as well as constraints. With regard to the former, divergence is enabled by the relative weakness of inter-governmental links. It is also supported by the opening up of governmental institutions in the devolved areas to new influences (Keating 2005). The reality of government has constrained the ability to develop innovative policy. The 'sheer weight of current policy commitments' (Jeffrey *et al.* 2010, p.11) in devolved policy areas has absorbed time and resources leaving less opportunity for local policy development. Another consequence has been what has been termed the 'photocopy model' of policy making (Keating *et al.* forthcoming) with near duplicate legislation introduced in Scotland, Wales and Northern Ireland to that for England (Keating *et al.* 2003). This is exacerbated by the practicalities of the 'weak policy capacity of the devolved governments' (Keating *et al.* forthcoming) particularly in Wales and Northern Ireland emerging as they do from the centralised state. Wales is recognised as most subject to this and attempts to address it and build policy capacity have been, and continue to be, made. London continues to hold the majority of policy resources, within and surrounding government. Whether politically driven and/or resource enabled in reality it is England where there has been 'more territorial policy innovation than the three devolved administrations combined' (Jeffrey *et al.* 2010, p.29).

One of the arguments for divergence in policy prior to devolution had been different political views of the people in the devolved communities. Scotland and Wales were more supportive of state provision; England for a mixed economy. However, research on public opinion suggests the contrary is often the case and public attitudes cluster around the centre of the political spectrum (Curtice 2010). This is in part the case where there are similar social and economic problems across the UK and 'shared values and policy preferences' (Jeffrey *et al.* 2010, p.11); and this has not prevented the politicians, not solely ciphers of the majority of public opinion, from pursuing alternative directions in devolved matters. Keating (2009) provides an explanation:

> Individually the differences on public service provision are often small but they point in a consistent direction, towards more universalism, less privatisation, less competition and more collaboration among government, professions and citizens. (Keating 2009, p.112)

These forces for divergence have produced difference in policy. However, this has been a more stuttering process than expected.

4.8 CONCLUSION

In this chapter we have described the conceptual and methodological challenges facing us as we have conducted our intra-country comparative study. We have highlighted that conducting inter- or intra-country comparative research is fraught with difficulty; understanding how something in one country appears and is understood by someone from another country takes a breadth and depth of understanding. We outlined our methodological approach by using a comparative qualitative case study involving a range of approaches to understand and tell a country-specific 'story'. We have also argued that methodological approaches usually more associated with inter-country comparison can also be applied to intra-country comparison.

In this context we have argued that it is not possible to understand developments in child protection across the UK without some insight into the story of how devolution is unfolding. Child protection in the context of devolution is not politically neutral. Rather, it is partly driven by political aims, which in part demonstrates difference to delineate one part of the UK from another. 'Unpicking' real difference from rhetoric is complex and has justified our case-by-case methodological approach.

We highlighted that early aspirations for devolution were that it would bring divergence of policy and opportunities for the different parts of the UK to find distinct political solutions to local problems. As yet, this has been a slower process to develop than anticipated, and forces exist both for and against the development of divergent policy. The net result is more constraint than divergence. We also argued that lack of divergence is partly explained by the unique position occupied by England. Because of its size, it has the bulk of the policy making capacity; and the corollary of this, the current relatively weak policy capacity of the devolved countries as they move out from underneath the influence of Westminster. This means that there remains a stronger tendency in the devolved countries towards bi-lateral links with England, rather than between each other, and there is more policy borrowing from England than from the devolved countries. In future chapters we explain the ways these tendencies have played out in relation to change and development in child protection across the UK.

Part 2

Child Protection Processes and Structures

Having looked at UK Child Protection systems from the wide vantage point of systems across the world, and discussed some of the meso-level factors which have tended to drive change in the systems of the UK (including devolution and the media); it is time to apply our case study, intra-country comparative approach to the key aspects of child protection systems in each part of the UK. In this part of the book, we compare and contrast the main features that make up the child protection systems in the UK. Once again our purpose is to hold a mirror to each of the systems to better understand the one we are operating in, and to better understand the whole. Essentially, we present a snapshot of child protection systems across the UK at March 2011. The past ten years of child protection in the UK has been a time of fast-moving reform and unprecedented change: a snapshot is difficult to capture! As we try, we are also aware that major change also lies ahead in the form of the Munro Review of Child Protection in England. The scale of change likely to result is difficult to read from our current vantage point.

Chapter 5

Policies and Procedures to Protect Children across the UK

5.1 INTRODUCTION

In this chapter we examine the broad legislative and policy frameworks underpinning child protection systems across the UK. Each part of the UK has its own separate overarching framework document setting out its own vision of how children should be cared for and protected.

Services to safeguard and protect children are underpinned by complex systems of legislation, guidance, regulations and procedures. These systems are not the same in different parts of the UK. Each part of the UK has undergone considerable reform of policy to safeguard and protect children over the last decade; with some parts of the UK introducing new legislation, policy and structures, to better protect children, strengthen local co-operation and increase accountability (Vincent 2010b). This chapter provides an overview of policies and structures to safeguard and protect children across the UK, concentrating in particular on the recent period of reform. It compares and contrasts legislation, policy, guidance and structures in different parts of the UK and identifies common themes and differences.

5.2 OVERARCHING CHILDREN'S POLICY AND OUTCOMES FRAMEWORKS

At the time of writing, it is no longer possible to separate policy and practice to safeguard and protect children from the wider policy context surrounding child welfare. In each part of the UK, as we outlined earlier, recent reform of child protection policy and practice has taken place within reform of children's services as a whole. Child protection is now viewed in all parts of the UK within a wider context of meeting children's needs and supporting families. There have been substantial changes in children's services in the last decade, not just in terms of the way that they are organised and delivered, but also in terms of the philosophy underpinning them. Each area of the UK has a host of policies to safeguard and protect children and young people and promote their general well-being; each has its own overarching children's policy framework within which all of these various policies fit together as shown in Box 5.1 (Vincent 2010b).

BOX 5.1 OVERARCHING CHILDREN'S POLICY FRAMEWORKS

England
Every Child Matters: Change for Children programme (HM Government 2004)

Wales
Children and Young People: Rights to Action (Welsh Assembly Government 2004)

Northern Ireland
Children and Young People – Our Pledge: A Ten Year Strategy for Children and Young People (Office of the First Minister and Deputy First Minister 2006)

Scotland
Getting it Right for Every Child (Scottish Government 2008a).

Integrating all policy relating to children together into one overarching policy document is a relatively new phenomenon in the UK. England and Wales were the first areas of the UK to produce an integrated policy framework. *Every Child Matters (ECM)*, introduced in 2004, was a response to Lord Laming's report into the death of Victoria Climbié (Laming 2003) and to *Safeguarding Children: A Joint Chief Inspectors' Report on Arrangements to Safeguard Children* (Department of Health 2002) which had similar findings to the *Laming Report* (Frost and Parton 2009). It was a strategy for integrated children's services to improve outcomes for all children. The *ECM* vision was to bring about a 'shift to prevention whilst strengthening protection' (Department for Education and Skills 2004, p.3). The priority was to intervene at a much earlier stage in children's lives, to identify problems before they became chronic, in order to prevent a range of problems in later life in relation to educational attainment, unemployment, crime and anti-social behaviour (Parton, Noyes and

Rose 2010). Practice would be determined by the needs of all children, there would be a continuum of services from early needs through to child protection risks and children and families would get a more joined up, co-ordinated response without the need for multiple assessments.

Children and Young People: Rights to Action in Wales was also a response to the *Laming Report* (2003). It represents a vision for all children in Wales and is similarly underpinned by a commitment to preventive services and early intervention. The Welsh Assembly Government also undertook a review of policies and practices for safeguarding vulnerable children in Wales. The review produced a report called *Keeping Us Safe* (National Assembly for Wales 2006).

Northern Ireland's ten year strategy document *Children and Young People – Our Pledge* followed a review of safeguarding which was also undertaken in response to the Laming recommendations. The review highlighted a number of shortcomings (DHSSPS 2006c) and resulted in an inspection of child protection arrangements and services in Northern Ireland. The inspection revealed inconsistency in structures, roles, systems and processes. One of the main objectives of reform in Northern Ireland has been to achieve consistency in the delivery of services to children and families. The ten year strategy document represents a shared vision for children and young people that is based on a whole child approach and a commitment to preventative and early intervention practice.

Scotland's overarching children's policy *Getting it Right for Every Child* (GIRFEC) followed a national audit and review of child protection (Scottish Executive 2002) and subsequent Child Protection Reform Programme which were undertaken after the publication of the report of the inquiry into the death of three-year-old Kennedy McFarlane (Hammond 2001). GIRFEC is a common, co-ordinated approach across all agencies that supports the delivery of appropriate, proportionate and timely help to all children as they need it. In common with the overarching children's policy frameworks in other parts of the UK the emphasis is on integrated support for children and on prevention and early intervention. The then Scottish Executive published the original *GIRFEC* Implementation Plan in June 2006 and the *GIRFEC* approach was piloted in a pathfinder local authority in order to inform future national guidance and best practice (Stafford and Vincent 2008). At the time of writing *GIRFEC* was being rolled out across Scotland with local authorities at various stages of implementation.

All areas of the UK are committed to promoting outcomes for children and young people and all of the overarching children's policy frameworks are underpinned by national outcomes as shown in Box 5.2.

BOX 5.2 NATIONAL OUTCOMES

England: There are five *Every Child Matters* outcomes: to be healthy; stay safe; enjoy and achieve; make a positive contribution; and achieve economic well-being.

Northern Ireland has the same *Every Child Matters* outcomes as England, with the addition of 'rights'.

Wales has seven core aims, developed from the principles of the United Nations Convention on the Rights of the Child: have a flying start in life; have a comprehensive range of education and learning opportunities; enjoy the best possible health and be free from abuse, victimisation and exploitation; have access to play, leisure, sporting and culture activities; be listened to, treated with respect and have their race and cultural identity recognised; have a safe home and a community which supports physical and emotional well-being; and not be disadvantaged by poverty.

Scotland has eight national outcomes: safe; healthy; achieving; nurtured; active; respected; responsible; and included.

Across the UK the aim is to improve outcomes for all children and to narrow the gap between those who do well and those who do not. In most parts of the UK child protection is part of an outcome around 'safety'. Only in Wales is 'free from abuse' stated as a specific outcome.

5.3 KEY LEGISLATION

Across the UK policy and practice to safeguard and protect children is underpinned by legislation. There is no separate legislation for child protection; rather, legislation covers child welfare in a broad sense, encompassing support for children in need as well as children in need of protection (Lindon 2008). The national Scottish inter-agency child protection guidance highlights the relevant legislation for protecting children including:

- duties conferred on services to investigate and respond to concerns about a child's welfare, as well as the responsibilities of local authorities to develop community planning processes with partner agencies

- overarching legislation (e.g. data protection) where some aspects are particularly relevant

- other legislation including laws relating to offences against children and young people and to civil law or administrative arrangements.

(Scottish Government 2010a)

Although all parts of the UK have undergone significant reform of child protection policy in recent years, legislative change has been relatively minor. The key legislation underpinning the child protection system in all parts of the UK remains the Children Acts which were introduced in the late 1980s and 1990s. These Acts define the thresholds for intervention in family life to protect children from abuse and neglect; and the definitions of 'significant harm' and 'children in need' within these Acts have not been amended (Owen 2009a). Significant harm is not well defined in legislation but in England, Wales, Scotland and Northern Ireland legislation stipulates that if statutory services have reasonable cause to suspect that a child is suffering, or likely to suffer 'significant harm' they have a duty to make child protection enquiries. If they do not suspect a child is suffering or likely to suffer significant harm they may still have a duty to assess the child's level of need and provide him or her with services but the case will not be investigated under child protection procedures (Vincent 2008b).

The key piece of legislation in England and Wales remains the Children Act 1989, although the Children Act 2004 has amended some of the provisions of the 1989 Act. The 2004 Act was largely a response to the Victoria Climbié inquiry which revealed that children's services had considerable problems identifying, agreeing and acting collaboratively and swiftly to prevent suspected harm and meet a child's needs (Pithouse forthcoming). In England the Children Act 2004 gave statutory force to the new shared vision of a child centred, outcomes led approach to child welfare services within ECM. It aimed to create clearer accountability between agencies, to enable better joint working to improve children's well-being and to secure a better focus on safeguarding children (Frost and Parton 2009; Luckock 2007; Rose 2009):

> The Children Act 2004 is primarily about new statutory leadership roles, joint planning, and commissioning of children's services, and how organisations ensure their functions are discharged in a way which safeguards children and promotes their welfare. (Owen 2009a, p.17)

The Children Act 2004 introduced:

- a new duty on agencies to co-operate to improve the well-being of children and young people (Section 10)

- a duty on key agencies working with children and young people to safeguard and promote their welfare (Section 11) through new statutory Local Safeguarding Children Boards (LSCBs) (Sections 13–16)

- the power to establish a national database or index (subsequently called Contactpoint), via secondary legislation and guidance, that would contain basic information about all children and young people to help professionals work together (Section 12)

- a requirement that all local authorities with children's services responsibilities appoint a Director of Children's Services and a Lead Council member responsible for, as a minimum, education and children's social service functions (Sections 18 and 19)

- the means by which local authorities, primary care trusts and others could pool budgets into a Children's Trust and share information to promote better joined up working (Section 10)

- an integrated inspection framework to assess how well services worked together to improve outcomes for children (Sections 20–25)

- the requirement for local authorities to produce a Children and Young People's Plan (Section 17 and schedule 5)

- the creation of a Children's Commissioner (Sections 1–9).

There are some differences between the application of the Children Act 2004 in England and Wales. For example, in England LSCBs have a duty to develop child death review panels but this duty does not apply in Wales.

Since 2007 Wales has had new powers to make its own primary legislation in relation to vulnerable children so further divergence from England is likely in terms of legislation. The Welsh Assembly is now able to seek legislative competence from the UK parliament. A number of areas of legislative competence have already been secured, including a Vulnerable Children Measure. The Children and Families (Wales) Measure 2009 is taking forward an agenda to eradicate poverty and provide greater support to children living in families with complex needs, where family members have difficulties with substance misuse, domestic violence, abusive behaviour or mental disorder. Work is now underway to enable a consolidation measure to be made that would bring together all the different parts of legislation affecting children into one new measure in Wales (Corbett and Rose 2010).

There has been some concern expressed in Wales that the emphasis on safeguarding in the 2004 Act potentially dilutes the 1989 Children's Act's specific and narrow focus on significant harm (Pithouse forthcoming; Vincent 2008a). Pithouse (forthcoming) points out that it will be for the Welsh Government to consider if such concerns are valid or not, and to institute new policy or guidance accordingly.

In Northern Ireland the Children (Northern Ireland) Order 1995 remains the primary piece of legislation in relation to the protection of children but the Safeguarding Board Act (Northern Ireland) 2011 allows for a single Safeguarding Board for Northern Ireland to replace Area Child Protection Committees (ACPCs).

The Children's Hearings (Scotland) Act 2011 has resulted in some reform of the Children's Hearings system. A concordat with local government in November 2007 heralded a new tone of facilitation between central and local government in Scotland, rather than direction from central government, and a new collaborative approach to policy development.

5.4 INTER-AGENCY CHILD PROTECTION GUIDANCE

Child protection procedures are set down both in law and in related guidance. An essential plank of child protection policy in all four parts of the UK is inter-agency guidance which sets out how individuals and organisations should work together to safeguard and protect children in accordance with legislation (Vincent 2008b). Each part of the UK has its own inter-agency child protection guidance as listed in Box 5.3.

BOX 5.3 INTER-AGENCY CHILD PROTECTION GUIDANCE

England
Working Together to Safeguard Children (DCSF 2010)

Wales
Safeguarding Children: Working Together Under the Children Act 2004
(Welsh Assembly Government 2006)

Northern Ireland
Co-operating to Safeguard Children (Department of Health, Social Services
and Public Safety 2003)

Scotland
The National Guidance for Child Protection (Scottish Government 2010a).

England and Wales both updated their inter-agency guidance following
the 2004 Children Act to take account of new statutory duties within
the Act (HM Government 2006a; Welsh Assembly Government 2006).
The English guidance was further updated in 2010 to take account of
Lord Laming's report *The Protection of Children in England: A Progress Report*
(2009). The revised and updated version of *Working Together to Safeguard
Children* (DCSF 2010) addresses 23 of Lord Laming's recommendations. It
provides a national framework within which agencies and professionals at
local level, individually and jointly, draw up and agree on their own ways
of working together to safeguard and promote the welfare of children.
It is made up of two parts: eight chapters of statutory guidance and four
chapters of non-statutory practice guidance. Nigel Parton has highlighted
the tendency for guidance to increase in length and complexity (Parton
2011): the 2006 version of *Working Together* was 231 pages while the
2010 version is 390 pages long. The English document is considerably
longer than the Northern Ireland guidance which is 122 pages long and
the new Scottish guidance which is 170 pages long, but only 56 pages
longer than the Welsh guidance which is 334 pages. In her interim
report, Eileen Munro (2011) stated that the review of child protection
in England acknowledged the importance of having a single set of rules
that all organisations, including professional bodies, voluntary and private
sector providers and government departments, could follow and be clear

about their respective responsibilities for protecting children from harm. She also pointed out, however, that the current guidance had become too long to be practical and this could be dangerous. In order to assess how *Working Together* can be simplified and improved, the review has assembled a group of representatives from relevant professional bodies to advise on how statutory guidance might better support the practical needs of the professions working to protect children and to consider what recommendations the review might make concerning *Working Together's* future form and content.

In addition to *Safeguarding Children: Working Together Under the Children Act 2004*, Wales also has the *All Wales Child Protection Procedures*. These are not statutory procedures and are not issued by the Welsh Assembly Government. Rather, they are the result of the former Area Child Protection Committees (ACPCs) taking the lead across Wales and commissioning one set of procedures to which all sign up to and work to on a voluntary basis:

> This approach has been continued by the LSCBs and is a model that has since been adopted in other parts of the UK, including London. It has been a major step forward in achieving a greater consistency of approach and indicative of what can be done differently in a country with a smaller number of local authorities working in a different relationship with the national government. (Corbett and Rose 2010, p.41)

In Northern Ireland the most up-to-date version of inter-agency guidance is *Co-operating to Safeguard Children* (Department of Health, Social Services and Public Safety 2003). This guidance was issued to take account of the recommendations in the 2003 *Laming Report* and is broadly similar to the 1999 version of *Working Together to Safeguard Children* (Department of Health, Home Office, and Department of Education and Employment 1999). At the time of writing Northern Ireland was reviewing its guidance to take account of the new Safeguarding Board Act (Northern Ireland) 2011.

In Scotland new guidance *The National Guidance for Child Protection in Scotland* (The Scottish Government 2010a) was published recently. The guidance replaced *Protecting Children – A Shared Responsibility: Guidance on Inter-agency Co-operation* (Scottish Office 1998).

a. Definitions used in the guidance

As outlined above significant harm was not well defined in legislation and the inter-agency guidance in all parts of the UK states that there are no absolute criteria on which to rely when judging what constitutes significant harm. All four sets of guidance state, however, that the concept will involve ill treatment, harm or lack of care which impacts on a child's health and development (Vincent 2008b). In England the most recent version of *Working Together* states that the test for likelihood of suffering harm in the future should be that either:

> The child can be shown to have suffered ill-treatment or impairment of health or development as a result of physical, emotional or sexual abuse or neglect, and professional judgement is that further ill-treatment or impairment are likely; or professional judgement, substantiated by the findings of enquiries in this individual case or by research evidence, is that the child is likely to suffer ill-treatment or the impairment of health or development as a result of physical, emotional, or sexual abuse or neglect. (DCSF 2010, p.167)

The new Scottish guidance states that:

> There are no absolute criteria for judging what constitutes significant harm. In assessing the severity of ill treatment or future ill treatment, it may be important to take account of the degree and extent of physical harm; the duration and frequency of abuse and neglect; the extent of premeditation; and the presence or degree of threat, coercion, sadism and bizarre or unusual elements. Sometimes, a single traumatic event may constitute significant harm, for example, a violent assault, suffocation or poisoning. More often, significant harm results from an accumulation of significant events, both acute and long-standing, that interrupt, change or damage the child's physical and psychological development. To understand and identify significant harm, it is necessary to consider:
>
> • The nature of harm, either through an act of commission or omission
>
> • The impact on the child's health and development, taking into account their age and stage of development
>
> • The child's development within the context of their family and wider environment
>
> • The context in which a harmful incident or behaviour occurred

- Any particular needs, such as a medical condition, communication impairment or disability, that may affect the child's development, make them more vulnerable to harm or influence the level and type of care provided by the family

- The capacity of parents or carers to meet adequately the child's needs; and

- The wider and environmental family context.

(Scottish Government 2011, p.15, para 43)

Both 'child protection' and 'safeguarding' are defined in the English and Welsh guidance, the new Scottish guidance defines 'child protection' but not 'safeguarding' and neither term is defined in the Northern Ireland guidance. *Working Together* (DCSF 2010) defines safeguarding and promoting the welfare of children as:

- protecting children from maltreatment

- preventing impairment of children's health and development

- ensuring that children are growing up in circumstances consistent with the provision of safe and effective care

- undertaking that role so as to enable those children to have optimum life chances and to enter adulthood successfully.

Child protection is defined as:

> ...the activity that is undertaken to protect specific children who are suffering, or are likely to suffer significant harm. (DCSF 2010, p.35)

While *Working Together* (DCSF 2010) describes child protection as being an essential part of safeguarding and promoting welfare it states that:

> However, all agencies and individuals should aim to proactively safeguard and promote the welfare of children so that the need for action to protect children from harm is reduced. (DCSF 2010, p.35)

The new Scottish guidance states that:

> 'Child protection' means protecting a child from child abuse or neglect. Abuse or neglect need not have taken place; it is sufficient for a risk assessment to have identified a *likelihood* or *risk* of significant harm from abuse or neglect. Equally, in instances where a child may have been abused or neglected but the risk of future abuse has not

been identified, the child and their family may require support and recovery services but not a Child Protection Plan. In such cases, an investigation may still be necessary to determine whether a criminal investigation is needed and to inform an assessment that a Child Protection Plan is not required. (Scottish Government 2010a, p.14, para 37)

The Scottish guidance also offers a definition of 'risk':

In the context of this guidance, risk is the likelihood or probability of particular outcome given the presence of factors in a child or young person's life. Risk is part and parcel of everyday life: a toddler learning to walk is likely to be at risk from some stumbles and scrapes but this does not mean the child should not be encouraged to walk... Risks 'may be deemed acceptable; they may also be reduced by parents/carers or through the early intervention of universal services. At other times, a number of services may need to respond together as part of a co-ordinated intervention. Only where risks cause, or are likely to cause, significant harm to a child would a response under child protection be required. Where a child has already been exposed to actual harm, assessment will mean looking at the extent to which they are at risk of repeated harm and at the potential effects of continued exposure over time. (Scottish Government 2010a, p.16, para 46)

A definition of risk is not offered in guidance in other parts of the UK. The English guidance has a definition of 'families at risk' but not of 'risk' generally, although the term is mentioned on many occasions throughout the document. The new Scottish guidance also includes an entire section on identifying and managing risk and a further section on indicators of risk. Although the Scottish guidance does not offer a definition of 'safeguarding' it does, on a number of occasions, refer to 'safeguarding and promoting the well-being of children' or to 'protecting children and safeguarding their welfare'.

5.5 KEY STRUCTURES FOR PROTECTING CHILDREN

In England, at present, under the Children Act 2004 every local authority must appoint a Director of Children's Services and a Lead Member for Children's Services and, at a minimum merge their education departments with the children's social care section of the old Social Services departments. The aspiration was that local authorities would set up a Children's Trust bringing together social services, education, health and other children's services in order to facilitate integrated front line practice. However, it was recognised that the nature and pace of change would vary. Updated guidance on the roles and responsibilities of the Director of Children's Services and Lead Member for Children's Services was published in July 2009.

The Children Act 2004 also required each local authority in England to establish an LSCB. Statutory LSCBs have wider responsibilities for the safeguarding of children than their predecessors in non-statutory ACPCs who had a much narrower child protection focus. They are key mechanisms for agreeing the way relevant organisations will co-operate to safeguard and promote the welfare of children and for ensuring the effectiveness of what these organisations do. While they have a role in co-ordinating and ensuring the effectiveness of individuals' and organisations' work they are not, however, accountable for their operational work with all board partners retaining their own existing lines of accountability. The decision to place LSCBs on a statutory footing and create Directors of Children's Services responsible for ensuring their effectiveness, was a response to Lord Laming's recommendation in his report following the death of Victoria Climbié (Laming 2003) that there should be a line of accountability from frontline services through to government. Published a year before the Laming Report, the *Joint Chief Inspectors' Report on Arrangements to Safeguard Children* (Department of Health 2002) had also been highly critical of ACPCs and concluded that there was a need to consider whether they should be established on a statutory basis to ensure adequate accountability and funding:

> In the majority of areas the ACPC was a weak body that was not exercising effective leadership of the safeguarding agenda across agencies effectively...local agencies did not generally accept that they were accountable to the local ACPC for safeguarding arrangements. (DCSF 2010, p.37)

Under the Children Act 2004, statutory membership of LSCBs in England must include local authorities, the police, NHS Trusts and health service providers in the NHS, probation and prison services, youth offending teams and bodies providing secure care for children and young people, and Connexions. Agencies with no statutory responsibility, but whom *Working Together* (HM Government 2006a) suggested should be included, were education services, early years and childcare services, housing services, youth services, cultural and leisure services, alcohol and drug services, the voluntary and independent sector, the armed services and faith communities.

Since 2004 the transparency and accountability of LSCBs has been strengthened even further. Under the Apprenticeship, Skills, Children and Learning Act 2009 from 1 April 2010 LSCBs are now required to produce and publish an annual report on the effectiveness of safeguarding in the local area, with the first annual reports due by 1 April 2011. They are also required to appoint two representatives of the local community to each LSCB and there is now statutory representation of schools. *Working Together* (DCSF 2010) also provides further clarity on the relationship between the LSCB and the Children's Trust Board, and makes it clear that the Chair of the LSCB should be independent.

The Children's Trust Board brings together all partners with a role in improving outcomes for children and has a wider role than the LSCB in the planning and delivery of children's services. From 1 April 2010 under the Apprenticeships, Skills, Children and Learning Act 2009, Children's Trust Boards are responsible for a joint strategy setting out how the Children's Trust partners will co-operate to improve children's well-being in the local area. All local areas must publish a Children and Young Person's Plan (CYPP) on or before 1 April 2011 and the LSCBs' activities must contribute to and fit within the framework established by the CYPP (Vincent 2008a). New guidance on Children's Trusts: Statutory Guidance on co-operation arrangements, including the Children's Trust Board and the Children and Young People's Plan was introduced around the same time as the revised version of *Working Together* (DCSF 2010).

In Wales, as in England, all local authorities are required to produce a Children's Plan. The local authority Children's Plan is the key mechanism for driving change and delivering the required outcomes in the Rights to Action document and related guidance (Pithouse forthcoming; Welsh Assembly Government 2007a) structures in Wales are, however, slightly different to those in England. Wales does not have Children's Trusts and in contrast to England has retained social services departments rather than integrating education and social care. The Welsh Assembly Government has stressed that it is not its role to tell local authorities how to structure themselves; this is a matter for local determination. Local authorities must, however, have in place a Director of Social Services at an appropriate senior level who is responsible for child and adult safeguarding arrangements. While all staff have responsibility to safeguard and promote the welfare of children the Director of Children's Services is the senior officer within the council who has final accountability for safeguarding.

> In Wales 'social services' is still the correct term, which marks the first point of divergence with England where 'children's social care' and 'adult social care' reflect major organisational and structural change in the last decade. (Corbett and Rose 2010, p.31)

Although Wales does not have Children's Trusts, Section 25 of the Children Act 2004 contained specific clauses for Wales making it a legal requirement to set up statutory children and young people's framework partnerships in all local authority areas, made up of local authority and health services and the voluntary sector. Under Section 26 of the 2004 Act, Children and Young People's Framework Partnerships are responsible for developing and delivering the Children and Young People's Plan and for driving the commissioning of services. As in England the 2004 Act required local authorities in Wales to identify a Lead Director for Children and Young People's Services and a Lead Member, together with their equivalents in NHS bodies. The role of the Lead Director for Children and Young People's Services in Wales is to take the lead in promoting and co-ordinating planning for children and young people. The Lead Directors of children and young people's services do not carry operational responsibility for the delivery of all children's services as they do in England (Corbett and Rose 2010). Guidance has been produced on the Lead Director role within the children and young people's partnerships and the role of the Director of Social Services is set out in a number of chief inspector's annual reports as well as in statutory guidance (National Assembly for Wales 2006; Welsh Assembly Government 2009). The guidance lays out recommended competencies for the appointment of the Director of Social Services.

As in England, statutory LSCBs replaced non-statutory ACPCs in Wales under the Children Act 2004. Statutory members of LSCBs in Wales are the local authority, police, probation, youth offending, health boards and trusts and governors of secure establishments or prisons.

Northern Ireland has somewhat different structures to those in England or Wales. In contrast to the rest of the UK local authorities in Northern Ireland do not have primary responsibility for planning and delivering children's services. Instead this is the function of integrated Health and Social Services (HSS) Boards. In 2007 the four existing Health and Social Services Boards were replaced by one Health and Social Care Board as the Commissioner of Services and the 18 community Health and Social Services Trusts were replaced by five integrated Health and Social Care Trusts, providing a mixture of community and hospital based services. Each HSS Board is required to produce a Children's Services Plan.

Until recently ACPCs operated in each HSS Board and were responsible for determining the strategy for safeguarding children and developing and disseminating policies and procedures. In addition, each Health and Social Services Trust had a Child Protection Panel to facilitate practice at a local level. These structures are now being replaced by a new single statutory Safeguarding Board for Northern Ireland (SBNI) which will have responsibility for strategic matters and five Safeguarding Panels, one in each joint Health and Social Services Trust, which will have a co-ordinating and operational role. These new arrangements represent a widening remit from traditional child protection responsibilities to broader safeguarding responsibilities as in England and Wales (Vincent 2008c). The Safeguarding Board Act (Northern Ireland) 2011 was passed in the Northern Ireland Assembly in March 2011 and the single, regional Safeguarding Board for Northern Ireland is expected to come into operation in Autumn 2011.

In Scotland, the way in which local child protection services are structured varies. There are some integrated children's departments but most local authorities have not integrated their social work and education departments and have retained Directors of Social Work. As in other parts of the UK local authorities have responsibility to produce an integrated children's services plan. Chief Officers are responsible for the leadership, direction and scrutiny of local child protection services. They are responsible for overseeing the commissioning of all child protection services and are accountable for this work and its effectiveness.

Scotland has non-statutory Child Protection Committees (CPCs) which are responsible for the strategic planning of local inter-agency child protection work and Chief Officers have strategic responsibility for their Child Protection Committee. CPCs were first established in 1991 and were reformed under the Child Protection Reform Programme but in contrast to the approach taken in England and Wales to reform ACPCs, Scotland opted for guidance for Chief Officers rather than statute (Scottish Executive 2005) and there are no plans to replace CPCs with statutory bodies. The 2005 guidance did, however, broaden the responsibilities of CPCs and strengthen accountabilities. CPCs are viewed as the principal stakeholder network for the Scottish Government in developing policies for the protection of children (Scottish Executive 2005; Tierney, Knight and Stafford 2010). CPCs now have a broader remit. They are responsible for the design, development, publication, distribution, dissemination, implementation and evaluation of child protection policy and practice in their local area. They no longer have a narrow child protection focus and although their name has not been changed as it has in England and Wales, their role is nevertheless very similar to the 'safeguarding' role of LSCBs and the proposed SBNI (Vincent 2008c). Each CPC must have an inter-agency lead officer and a dedicated Child Protection Training Officer. The CPC chair is a matter for local discretion. The chair can, but does not have to be, independent and the membership of CPCs is not specified in the 2005 guidance.

CPC members who were interviewed by Daniel, Vincent and Ogilvie-Whyte (2007) for A Process Review of the Child Protection Reform Programme felt that the 2005 guidance had led to CPCs having more significance and influence and allowed them to be more effective. Some respondents felt, however, that CPCs should have been put on a statutory footing in the same way that they had been in other parts of the UK. One CPC member said:

> For some reason there was a resistance in the Child Protection Reform Programme for doing that, quite where that resistance was coming from I'm not clear…so eventually we ended up with CPC national guidance which was not rooted in legislative provision, which I think is a major disappointment and probably, a major own goal. (Daniel *et al.* 2007, p.43)

Scotland's unique Children's Hearings system further sets it apart from systems to protect children in other parts of the UK. The Children's Hearings system is at the heart of the legal framework for children in Scotland. While social work departments and the police have a statutory duty to investigate and take action to protect children where there is reasonable cause to suggest they are suffering, or likely to suffer significant harm, as in other parts of the UK, offence and care and protection cases must be referred to the Scottish Children's Reporter's Administration (SCRA) if compulsory measures of care are needed. Anyone, not just professionals, can contact a Children's Reporter if they have concerns about a child (Stafford and Vincent 2008).

The Children's Hearings system was established in 1971 following the recommendations of the Kilbrandon Committee in 1964. The Committee considered arrangements for children and young people who were in need of care and protection as well as those who were deemed to be beyond parental control. It concluded that there was no meaningful distinction between children for whom there are child protection concerns and children who have committed offences and recommended that both types of case be dealt with in one system (Stafford and Vincent 2008). This separation had no precedent in UK law. With the establishment of the Children's Hearings system courts were only involved in establishing the facts of a case if they were disputed. Otherwise, decisions about the appropriate measures for a child are made by a lay panel and based on the needs of the child (Murray and Hill 1991).

The Children's Hearings system has changed very little since its inception. Over time, however, as with the child protection system as a whole, there has been a huge increase in the number of referrals to the Children's Hearings system on care and protection grounds, and growing concerns about the system becoming overloaded. Furthermore, the report of the audit and review of child protection in Scotland (Scottish Executive 2002) suggested that the Children's Hearings system effectively added an additional layer to the child protection system when compared to systems in other parts of the UK and recommended changes to the system:

> The three main aspects of child protection – protection services, criminal justice and children's hearings are not well aligned. Professionals should be able to respond to children's needs in a holistic way, in the spirit of the Children (Scotland) Act 1995 within a single coherent system for meeting children's needs... The interfaces between children's services and the Hearing systems need to be improved to address the weaknesses identified in this report. (Scottish Executive 2002, quoted in Stafford and Vincent 2008, p.57)

The reasons for referral to the Children's Reporter and the grounds for registration can, and often do, differ from those used for registering children in need of protection. Different sets of procedures, reports and information are required for the different purposes; different meetings are required, such as the hearings, case conferences, and review meetings. The grounds upon which a child can be referred to a children's hearing are defined in law and are as follows. A child can be referred to a hearing if he or she:

a.   is beyond the control of any relevant person

b.   is falling into bad associations or is exposed to moral danger

c.   is likely to suffer unnecessarily, or be impaired seriously, in his health or development, due to lack of parental care

d.   is a child in respect of whom any of the offences mentioned in Schedule 1 of the Criminal Procedure (Scotland) Act 1995 (offences against children to which special provisions apply) has been committed

e.   is, or is likely to become, a member of the same household as a child in respect of whom any of the offences referred to in (d) above

f.   is, or is likely to become, a member of the same household as a person who has committed any of the offences referred to in (d) above

g.   is, or is likely to become, a member of the same household as a person in respect of whom an offence under sections 1 to 3 of the Criminal Law (Consolidation) (Scotland) Act 1995 (incest and intercourse with a child by step-parent or person in position of trust) has been committed by a member of that household

h.   has failed to attend school regularly without reasonable excuse.

(Scottish Executive 2002, p.69)

The Scottish Executive responded to the recommendations around the Children's Hearings system in *It's Everyone's Job to Make Sure I'm Alright* by undertaking a review of the Children's Hearings system which was subsequently undertaken alongside review of children's services as a whole. A Draft Children's Hearings Bill was published in June 2009 aimed at strengthening and modernising the Children's Hearings system while retaining the original ethos and principles. The Bill was passed in November 2010 and received royal assent on 6 January 2011. The provisions of the Children's Hearings (Scotland) Act 2011 are expected to be fully implemented by summer 2012.

5.6 INSPECTION PROCESSES

Inspections of children and young people's services are designed to ensure quality and transparency of quality in services. Inspections can also highlight the strengths and weaknesses of safeguarding in local authority areas. These inspections are important as they are routine and not done on the back of a crisis but can flag up areas for improvement. Inspection is also a key point at which public bodies, children's services and the general public interface around issues of child protection. Box 5.4 lists some key child protection inspection framework documents.

BOX 5.4 KEY CHILD PROTECTION INSPECTION FRAMEWORK
DOCUMENTS

England
Inspections of Safeguarding and Looked After Children (Ofsted 2009a)

Unannounced Inspections of Contact, Referral and Assessment from 1 Sep 2010
(Ofsted 2010)

*Comprehensive Area Assessment: Annual Rating of Council Children's Services
for 2009* (Ofsted 2009b)

Northern Ireland
Our Children and Young People: Our Shared Responsibility. Inspection of
Child Protection Services in Northern Ireland (Department of Health,
Social Services and Public Safety 2006a)

Standards for Child Protection Services (Department of Health, Social
Services and Public Safety 2008a)

Scotland
*How Well Do We Protect Scotland's Children? A Report on the Findings of the
Joint Inspections of Services to Protect Children 2005–2009* (HMIE 2009a)

How Well Do We Protect Children and Meet their Needs? (HMIE 2009b)

*A Common Approach to Inspecting Services for Children and Young People:
Consultation Report* (HMIE 2009c)

Wales
*Safeguarding and Protecting Children in Wales: A Review of the Arrangements
in Place Across the Welsh National Service* (Healthcare Inspectorate Wales
2009)

Within each area of the UK, safeguarding inspections sit within a larger
framework of the inspection of children and young people's services
and form an integral component of measuring outcomes against national
frameworks (as specified earlier in this chapter). The mechanism for
inspections usually includes a team (often from multiple government or
independent bodies) that conduct local area (usually local authority area)
inspections. The inspections include observation of services, meetings

with service users often including children and parents, review of key documents, guidance, plans and records, as well as meetings with children's service workers. In addition to local area inspections, each nation will often produce thematic reports on child protection and safeguarding among specific populations such as children with disabilities or children in care.

While each part of the UK utilises slightly different processes and inspectorates for child protection inspections, the four nations look to inspections to provide the same end result of providing an open and transparent process for the inspection of services for children and young people. These inspections can lead to improvement of services and provide the public with assurances that the services given to children and young people are of the highest quality and comply with and have an understanding of safeguarding and child protection.

In England, the safeguarding component of inspections includes several key elements:

- findings from safeguarding and looked after children's inspections

- unannounced inspections of contact, referral and assessment

- assessment and referral arrangements for children in need and children who may be in need of protection

- evaluations of Serious Case Reviews (SCRs)

- safeguarding and looked after children findings from joint area review inspections

- findings from triggered inspections.

(Ofsted 2009)

This framework on the inspection of safeguarding and looked after children's services replaced the previous Joint Area Review from April 2009. These earlier inspections formed the Comprehensive Area Assessment (CAA) and were carried out by the Office for Standards in Education, Children's Services and Skills (Ofsted) and the Care Quality Commission and in some cases with Her Majesty's Inspectorate of Constabulary. This new inspection regime will take place in all local areas over the course of a three-year period from April 2009 to 2012. The framework was reviewed and revised in September 2010. One new component of the framework is the unannounced inspections of contact, referral and assessment. These unannounced inspections are not a full inspection of safeguarding – rather they are an inspection of front-line practice in relation to contact, referral and assessment processes for children in need and children who may be in need of protection (Ofsted 2010). All local authority areas will have an unannounced inspection of contact, referral and assessment arrangements in any one 12-month period. In addition to this child protection inspection framework, pilot inspections have been carried out in the Children and Family Court Advisory and Support Service (Cafcass).

In Northern Ireland, the Department of Health, Social Services and Public Safety (DHSSPS) embarked on inspections in 5 of the 11 community Health and Social Service Trusts between 2002 and 2006. These inspections came as the result of a recommendation from the Laming report that nations conduct an audit of child protection services against key themes identified for safeguarding.

In 2008, DHSSPS produced the Standards for Child Protection Services. The child protection standards are applicable to all public bodies, organisations, professionals and persons who provide statutory services to children. They also establish a framework of best practice in child protection for voluntary, community and independent sector organisations and practitioners (including counsellors and therapists working in a private capacity) who work with or have significant contact with children and young people. The child protection standards give inspecting bodies, other agencies and communities guidelines and standards for planning, commissioning, providing, quality assuring and auditing child protection services, which meet statutory and governance requirements.

In Scotland, a joint inspection bill was passed in 2006 which set up a partnership between the following agencies for child protection inspections:

- Her Majesty's Inspectorate of Education (HMIE)

- Social Work Inspection Agency (SWIA)

- Her Majesty's Chief Inspector of the Constabulary (HMCIC)

- The Care Commission, and

- National Health Service Quality Improvement Scotland (NHS QI).

This legislation and the accompanying framework places emphasis on self-evaluation of organisations in addition to the formal inspection process.

More recently, the Public Services Reform (Scotland) Act 2010 created two new bodies to coordinate and deliver efficient and effective scrutiny of health and social care, social work and child protection. From 1 April 2011, the new unified independent body called the Social Care and Social Work Improvement Scotland or SCSWIS, is responsible for inspection of child protection and integrated children's services. This new body replaces the Care Commission, the Social Work Inspection Agency and the part of HMI that is responsible for child protection inspections. Inspections will still be carried out in all 32 local authority areas. This new body will set national performance indicators and targets and will carry on and complete the joint inspection programme for child protection.

In addition, SCSWIS will focus scrutiny on particular themes and issues which include responding to emerging national themes and risks, carrying out pilot projects, and looking at potential themes several of which have already been identified:

- integrated children's service inspections
- inspecting services for children living in families affected by drug misuse
- outcomes for children looked after away from home
- vulnerable adults
- offenders
- out of hours services.

In Wales, the Social Services Inspectorate for Wales (SSIW) and the Wales Audit Office (WAO) conduct joint reviews of social services every five years in each of the 22 local authority areas. These reviews examine children's services and safeguarding of children in addition to looking at other social services. In addition, SSIW conducted seven specific child protection inspections during 2001.

In addition to SSIW and WAO, the Healthcare Inspectorate Wales (HIW) has a specific statutory responsibility to safeguard and promote the rights and welfare of children in exercising its role in relation to the inspection and investigation of NHS organisations. HIW builds safeguarding and child protection into every review, whether it be a review of the governance arrangements of an organisation or of a specific service such as maternity or mental health with the aim of answering two key questions:

1.   Are all those working in healthcare organisations aware of their responsibilities in relation to child protection and safeguarding, and do they know how to properly deal with suspected child protection/safeguarding issues?

2.   Are children and young people safe when accessing health services or visiting healthcare premises?

5.7 CONCLUSION

In this chapter we have looked at the broad legislative and policy frameworks underpinning the child protection systems of the UK. Across the UK, services to safeguard and protect children are underpinned by complex systems of legislation, guidance, regulations and procedures. These are different in each part of the UK and we examined the extent of these differences.

Our analysis has suggested that while each part of the UK has undergone significant reform of child protection *policy* over the past ten years, *legislative* change in the context of devolution has been relatively minor.

With regard to legislation, there are broad similarities between the Acts. All of them define the thresholds for intervention in family life to protect children. In each part of the UK the threshold for intervention remains 'significant harm'. The concept of 'significant harm' is not well defined. The concept 'children in need' also exists across the UK.

Turning to the broad policy frameworks underpinning child protection across the UK, a central plank of child protection in each part of the UK is the multi-agency guidance for professionals working together to support children. Once again, each part of the UK has such guidance. Common to all the UK inter-agency guidance has been the tendency for the guidance to become longer and more complex (Parton 2011). All of the guidance contains definitions of abuse. Definitions are broadly similar with some differences in detail. Thus, while each part of the UK has separate inter-agency guidance and while there are differences, their content covers the same broad areas.

With regard to the main structures underpinning child protection in each part of the UK, once again, the overall structures are similar, with some differences in content. All parts of the UK have LSCBs or Child Protection Committees (CPCs). Since 2004, legislation and policy has introduced shifts in LSCBs/CPCs away from having a narrower child protection to a broader safeguarding role, and change has been in the direction of tightening arrangements and making LSCBs/CPCs more accountable. There are differences in arrangements for setting them up and not all of them are set up on a statutory basis. All are moving in the direction of increased responsibility and accountability.

Many of the child protection structures in England are legally prescribed and nationally applied. For example, Children's Trusts, LSCBS, the appointment of Directors of Children's Services, and the publication of Children's Plans are all governed by statute. In other parts of the UK, especially Scotland, while many of these structures exist, and while the devolved parts of the UK have looked to England to inform their development, they are not legally prescribed and in some cases have not been rolled out nationally.

Wales does not have Children's Trusts; instead, they have retained social services and each local authority must have a lead Director responsible for Children's Services. There is a requirement to produce a Children's Plan. All-Wales Child Protection guidance has been commissioned and produced under the auspices of the LSCBs in Wales. In Northern Ireland, Local Authorities do not have responsibility for children's services, rather it is the function of the Integrated Health and Social Services Boards. Northern Ireland now has a single statutory Safeguarding Board.

In Scotland there is no national requirement for integrated children's departments. There is no statutory basis for CPCs in Scotland although Chairs of CPCs are increasingly coming together as a group on a more formalised basis and are becoming an important mechanism for developing and implementing child protection policy in Scotland and they were heavily consulted and involved in the production of the 2010 National Child Protection Guidance.

Arrangements for inspecting child protection services differ throughout the UK. Within each part of the UK, inspecting child protection services sits within a wider framework for inspecting children's services and forms an integral component of measuring outcomes for children against national standards. All of the inspectorates produce overview reports based on individual inspections. While there are differences in processes for inspection, all four look to inspection to provide the same end results and aspire to improvement in services and public assurances of quality.

We have highlighted that a major similarity between parts of the UK is that it is now no longer possible to separate policy and practice to safeguard and protect children from wider policy context surrounding children's welfare as a whole. In each case child protection is embedded in wider systems of welfare. Each part of the UK has its own overarching policy framework for children's services: The first of these was developed in England following the Laming inquiry into the death of Victoria Climbié. Similar strategy documents were developed in Wales, Northern Ireland and Scotland. Those developed in the devolved countries borrowed heavily from *ECM* in England. These documents are similar in broad aims, scope, structures and aspirations for children. All of them are underpinned by broad national outcomes and aspirations for children, with some differences in the national outcomes specified. They all provide a strategy to support the integration of children's services and improve outcomes; and they stress the importance of early intervention and provide a continuity of services from early intervention through to child protection and risk.

Thus in terms of the wider legislation, structures and processes which underpin the child protection systems in the UK, each part has its own clear and separate vision for what it wants to achieve for children and its own distinctive policy for achieving it. While there are some differences in structures and polices to safeguard and protect children, there are many parallels. All parts of the UK approach the protection of children in broadly similar ways. While there is legislative difference, much of this was in place before devolution was introduced. The purpose of much of the legislative and policy reform across the UK has been to increase levels of accountability as a result of high profile child death and child abuse cases.

Chapter 6

Managing Individual Cases where there are Child Protection Concerns

6.1 INTRODUCTION

In this chapter we shift from comparing wider structures, mechanisms and processes for managing child protection, to zoom in on examining arrangements to protect individual children who may be at risk of child abuse and neglect. We examine the different processes and mechanisms that exist across the UK to respond to referrals and investigate concerns. We compare emergency protection measures, look at arrangements for information sharing, for registration, review and de-registration of children at risk of abuse.

As outlined in the previous chapter, each area of the UK has its own inter-agency guidance setting out the procedures for handling individual cases if there are concerns about a child. The main aim of this guidance is to encourage professionals and organisations to work together when there are child protection concerns. Alongside central government guidance, organisations usually have their own local procedures. Everyone who works with, or has contact with, children or with parents or carers (for example, those working in education, health, social care, the police, early years services, youth justice, in adult mental health, substance misuse, criminal justice or housing agencies), is expected to be familiar with national inter-agency guidance as well as their own individual agency guidance and to know what to do about concerns about the welfare of a child.

The broad stages of the child protection process – referral, investigation and assessment, case conference, and case management and review are the same in each part of the UK but within these broad stages there are some distinctive features (Vincent 2010b). This chapter outlines the various stages of the child protection process, highlighting

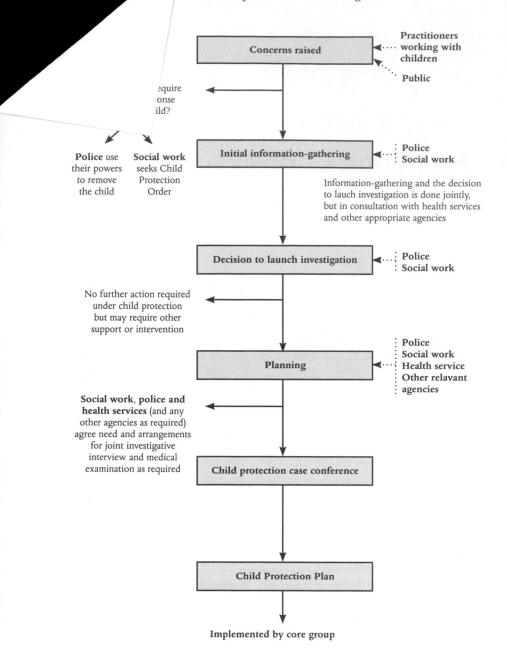

FIGURE 6.1 RESPONDING TO CHILD PROTECTION CONCERNS (SCOTTISH GOVERNMENT 2010A)

similarities and differences across the UK. Figure 6.1, which is tak
the Scottish Government's new inter-agency child protection guid
a useful illustration of how an individual case progresses when th
child protection concerns. It summarises what happens in Scotlan but
could just as easily be used to describe how an individual case proceeds
in England, Wales and Northern Ireland. The main difference would be
that social work services would need to be substituted with children's
social care in England and social services in Wales and Northern Ireland.

6.2 RESPONDING TO CONCERNS AND MAKING A REFERRAL

In all four parts of the UK the child protection process begins when a
professional, a family member, the child him/herself, or a member of the
public has a concern about the welfare of a child. Referral is the first stage
of the child protection process in all four areas of the UK. Anyone who
has concerns about the safety or welfare of a child can make a referral to
statutory services:

- local authority children's social care services, the police or the
  National Society for the Prevention of Cruelty to Children
  (NSPCC) in England

- social services, the police or the NSPCC in Wales and Northern
  Ireland

- social work services, the police, or the Children's Reporter in
  Scotland.

The UK approach contrasts with that taken in some other countries such
as the US and Australia where there are mandatory reporting requirements
and professionals are legally obliged to refer to statutory agencies when
they have concerns about a child.

The agencies listed above have a duty, (or in the case of the NSPCC
are mandated under the various Children Acts for England, Wales and
Northern Ireland), to respond to reports from professionals and the public
and to take action to protect children. If the police are the first agency to
receive information about a child they normally refer their concerns to
children's social care, social services or social work services. Children's
social care, social services or social work services screen referrals made
to them and respond to them as they see fit. Most referrals are received
by telephone. In some parts of the UK statutory services have to respond
within set timescales:

- In Northern Ireland inter-agency guidance (DHSSPS 2003) states that telephone referrals from professionals should be followed up in writing within 24 hours; in England and Wales within 48 hours (DCSF 2010; Welsh Assembly Government 2006); the new Scottish guidance does not specify that referrals should be followed up in writing (Scottish Government 2010a).

- The English and Welsh guidance also states that local authority children's social care/social services should decide how to respond to a referral and record their next steps of action within one working day following discussion with other agencies. The Scottish guidance states that local authorities should make initial enquiries and consult with other agencies but no timelines are given.

All parts of the UK publish statistics on the number of children for whom there are concerns.[1] A 'referral' is, however, defined differently in different parts of the UK. Indeed there is evidence to suggest that data may not even be consistent within one area of the UK. The Scottish Government warns, for example:

> It should be noted that different local authorities may classify child protection referrals differently. For example, some local authorities start the referral process at different points and some local authorities do not include unborn children. As a result of these differences, comparisons across years and across local authorities should be made with caution. (Scottish Government 2010b, p.7)

Table 6.1 highlights the number of referrals in each part of the UK but because of variations in how a 'referral' is defined this data is not comparable. Scotland publish data on the number of child protection referrals over the year, while in England and Wales a referral is defined as 'a request for services to be provided' (Department for Education 2010, p.9; Welsh Assembly Government 2010b, p.2) by children's social care or the social services department in respect of a case where the child is not previously known to the council, or where the case was previously open but is now closed; a child cannot be referred if his or her case is already open. In England and Wales referrals, therefore, include all

---

1   All statistics for England used in this chapter are taken from Department for Education (2010b); statistics for Wales are taken from Welsh Assembly Government (2010b) and Welsh Assembly Government (2010a); all statistics for Scotland are taken from Scottish Government (2010b); statistics for Northern Ireland are taken from DHSSPS (2010b), DHSSPS (2010a) and DHSSPS (2010c).

concerns about the welfare of a child, not just child protection concerns. Northern Ireland usefully publish both the total number of referrals to social services and the number of 'child protection' referrals which they define as 'those referrals for which the initial assessment indicates that there may be child protection issues' (DHSSPS 2010a, 2010b, p.12) and it is interesting to see that child protection referrals account for only a very small proportion of the total number of referrals to social services (Vincent 2008a).

TABLE 6.1 NUMBER OF REFERRALS

Area of the UK	Number of referrals (figures for England, Wales and Scotland for the year ending 31 March 2010; figures for Northern Ireland for the year ending 31 March 2009)
England	603,700 requests for services to be provided
Wales	49,000 requests for services to be provided
Scotland	13,523 child protection referrals
Northern Ireland	28,440 referrals to children's social services 3825 child protection referrals

Although referral data is not comparable across the UK, the number of referrals, however they are counted, has increased in all parts of the UK in recent years:

- In England the number of requests for services to be provided fluctuated in the five years up to 2009, then increased in 2009–10.

- In Wales the number of requests for services to be provided increased by 5% between 2008–09 and 2009–10.

- In Scotland the number of child protection referrals increased by 6% between 2008–09 and 2009–10.

- In Northern Ireland the number of child protection referrals increased by 25% between 2007–08 and 2008–09.

The recent increase in the number of referrals in England has been attributed to professional reaction following the death of Peter Connelly. Professionals were castigated in the media for failing to recognise that Peter was being maltreated (Munro 2011) and this appears to have had an impact on recent practice with professionals choosing to err on the side of caution. Northern Ireland usefully publishes data on the source of child protection referrals. In the quarter ending 31 March 2010:

- 43% of referrals originated from social services

- 8% originated from schools or education welfare officers

- 13% originated from the police

- 5% originated from health

- 9% originated from relatives/neighbours/friends

- 22% originated from other sources (e.g. voluntary organisations, anonymous, self).

Unfortunately data on the source of referrals is not available in other parts of the UK. It would be useful if data were available so we could establish whether there has been an increase in the proportion of referrals from universal services in line with the strengthened role envisaged for these services in recent policy reforms across the UK.

6.3 INITIAL INVESTIGATION AND ASSESSMENT

Referrals may result in a number of different routes being taken, including:

- no further action

- referral to another service for family support if the child is considered to be in need but not at risk of significant harm

- further investigation.

The police must be informed if a concern may constitute an offence. Inter-agency guidance in all parts of the UK stipulates that whenever there is reasonable cause to suspect a child is suffering significant harm or likely to suffer significant harm, a strategy discussion involving social care, social work or social services, the police and other appropriate agencies should be initiated by social care, social work or social services at the earliest opportunity.

Statutory agencies usually undertake some sort of initial investigation to determine what response should be made in relation to a referral. Initial investigation is normally undertaken by a social worker but may involve the police, as well as health and education. Information may be gathered by undertaking an initial assessment.

In Scotland, if initial investigation suggests a child may be in need of compulsory measures of care, information may be passed to the Children's Reporter. On receipt of information from any source about a case which may require a Children's Hearing to be arranged, the Children's Reporter will also undertake an initial investigation (the Scottish Children's Hearings system is explained in more depth in the previous chapter). This may entail asking for information from other agencies, or asking the social work service to undertake an assessment or prepare a background report. Following initial investigation, if a Children's Reporter feels a child may be in need of compulsory measures of supervision he or she will arrange a children's hearing.

If initial investigation suggests that a child may have suffered significant harm, or is at risk of suffering significant harm, social work, social services or local authority children's social care must undertake a joint investigation. In England, Wales and Northern Ireland the NSPCC also has the power to investigate as does the Reporter to the Children's Hearing System in Scotland. Assessment is part of the process of joint investigation and each part of the UK has developed tools for undertaking comprehensive assessments (assessment frameworks are outlined in more depth in the next chapter). If parents refuse access to a child for the purpose of assessment, agencies may apply for a Child Assessment Order in all parts of the UK. If granted by a court, a Child Assessment Order directs parents or carers to co-operate with an assessment. A Child Assessment Order does not, however, take away the child's own right to refuse to participate in an assessment providing he or she is of sufficient age and understanding.

England and Wales publishes data on the number of initial assessments undertaken (see Table 6.2). An initial assessment is defined in England and Wales as 'a brief assessment of any child who has been referred to social services with a request that services be provided' (Department for Education 2010b; Welsh Assembly Government 2010b). The number of initial assessments undertaken has increased gradually in England and Wales over the last few years.

TABLE 6.2 NUMBERS OF INITIAL ASSESSMENTS AND CORE ASSESSMENTS COMPLETED IN YEAR ENDING 31 MARCH 2010

	England	**Wales**
Initial assessments completed	395,300	24,380
Core assessments completed	137,600	7782

The 2006 version of inter-agency guidance for England (HM Government 2006a) and the inter-agency guidance for Wales (Welsh Assembly Government 2006) both stated that initial assessments should be completed within seven working days to determine whether or not a child was in need and whether there was reasonable cause to suspect the child was suffering or likely to suffer significant harm. The latest version of *Working Together* (DSCF 2010) extended the timescale for the completion of an initial assessment from seven to ten working days from 1 April 2010. In Northern Ireland inter-agency guidance states that an initial assessment must be completed within seven days, and an initial plan must then be developed. England and Wales both publish data on the percentage of initial assessments which are undertaken within the relevant timescales: in England 67.3 per cent of initial assessments were completed within seven working days in the year ending 31 March 2010 (slightly less than in the previous year); and in Wales 65 per cent (also a slight decrease).

Scotland and Northern Ireland do not publish data on the number of initial assessments undertaken. Northern Ireland does, however, publish data on the outcome of referrals to children's social services. Eighty per cent of children referred to social services in the year 2008–09 were allocated for further action (service or assessment), an increase of just over 20 per cent compared to figures for 2007–08; there was a fall of 41 per cent in the number of children referred where no action was required. There was, however, a significant increase in the number of children referred for whom no action was possible due to unmet need from 58 in 2007–08 to 580 in 2008–09. The Northern Ireland publication also includes data on the number of child protection investigations completed over the year. The number of investigations increased by almost a quarter between 2007–08 and 2008–09.

6.4 EMERGENCY PROTECTION

Sometimes emergency action needs to be taken to protect a child. Emergency procedures to protect children believed to be in immediate danger exist in all four parts of the UK and may be invoked at any point in the child protection process. (See Appendix for a comparison of emergency protection measures in each part of the UK.) Emergency procedures are similar across the UK. All four areas of the UK have:

- Emergency Protection Orders (known as Child Protection Orders in Scotland)

- police protection powers

- Exclusion Orders.

Emergency Protection Orders/Child Protection Orders and police protection powers were introduced under the various Children Acts in the UK. Emergency Protection Orders/Child Protection Orders can be made by a court if there are reasonable grounds to believe the child is, or is likely to, suffer significant harm if he or she is not removed to, or allowed to stay in, a place of safety. The order requires a person to produce the child, authorise the child's removal to a place of safety, or authorise the prevention of the child's removal if he or she is already in a place of safety. Police protection powers enable a police officer to remove a child to a place of safety without court authorisation, for a specified period of time, providing certain criteria are met.

Child Protection Orders (CPOs) apply in Scotland and Emergency Protection Orders (EPOs) in England, Northern Ireland, and Wales, the contents of which are similar in all of these jurisdictions with a few notable exceptions:

1. The duration of a CPO in Scotland lasts no longer than eight days and a hearing must take place on the eighth working day after an order was implemented. In England, Wales and Northern Ireland, this can be extended by seven days. Thus, the duration of a CPO is eight days in Scotland and potentially 15 days elsewhere in the UK.

2. A CPO has the same impact in every country as it authorises the removal of the child by the applicant or prevents the removal of the child from a place he is being accommodated. In Scotland, however, a CPO can also prevent the disclosure of a child's location to any person classified in the order.[2]

3. Within Scotland, an initial hearing must be heard on the second day after the implementation of the order to determine whether the CPO should be continued until the hearing on the eighth day.[3] There is no such provision in England, Wales or Northern Ireland.

---

2   CA Act 1995 s.57(4)(d).

3   CA Act 1995 s.59(2) & (3).

4.   In Scotland, a child, parent or other relevant person may apply to vary or to set aside a CPO either before the initial hearing or before two days have passed since the hearing sat.[4] In England and Northern Ireland, a child, parent or relevant person may apply to have the order discharged after 72 hours have passed since the implementation of the order but only if they did not receive notice and were not present at the original hearing where the Emergency Protection Order (EPO) was granted.[5]

5.   In Scotland, with regard to alternative short term procedures, in addition to the police powers available are powers available to justices of the peace. Under the legislation, a justice of the peace may use any of the CPO powers where application to a Sheriff is not possible.[6] In England and Northern Ireland, this power derives solely with the police.

6.   In England, an EPO automatically gives the applicant parental responsibility for the child.[7] In Scotland, a CPO has the same impact as an EPO in England, however, the provision is worded slightly differently. Instead of handing the applicant automatic parental responsibility, the provision allows for the applicant to apply for a direction in relation to the exercise or fulfilment of any parental responsibilities or parental rights in respect of the child concerned, if the person considers such a direction necessary to safeguard the welfare of the child.[8]

7.   In England, there are extra powers available to ask people to disclose information about a child's whereabouts if he cannot be found and to search premises to find a child with respect to whom an EPO has been made. A court may also allow for a search of another child on premises with respect to whom an EPO ought to be made.[9] These additional powers are not specifically mentioned within Scottish legislation.

8.   In Scotland, where a police constable has used powers provided to him by the 1995 Act and removed a child to a place of safety, he

4   CA Act 1995 s.60(8).

5   CA Act 1989 s.45.

6   CA Act 1995 s.61(3).

7   CA Act 1989 s.44(4)(c).

8   CA Act 1995 s.58(4).

9   CA Act 1989 s.48.

can only keep the child in that place for 24 hours.[10] In England, where a constable removes a child in a case of emergency, he may keep the child in police protection for 72 hours.[11]

9. In England and Wales a local authority shall make initial inquiries to ascertain whether they should take any action to safeguard or promote the child's welfare. They do this if they discover that a child is subject to an EPO or they have obtained an EPO with respect to the child.[12] In Scotland, the procedure is different due to the Children's Hearing system (i.e. there is an initial hearing to decide whether to continue the CPO, and if it is continued, a Children's Hearing will follow), as such the same duties are not included in the legislation.

The Cleveland Inquiry Report, published in England in 1988, identified a major problem with Place of Safety Orders (POSOs). These were seen to have given too many powers to professionals to intervene in family life, and with too little accountability. This became a major focus for the Children Act 1989 which tightened them up considerably. From then, the length of time a child could be removed from home without a court order was reduced from a maximum of 28 days to eight days (with a possible seven day extension). This was also identified as a major problem in the Report of the Orkney Inquiry in 1991.

Exclusion Orders were introduced so that children did not always have to be removed from home in emergency situations. They permit the exclusion of an alleged abuser from the home. Scotland was the first part of the UK to introduce exclusion orders under the Children (Scotland) Act 1995. Exclusion orders were not included in the Children Act 1989 in England and Wales (McGhee and Francis 2003) or in the Children (Northern Ireland) Order 1995. They were introduced in England and Wales under an amendment to the Children Act 1989 which was made under the Family Law Act in 1996 and under the Family Homes and Domestic Violence (Northern Ireland) Order 1998 in Northern Ireland. Data on the number of protection orders or exclusion orders are not published in child protection statistical bulletins in any part of the UK.

---

10 CA Act 1995 s.61(6).

11 CA Act 1989 s.46(6).

12 CA Act 1989 s.47.

6.5 CASE CONFERENCE

Initial investigation may indicate that a child is a 'child in need' as defined by the various Children Acts in each part of the UK, but that there are no substantiated concerns that he or she is suffering or likely to suffer significant harm. Following initial investigation, if a child is, however, still considered to have suffered, or to be at risk of suffering significant harm, then local authorities in all parts of the UK may decide to convene an initial child protection case conference. A case conference can also be convened prior to a child's birth if there is reason to suspect an unborn child may be likely to suffer significant harm. In England, Wales and Northern Ireland a case conference must be convened within 15 days of the strategy discussion; in Scotland the new guidance specifies that a case conference should be convened no later than 21 days from notification of the concern. The Scottish guidance issued in 2010 also states that participants should be given a minimum of five days notice of the decision to convene a Child Protection Case Conference (CPCC) whenever possible. Timescales are not specified in other parts of the UK although the English guidance states that:

> Those attending should be notified of conferences as far in advance as possible, and the conference should be held at a time and place likely to be convenient to as many people as possible. (DCSF 2010, p.171)

Case conferences bring together professionals involved with the family as well as family members and, if he or she is older, the child. At the conference professionals determine whether the child has suffered or is likely to suffer significant harm in the future and whether or not he or she should be the subject of a child protection plan. There are some variations in inter-agency guidance across the UK in terms of how case conferences should operate, including slight differences around the provision of written reports and around minuting:

- In England and Wales the guidance states that a copy of the minutes must be sent to everyone invited as soon as possible and that conference decisions must be shared within one day.

- In Northern Ireland the guidance states that the minutes be sent to all invitees within 14 days.

- The Scottish guidance states that the minutes should be sent out within 15 calendar days and that the chair should produce a record of key decisions and agreed tasks for circulation within one day of the meeting; it also states that participants should receive a copy of the agreed Child Protection Plan within five calendar days of the case conference.

- The English and Welsh guidance state that the minutes are confidential and not to be shared with third parties without the consent of the chair or key worker; this is not specified in the Scottish or Northern Ireland guidance (Vincent 2008b).

All areas of the UK publish data on the number of initial case conferences that are convened in a year (see Table 6.3).

TABLE 6.3 NUMBER OF INITIAL CASE CONFERENCES

Area of the UK	Number of conferences
	(figures for England, Wales and Scotland for the year ending 31 March 2010; figures for Northern Ireland for the year ending 31 March 2009)
England	43,100
Wales	3687
Scotland	4660
Northern Ireland	2159

The number of initial case conferences in Scotland increased by ten per cent between 2008 and 2009 yet the number of referrals only increased by three per cent over the same period. In 2009–10 this pattern reversed – the number of initial case conferences reduced slightly while the number of child protection referrals went up: while 37 per cent of all referrals resulted in a case conference in 2008–09, the proportion fell to 34 per cent in 2009–10. In Northern Ireland there was an even larger increase of more than 20 per cent, in the number of initial case conferences held between 2008 and 2009. However, in contrast to Scotland, the number of child protection referrals increased at an even greater rate than the number of case conferences – by 25 per cent. In Wales there was a substantial increase in the number of initial child protection case conferences held in 2009–10 compared to 2008–09. The number of referrals also increased but at a slower pace than the number of conferences.

Northern Ireland and Scotland both publish data on the outcome of case conferences. In Northern Ireland 84 per cent of children who were the subject of an initial case conference in the year ending 31 March

2009 became registered compared to 76 per cent in Scotland in the year ending 31 March 2010.

6.6 REGISTRATION

Wales, Scotland and Northern Ireland have child protection registers which are maintained by social work/social services. A child's name is placed on the register if the case conference concludes that there are reasonable grounds to suspect he or she has been suffering or will suffer abuse or neglect or is at risk of suffering abuse or neglect. In England the child protection register was phased out and replaced by the Integrated Children's System (ICS) in April 2008. Although England no longer has a child protection register, registration still exists in the sense that children are recorded on the ICS as having a child protection plan. Across the UK registration, therefore, provides a central point of enquiry for professionals who are concerned about a child's safety or welfare, regardless of whether or not there is actually a child protection register.

The decision to register a child is taken by a child protection case conference when there are reasonable grounds to suspect he or she has been suffering or will suffer abuse or neglect, or is at risk of suffering abuse or neglect, and agencies need to work together to protect the child. If a child is registered a child protection plan must be developed for him or her in all parts of the UK. Where a child becomes the subject of a child protection plan the case conference has to consider how professionals and the family should work together to protect the child. This involves appointing a lead professional, key worker or a case coordinator, depending on which part of the UK the child lives, who is usually a social worker, to take responsibility for the case and for completing a core or comprehensive assessment of the child's needs. In addition, a core group of professionals and family members are appointed to implement the child protection plan. The Welsh and English guidance states that the first meeting of the core group should take place within ten working days of the initial child protection conference. The new Scottish guidance specifies that the initial core group meeting should be held within 15 calendar days of the initial child protection conference. Time scales are not given in the Northern Ireland guidance.

England and Wales both publish data on the number of core assessments undertaken (see Table 6.2, p.115), Scotland and Northern Ireland do not. A core assessment is defined in England as 'an in-depth assessment which addresses the central or most important aspects of the child's needs' (Department for Education 2010b, p.13). There are several junctures at which a core assessment may start, depending on the child's circumstances, and the existence of child protection concerns is not a prerequisite. The number of core assessments undertaken has increased gradually in England and Wales over the last few years. In England and Wales inter-agency guidance states that core assessments should be completed within 35 working days. In Northern Ireland the guidance states that a second stage of assessment should be completed within 15 days. England and Wales publish data on the percentage of core assessments completed within the specified timescales: 78.1 per cent of core assessments were completed within 35 working days in England in the year ending 31 March 2010 (a similar proportion to 2009), and 63 per cent in Wales (a slight increase compared with 2009 figures).

All four areas of the UK publish data on registration. Table 6.4 outlines the number of registrations as at 31 March 2010 by gender.

TABLE 6.4 NUMBER OF REGISTRATIONS, BY GENDER

	England	**Wales**	**Scotland**	**Northern Ireland**
Total registrations as at 31 March 2010	39,100	2730	2518	2357[13]
Boys as % of total	51	51	51	Not available
Girls as % of total	48	49	48	Not available

Table 6.5 illustrates the number of registrations over the period 2002 to 2010. In England and Wales the number of registrations has increased since 2002, and there were particularly large increases between 2008 and 2010. In Scotland and Northern Ireland numbers similarly increased until 2009 but decreased in 2010 by six per cent in Scotland and five per cent in Northern Ireland.

---

13   At the time of writing the number of registrations as at 31 March 2010 for Northern Ireland had been published; however, data disaggregated by gender was not yet available.

TABLE 6.5 NUMBER OF REGISTRATIONS OVER PERIOD 31 MARCH 2002–10

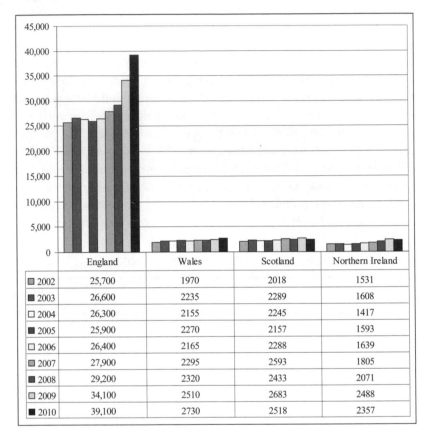

	England	Wales	Scotland	Northern Ireland
2002	25,700	1970	2018	1531
2003	26,600	2235	2289	1608
2004	26,300	2155	2245	1417
2005	25,900	2270	2157	1593
2006	26,400	2165	2288	1639
2007	27,900	2295	2593	1805
2008	29,200	2320	2433	2071
2009	34,100	2510	2683	2488
2010	39,100	2730	2518	2357

In all parts of the UK registration data are disaggregated by age, as well as gender, but the age groups that are used are not directly comparable:

- In Scotland data is broken down into unborn children; children aged 0–4; 5–10; 11–15; and 16 and over.

- In Northern Ireland, under 1; 1–4; 5–11; 12–15; and 16 and over.

- In England and Wales, under 1; 1–4; 5–9; 10–15; and 16 plus.

Data can only, therefore, be compared across the UK for under 5s, 5–15s and over 16 year olds. Table 6.6 shows that children and young people who are registered are somewhat older in Northern Ireland than in the rest of the UK. Just over a third of children are under five in Northern

Ireland compared to over half in Scotland, and a significantly higher proportion of children are 16 and over in Northern Ireland. The figures for 2009 have, however, been used for Northern Ireland because 2010 figures were not available at the time of writing and it is possible that the difference would have been less marked if 2010 data had been used. Children in Northern Ireland also tend to stay on the child protection register for a longer period than children in other areas of the UK (see Table 6.10, p.130) and it is possible that a high proportion of the young people aged 16 and over who were on the register at 31 March 2009 had been on the register since before they were 16. Indeed the Northern Ireland annual statistical publication also breaks down the number of children who were registered in the year ending 31 March 2009 by age and this shows that just four per cent of young people who became registered over the year were 16 and over.

TABLE 6.6 REGISTERED CHILDREN, BY AGE

Registered children by age (as at 31 March 2010 for England, Wales and Scotland; 31 March 2009 for Northern Ireland)	England	Wales	Scotland	Northern Ireland
Under 5s as % of total	43	45	52	35
5–15 as % of total	54	52	48	58
16 and over as % of total	2	2	0	7

England and Wales publish the rate of registrations per 10,000 population under 18. At 31 March 2010 43 per 10,000 children were registered in Wales and 35.5 per 10,000 in England. The rate has increased considerably in both areas since 2007. Scotland report the rate per 1000 population aged 0 to 15 so their figures are not directly comparable. However, as outlined above, Scotland has a very small proportion of over 16s on the child protection register so the figures are not likely to be substantially different. 2.8 per 1000, or 28 per 10,000 population aged 0 to 15 were registered in Scotland at 31 March 2010. Rates in Scotland have remained fairly stable in comparison to England and Wales where rates have increased significantly. Annual data for 2010 were, at the time of writing, not yet available for Northern Ireland, but in the quarter ending 31 March 2010 Northern Ireland had a much higher rate of

children on the child protection register than the other areas of the UK
– 54.6 children per 10,000 population aged under 18. Northern Ireland
continued to publish quarterly data after 31 March 2010 which shows
that the rate has continued to increase – 56 children per 10,000 under
18 were registered in the quarter ending 30 June 2010 and 58.5 per
10,000 in the quarter ending 30 September 2010.

All four parts of the UK publish data on re-registrations (see Table
6.7). Across the UK between 12 per cent and 16 per cent of registrations
have previously been registered. At the time of writing 2010 figures were
not yet available for Northern Ireland but there was a significant fall in
the percentage of re-registrations in Northern Ireland between 2007 and
2009.

TABLE 6.7 RE-REGISTRATIONS

Area of the UK	Percentage of registrations previously registered (year ending 31 March 2010 for England, Wales and Scotland; year ending 31 March 2009 for Northern Ireland)
England	13.4
Wales	16
Scotland	16
Northern Ireland	12

In England, Wales and Northern Ireland if a case conference decides that
a child should be registered the category of abuse (neglect, physical abuse
or injury, sexual abuse, or emotional abuse) the child has suffered, or is
likely to suffer, must be determined. Under the new guidance in Scotland,
it is no longer necessary to identify a category of registration relating to
the primary type of abuse or neglect, as was previously the case. Instead,
the key areas of risk to the child should be recorded to enable the child
protection plan to be more explicitly linked to the individual child. It
was felt that the four categories of neglect, physical abuse, sexual abuse
and emotional abuse were too restrictive. For example, it was argued that
a child could be neglected because of concerns around domestic abuse
or substance misuse and that neglect might impact on a child's health
and emotional well-being. This new approach fits with the emphasis
within *Getting it Right for Every Child* (GIRFEC) on meeting all the needs
of individual children, not just their needs for protection.

Although professionals no longer have to specify a category of
abuse for registration purposes, definitions of abuse and neglect are still

outlined in the new guidance in Scotland. The definitions of abuse and neglect which are used in inter-agency guidance across the UK are similar but there are some minor variations:

- In England and Wales the definition of physical abuse specifically mentions that a parent or carer may fabricate or induce illness in a child; the Scottish definition also includes fabricated or induced illness by a carer; however, this is not covered in the guidance in Northern Ireland.

- In Northern Ireland and Wales, but not England and Scotland, the guidance specifically states that domestic abuse, parental mental health problems and parental substance misuse may expose children to emotional abuse.

- The English definition of sexual abuse states that sexual abuse is not solely perpetrated by adult males. Women and other children can be perpetrators; this is not found in the definitions of sexual abuse in other parts of the UK.

- The English definition of neglect states that neglect may occur during pregnancy as a result of maternal substance misuse; this is not found in the definitions of neglect in other parts of the UK.

All parts of the UK currently publish statistics on registration by category of abuse (see Table 6.8) and it remains to be seen whether Scotland will still be able to do so now that professionals no longer have to identify a category for registration purposes. Registration data by category of abuse is one of the few statistics that can be compared across the UK and it would be a loss if such data were no longer comparable. In all four areas of the UK the highest proportion of registrations are for neglect. However, Northern Ireland has a lower proportion of registrations for neglect than other areas because it has a far higher number of 'mixed' registrations (registrations for more than one category of abuse), and mixed registrations frequently include neglect with one or more other forms of abuse. If the number of mixed registrations including neglect are added to the number of registrations for neglect alone in Northern Ireland then half of all registrations are for neglect which is comparable to the proportion in other parts of the UK. Northern Ireland also has a lower proportion of registrations for emotional abuse and a higher proportion for physical abuse than the other three parts of the UK.

TABLE 6.8 REGISTRATIONS BY CATEGORY OF ABUSE (2009–10
FOR ENGLAND, WALES AND SCOTLAND; 2008–09 FOR NORTHERN
IRELAND)

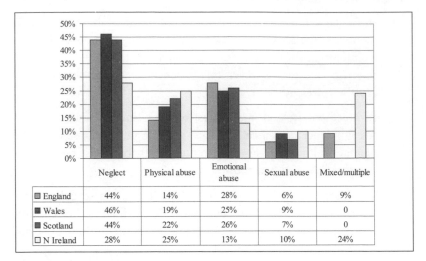

	Neglect	Physical abuse	Emotional abuse	Sexual abuse	Mixed/multiple
England	44%	14%	28%	6%	9%
Wales	46%	19%	25%	9%	0
Scotland	44%	22%	26%	7%	0
N Ireland	28%	25%	13%	10%	24%

In England, Wales and Scotland there has been an increase in the
proportion of registrations for neglect and emotional abuse over the
period for which data is available and a decrease in the number of
registrations for physical abuse and sexual abuse. The proportion of
registrations for emotional abuse increased particularly substantially in
Wales and Scotland between 2007 and 2009. The picture for Northern
Ireland is again somewhat different to the rest of the UK because of the
high proportion of mixed registrations.

Where it is concluded that a child has suffered, or is likely to suffer,
significant harm in the future, the case conference may consider the
evidence and decide whether any legal action should be taken, whether,
for example, care proceedings should be initiated. In Scotland the case
conference will also decide whether or not to refer the child to the
children's reporter.

6.7 REVIEW AND DE-REGISTRATION
In all areas of the UK the first child protection case conference review
should take place three months after the initial conference and then at
six month periods if the child remains on the register and/or continues
to have a child protection plan. The purpose of reviews is to establish
whether the child is continuing to suffer, or is likely to suffer, harm and to

monitor the progress of the child protection plan. Decisions to de-register children are made at review conferences. A child will be de-registered once he or she is considered to be no longer in need of a child protection plan, because the reasons for registration no longer apply, and he or she is no longer considered to be at risk of harm. A child may also be de-registered if he or she reaches the age of 18 or dies. De-registration may not necessarily lead to withdrawal of services since the child may continue to require support to meet his or her needs and promote his or her well-being.

England and Wales publish data on the proportion of cases which should have been reviewed over the year which were reviewed – 96.8 per cent in England at 31 March 2010 (slightly less than in 2009), and 96 per cent in Wales (also a slight decrease). Scotland and Northern Ireland do not publish data on case review.

All four areas of the UK publish data on the number of de-registrations. In England de-registrations refer to the number of children whose child protection plans were discontinued, in Wales, Scotland and Northern Ireland the number who were removed from the child protection register (see Table 6.9).

TABLE 6.9 DE-REGISTRATIONS

Area of the UK	Number of de-registrations
	(for England, Wales and Scotland year ending 31 March 2010; for Northern Ireland year ending 31 March 2009)
England	37,900
Wales	3150
Scotland	3826
Northern Ireland	1401

The statistical publications in all parts of the UK disaggregate the number of de-registrations by length of time on the register (see Table 6.10). Children in Northern Ireland spend longer on the child protection register before they are de-registered than children in England, Scotland or Wales. More than half of children in Northern Ireland had been on the register for over a year in 2009 compared to one-third of children in England and around one-fifth of children in Scotland and Wales in 2010. As outlined above, however, 2010 data were not available for Northern Ireland at the time of writing and it is possible that these variations may have narrowed.

TABLE 6.10 DE-REGISTRATION, BY LENGTH OF TIME ON REGISTER

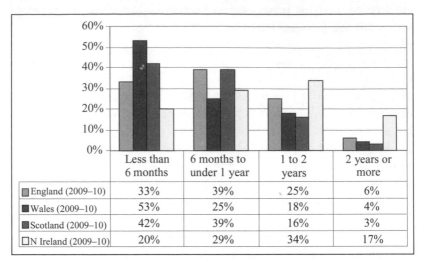

	Less than 6 months	6 months to under 1 year	1 to 2 years	2 years or more
England (2009–10)	33%	39%	25%	6%
Wales (2009–10)	53%	25%	18%	4%
Scotland (2009–10)	42%	39%	16%	3%
N Ireland (2009–10)	20%	29%	34%	17%

Numbers of de-registrations have increased across all parts of the UK in recent years in line with increased numbers of registrations in most areas.

6.8 SHARING INFORMATION WHERE THERE ARE CHILD PROTECTION CONCERNS

In order to be able to respond to concerns about children, professionals need to understand when it is necessary to share information and what they should do with it. While the need for effective information sharing between professionals working with children and families where there may be child protection concerns is recognised, in practice this proved challenging particularly where cases may be complex and involve a wide range of professionals and agencies. This section of the book considers the guidance on information sharing that exists across the UK.

a. Guidance on information sharing

Across the UK legal frameworks exist governing the unlawful use of confidential information and there are codes for individual professions. The legal basis for this is:

- The Human Rights Act 1998. Article 8 specifically recognises the right to respect for private and family life (HM Government 2009a).

- The Data Protection Act 1998 prevents personal information being used for purposes other than that for which it has been collected (Scottish Government 2010e).

- The common law duty of confidentiality applies to situations when a person shares information with another in circumstances where it is reasonable to expect that the information be kept confidential (Welsh Assembly Government 2007b).

In addition, all disclosures must be within a public body's statutory powers (Scottish Executive 2007a).

b. Sharing information with consent

While children and families have the right to confidentiality as a norm, where there are child protection concerns, there are necessary limits to this. The Northern Ireland guidance highlights that consent will normally be sought before personal information is disclosed (DHSSPS 2003). In Scotland children and families have the right to know the information that is being exchanged and where possible their consent should be sought (Scottish Government 2010a). Wales states consent is the basis upon which there is disclosure (Welsh Assembly Government 2007b). The English guidance deals in some detail with the issue of informed consent and also makes it clear that where possible the wishes of those who do not consent to share information should be adhered to (HM Government 2009b). Informed consent by children and young people is specifically referred to in the guidance of England and Northern Ireland. In England, where a young person has the capacity to understand and make their own decisions they are able to give or refuse consent to information sharing. This is expected in relation to children over 12 and enshrined in law for those over 16. In the case of the latter, their wishes should be the basis for making a decision even when a parent disagrees.

A parent has the right to consent where it is judged a child is not competent to do so (HM Government 2009b). However, even in these cases the child's views should still be sought and be taken into account. The code in Northern Ireland also deals with children who lack capacity to consent (DHSSPS 2009). Where children and young people do not wish information to be shared, professionals should try to gain their agreement to inform parents. When agreement is not obtained information can be shared with parents where it is considered necessary in the child's best interests (DHSSPS 2009).

c. Sharing information without consent

There are two instances where information may be shared without consent. The first is where there is a court order or statutory obligation to disclose (HM Government 2009b; Welsh Assembly Government 2007b). The guidance for England notes that this is the case unless the organisation is mounting a challenge to such an order (HM Government 2009b). The second basis for sharing without consent is if it can be 'justified in the public interest' to protect a child or to prevent or detect a crime (HM Government 2009b, p.21).

The guidance in England states that 'it is critical that where you have reasonable cause to believe that a child or young person may be suffering or may be at risk of suffering significant harm, you should always consider referring your concerns to children's social care or the police, in line with your Local Safeguarding Children Board (LSCB) procedures' (HM Government 2009a, p.7). The Wales guidance reflects the position that 'most practitioners in children's services understand that they have a duty to share information when they or others have evidence that a child is being or is at risk of being, abused or neglected' (Welsh Assembly Government 2007a, p.295). The Northern Ireland guidance stares that there are many instances where sharing information is an important aspect of safeguarding children and that disclosure is 'usually justified' where doing so would be in the best interests of the child and it is 'impractical' or 'inappropriate' to gain consent (DHSSPS 2009, p.8). In Scotland the child protection guidance states 'Where there are concerns about harm, abuse or neglect, these must be shared with the relevant agencies, so they can decide together whether the harm is, or is likely to be, significant' (Scottish Government 2010a).

Across the UK, it is the responsibility of professionals to judge when, what and with whom confidential information is to be shared for the purpose of protecting a child. Where sharing information without consent is considered, individuals should discuss the matter with an appropriate person able to give advice such as their manager or a trusted colleague.

> The key factors in deciding whether or not to share confidential information are necessity and proportionality, i.e. whether the proposed sharing is likely to make an effective contribution to preventing the risk and whether the public interest in sharing information overrides the interest in maintaining confidentiality. (HM Government 2009a, p.21)

The Northern Ireland Code expands the explanation about the need for public interest to 'exceptionally prevail' over an individual's right to privacy against the benefits of disclosure (DHSPPS 2009, p.18).

However, decision making in this area can be complex, as child protection information gained from public sources can be imprecise and ambiguous (Clark and McGhee 2008). In addition, inadequacies in information sharing in child protection have also been highlighted in inquiries and reviews into child deaths (Vincent 2010a).

Whilst acknowledging the difficulty in this area it does set limits and states that 'health and social care staff could be found to be negligent if a disclosure was not made but a public interest justification could clearly be made and harm resulted' (DHSSPS 2009, p.18).

Information that is passed on, should be proportionate and relevant for the reason stated and sent only to those with legitimate need to know (HM Government 2009b; Scottish Government 2010a).

> The amount of confidential information disclosed, and the number of people to whom it is disclosed, should be no more than is strictly necessary to meet the public interest in protecting the health and well-being of a child. The more sensitive the information is, the greater the child-focussed need must be to justify disclosure and the greater the need to ensure that only those processionals who have to be informed receive the material (the need to know basis). (Welsh Assembly Government 2007a, p.301)

The Northern Ireland guidance raises the possibility of disclosure of parts of the information to assist in assessing the level of harm and to inform a decision about whether further information should be released. The caveat to this is that there should be no delay in passing on information 'if this would increase the risk of harm to the child' (DHSSPS 2009, p.28).

Individuals should be informed where possible prior to the information being shared and even where they have not given consent. This includes children who should be told that information will be shared, the nature of the information to be shared and who it will be sent to. However, in Wales it is cautioned that this should not be done if it 'would adversely affect the purpose for which the information is to be shared' (Welsh Assembly Government 2007a, p.296).

d. When consent should not be sought

The Scottish guidance acknowledges there may be instances where it is not appropriate to attempt to obtain consent (Scottish Government 2010a). This is expanded in the Wales guidance which states that 'you should gain consent to share information unless it is not safe or possible to do so, or if it would undermine the prevention or detection of a crime' (Welsh Assembly Government 2007, p.301). Northern Ireland states that where prior notification to share 'would prevent achieving the justified aim of the disclosure and where doing so would put the safety of the member of staff or another person at risk' (DHSSPS 2009, p.19). English guidance also states

> some circumstance where you should not seek consent from the individual or their family, or inform them that the information will be shared. For example if doing so would:
>
> • place a person (the individual, family member, yourself of a third party) at increased risk of significant harm if a child or serious harm if an adult
>
> • or prejudice the prevention, detention or prosecution of a serious crime
>
> • lead to an unjustified delay in making enquiries about allegations of significant harm to a child, or serious harm to an adult.
>
> (HM Government 2009a, p.21)

Complex child welfare cases generally involve more than one public service. Effective information sharing is an integral part of being able to protect children. Across the UK, the norm is that information shared across agencies is done with the consent of children and families. Where this is not possible, guidance suggests that it is possible to share information without consent. However, caution is needed to ensure this is appropriately done.

6.9 PROTECTING CHILDREN IN SPECIFIC CIRCUMSTANCES

Inter-agency guidance in all parts of the UK includes general guidance for managing cases but also provides supplementary guidance on how to protect children in specific circumstances where they may be particularly vulnerable. Table 6.11 provides a comparison of the specific circumstances which are covered in the guidance in different parts of the UK. The list of specific circumstances which are covered has increased as inter-agency guidance has been updated over the years. In 2008, the Centre produced a briefing paper comparing inter-agency guidance across the UK in 2008 (Vincent 2008b). Since this paper was written England has updated their guidance and added information on parental mental illness, parental learning disability, children in hospital, children affected by gang activity, children affected by violent extremism, children with families whose whereabouts is unknown, and children who go missing from education. Parton (2011) has commented on the growth in the length and complexity of the guidance in England which has arisen partly because of the addition of lengthy supplementary guidance on a range of specific protection issues. When the Centre published their paper in 2008 the most up-to-date version of inter-agency guidance in Scotland was ten years old (Scottish Office 1998) and the only specific circumstances which were covered were stranger abuse, children living away from home, organised abuse, abuse of children with disabilities, and abuse by children and young people and children on international visits. As can be seen in Table 6.11 the new Scottish guidance now covers a much wider set of specific circumstances.

Governments across the UK, and particularly in the case of England, have tended to write supplementary guidance to cover any potential circumstance in which a child might be harmed. There is, however, no evidence to suggest that children will be protected simply because guidance exists on that issue and there will always be new risks emerging that have not been covered.

6.10 CONCLUSION

In this chapter we shifted from comparing wider structures and mechanisms and processes for managing child protection to examining arrangements throughout the UK to protect individual children at risk of abuse and neglect – arrangements for responding to referrals, investigating child protection concerns, for protecting children in an emergency, for registering, reviewing and de-registering children at risk of abuse.

We have argued that there are similar arrangements in place for initiating investigations into child protection concerns in each of the four parts of the UK. However, the child protection system in Scotland adds another dimension to this where a decision needs to be made about whether or not a child might be in need of compulsory measures of care and whether or not a referral to the Reporter to the Children's Hearing System is required.

TABLE 6.11 PROTECTION OF CHILDREN IN SPECIFIC CIRCUMSTANCES

Circumstance	England	Northern Ireland	Wales	Scotland
Domestic violence/abuse	X	X	X	X
Parental mental illness	X	X	X	X
Parental substance misuse	X	X	X	X
Fabricated or induced illness	X		X	X
Parental learning disability	X		X	X[14]
Children living away from home	X	X	X	X
Allegations of abuse by a professional carer/volunteer	X	X	X	X[15]
Organised/complex abuse	X	X	X	X
Stranger abuse		X		X[16]
Historic abuse	X[17]			X
Abuse of children with disabilities	X	X	X	X
Abuse by children and young people	X	X	X	X
Bullying	X	X	X	X
Sexually exploited children	X	X	X	X[18]
Risks posed by ICT	X	X	X	X
Sudden unexpected death in infancy		X		X
Female genital mutilation	X		X	X
Forced marriage and honour based violence	X		X	X
Lack of parental control	X		X	
Race and racism	X		X	X[19]
Child abuse linked to belief in possession or witchcraft or in other ways related to spiritual or religious belief	X		X	
Children with families whose whereabouts is unknown	X		X	

14 Mentioned briefly in section on disabled parents and carers.

15 *Interim Guidance on Best Practice in Responding to Allegations against Foster Carers* is mentioned in the section on children who are looked after away from home.

16 The children who go missing section mentions stranger abduction.

17 Mentioned in sections on organised abuse and allegations of abuse against a person working with children.

18 Mentioned in sections on children who go missing, children and young people who place themselves at risk, ritual abuse by organised networks and child trafficking.

19 Mentioned in section on children and young people experiencing mental health problems.

Circumstance	England	Northern Ireland	Wales	Scotland
Children who go missing from education	X		X	X[20]
Children and young people who go missing	X	X[21]	X	X
Children living in temporary accommodation	X		X	
Migrant children	X		X	
Child victims of trafficking	X		X	X
Unaccompanied asylum seeking children	X		X	
Children in hospital	X		X	
Visiting of psychiatric patients by children	X	X	X	
Children of prisoners	X[22]	X	X	
Children in custody		X	X	
Children who are privately fostered	X		X	
Children affected by gang activity	X			
Children affected by violent extremism	X			
Non-engaging families	X[23]		X[24]	X
Children and young people experiencing mental health problems	X[25]		X[26]	X
Children and young people who place themselves at risk	X[27]			X
Under age sexual activity	X		X	X

Across the UK there is guidance which stipulates timescales for initial assessment and these vary across the UK. Slightly different statistical data is published in the four parts of the UK about referrals and this makes UK-wide comparison problematic.

Measures to protect children in emergency child protection situations also exist in all parts of the UK and have in common: Emergency Protection Orders (Child Protection Orders in Scotland); Police Protection Powers; Exclusion Orders. Data on numbers of protection orders or exclusion

20 Mentions home educated children in section on children who are missing and children missing from education mentioned in section on responsibilities for education.

21 Children who run away from institutions mentioned in section on institutional care.

22 Only mentioned very briefly in a section on sources of stress for children and families.

23 Does not specifically mention non engaging families but has a whole chapter on working effectively with children and their families, including a section on working with fathers.

24 As in England there is a chapter on working with children and families.

25 Mentioned in chapter on the impact of maltreatment.

26 As in England mentioned in chapter on impact of maltreatment.

27 Self destructive behaviour mentioned in section on the impact of maltreatment.

orders are not published in any part of the UK. Exclusion orders exist in each part of the UK but are rarely used.

Multi-agency case conferences are convened to consider individual child protection cases in each part of the UK. While there are differences in detail and timescales, processes are similar and their role is consistent across the UK: to determine what has happened to the child, determine future risk and plan for the future. All parts of the UK have procedures in place for providing written reports and minute taking, although these differ in detail. While there are only small differences in arrangements for case conferences and while all parts of the UK publish data on case conferences it is not necessarily the same and difficult to make UK comparison.

All parts of the UK have arrangements in place for registration, review and de-registration. Once again these arrangements across the UK have remained relatively unchanged over time and similar in each part of the UK. Decisions to register are taken by the child protection case conference. If a child is registered it is specified that a clear plan is necessary for how professionals will work together to protect the child. Once again, the process and aims of holding case conferences have been around since the system was set up and are similar in each part of the UK. There are differences in detail mainly in relation to planning arrangements and timescales. Once again, despite very similar systems across the UK, there are differences in the way statistical information is gathered and published making it difficult to compare rates of registration across the UK.

With regard to arrangements for registration, while Scotland, Wales and Northern Ireland have retained the Child Protection Register, England has not. In England registration was replaced with the Integrated Children's System (ICS). However, this does record children who have a child protection plan. Across the UK, registration is still the central point of inquiry for professionals where there are concerns about a child's safety. All four parts of the UK publish data on registration.

Each part of the UK has its own code governing arrangements for professionals sharing information between themselves and agencies where there are concerns about a child. Again, these are broadly similar throughout the UK with some differences in detail. All share as the norm child and family rights to confidentiality and specify conditions in which information can be shared with or without consent. These circumstances are broadly the same with some differences in specific wording.

All parts of the UK have guidance for managing cases where children may be particularly vulnerable. It has been argued that the guidance produced to take account of new understandings of specific harm to children and widening definitions of abuse account almost entirely for the growth in size and complexity of policy documents produced as lengthy supplementary guidance to the main guidance (Parton 2011). While this tendency towards longer and more complex guidance is evident throughout the UK, it has perhaps been less so in the devolved countries than in England. New national guidance in Scotland has developed some Scotland-specific supplementary guidance; in others it contains direct links to the equivalent English supplementary guidance.

Thus while there are distinctive features in relation to arrangements to protect individual children, the broad stages of the system are similar throughout the UK and have remained relatively unchanged since the system was set up. We included a table earlier in the book reproduced from the new National Child Protection Guidance in Scotland in 2010 outlining the various stages in a child protection investigation; while there are some differences in, for example, timescales for responding and some differences in what constitutes a referral, the broad stages correspond and the diagram could equally apply to any part of the UK.

While the processes are very similar, and differences between them small, there are subtle differences in definitions of abuse used. This means that data collected about child abuse differs across the UK and while the systems are very similar, data is collected in ways which make it difficult to compare referral rates, make UK-wide comparison or draw UK-wide conclusions.

Despite recent reform being about prevention and early intervention, in line with the shift towards family support orientation, there remains a clear point in all four parts of the UK where more traditional child protection processes come into play. Despite the burgeoning number of policy documents and guidance emanating from central government, there has been remarkably little change in procedures for managing individual cases where there are child protection concerns. Despite the new emphasis on meeting need early, there is little evidence to suggest that these developments have brought fewer children into the system at this point. Whatever changes professionals experience in managing individual cases as a result of bureaucratic demands, the experience is unlikely to have changed much for the children and families entering the child protection system at the point of investigation.

Once again we highlight that while there are distinctive features between different parts of the UK, currently the broad stages are similar and include: referral, investigation, case conference, management and review.

Chapter 7

Assessment Frameworks

7.1 INTRODUCTION

In this chapter we examine the frameworks for assessing children's needs, including their child protection needs. Currently, each part of the UK is at a different stage in the development and introduction of national comprehensive assessment tools or frameworks for assessing the needs of children including those who may be in need of protection.

Practitioners undertake assessments in order to identify children's needs. The assessment process consists of two related tasks: the gathering of information to find out what is happening to a child and family; and analysis of that information in order to gain a better understanding of *why* things are happening. The understanding that a professional acquires through undertaking a holistic assessment is used to inform decisions about action to be taken, and to plan services around the individual needs of the child and family (Rose 2009; Seden 2007).

Over the last decade all parts of the UK have introduced assessment frameworks which outline the domains to be considered in an assessment of children's needs, guiding practitioners towards useful analyses and encouraging them to draw on a range of evidence in making decisions (Crisp *et al.* 2007; Milner and O'Byrne 2002). Assessment frameworks were introduced to address concerns in inquiries, inspection reports and research studies: comprehensive assessments of need were not undertaken at all or were not sufficiently analytical; children had to undergo numerous assessments because agencies worked in silos, and failed to communicate effectively with one another; or that following assessment children and families were not receiving the services that were required to address their needs and prevent difficulties escalating (Luckock 2007; Reder, Duncan and Gray 1993; Seden 2007). There is an underlying assumption that the introduction of assessment frameworks will systematise practice, thereby improving services and contributing to more effective outcomes for children and young people (Crisp, *et al.* 2007).

This chapter considers the development of frameworks to assess children's needs across the UK. It explores similarities and differences in the assessment frameworks which have been introduced in England and Wales, Scotland and Northern Ireland and considers available evidence on the impact these assessment frameworks have had on practice.

7.2 ENGLAND AND WALES

a. The *Orange Book*

In England *Protecting Children: a guide for social workers undertaking a comprehensive assessment* (Department of Health 1988) was introduced in 1988 to assist social workers undertaking comprehensive assessments for long term planning for children where child abuse had been confirmed, or was strongly suspected. The guide was created in response to increasing evidence that practitioners were experiencing difficulties in undertaking assessments (Luckock 2007; Parton 2006; Rose 2009). The guide, which became known as the *Orange Book*, was underpinned by a developmental approach. It was distributed in Wales and England and was also widely used by practitioners in Scotland and Northern Ireland. It remained in place for 12 years. However, a number of research studies published during this time revealed that the quality of assessment practice remained variable; child protection plans were still not always informed by comprehensive assessments, and there was a tendency for practitioners to use the guide more as a checklist than an analytical tool (Katz 1997; Rose 2009).

b. The Framework for the Assessment of Children in Need and their Families

The Framework for the Assessment of Children in Need and their Families, introduced by the Department of Health in 2000, and the National Assembly for Wales and Home Office in 2001, replaced the *Orange Book*. It was developed in response to the findings from a programme of research on child protection (Department of Health 1995), as well as a series of government inspections which highlighted inadequacies in assessment. It was designed to support the implementation of Quality Protects, the government's programme to modernise the management and delivery of children's services (Department of Health 1998). It took an ecological approach to assessment and drew heavily on the wealth of research and accumulated practice experience about the developmental needs of children (Department of Health 2000). It centred on an assessment triangle consisting of three domains representing the key aspects of a child's world – the child's developmental needs, the capacity of parents or carers to support their child's development and respond appropriately to their needs, and wider family and environmental factors that may have an impact on a child's development and on the capacity of their parents or carers (Rose 2009). Each domain had a number of dimensions. By taking account of 'the inner world of the self and the outer world of the environment' (Schofield 1998, p.57), the Assessment Framework provided:

> ...a systematic way of analysing, understanding and recording what is happening to children and young people within their families and the wider context of the community in which they live. (Department of Health 2000, p.viii)

A number of principles underpinned the assessment framework, for example that assessments should:

- be child centred
- be rooted in child development
- build on strengths as well as identify difficulties
- be multi-disciplinary
- be an ongoing process
- be evidence based.

(Horwath 2002; Luckock 2007)

Another principle was that professionals should be able to recognise and work with diversity. The guidance accompanying the Assessment Framework emphasised that a diversity of family styles must be recognised and noted that additional specialist help might be needed if the child's first language was not English. There was specific guidance in relation to assessing the needs of children from black and ethnic minorities as well as disabled children (Crisp 2007 *et al.*; Seden 2007).

The Assessment Framework was supported by practice guidance, questionnaires and scales, assessment record forms and a training pack, all designed to ensure widespread understanding of the approach and enable the principles behind the Framework to be translated into practice (Rose 2009). The Department of Health stressed, however, that these resources could not replace professional skills, rather they were tools to assist social workers and other colleagues in the process of assessment, recording and decision making (Department of Health 2000).

The assessment process consisted of three stages – referral, initial assessment and core assessment, with timescales attached to each stage:

- within one working day of a referral social services departments should make a decision about what response was required

- if they considered more information was required then this constituted an initial assessment which should be completed within seven working days. The purpose of an initial assessment was to address the three domains of the Assessment Framework and determine if the child was in need, the nature of any services required and whether a further in depth core assessment should be undertaken

- a core assessment had to be undertaken in 35 days from the point that the initial assessment ended.

(Parton 2006)

c. The impact of the assessment framework on practice

A number of research studies have explored the implementation of the Assessment Framework and its impact on practice. A study of early implementation in 24 local authorities (Cleaver and Walker 2004) highlighted both positive and negative impacts. Positive impacts included improved initial and core assessment, increased inter-agency collaboration, and most significantly, increased involvement of children and families in the assessment process. On the negative side, a considerable proportion of social workers expressed anxiety about their ability to undertake assessments, particularly in terms of analysis of the information and working collaboratively with other agencies, and social workers and managers reported increased workloads. Parents and carers interviewed by Corby, Millar and Pope (2002) in a study in a local authority in north-west England were generally positive about their involvement in assessments but social workers were concerned that staffing resources were being stretched to ensure time limits were met.

Horwath (2002) explored the extent to which the Assessment Framework had improved assessment practice in cases of neglect. She concluded that the principles behind the Framework were not being achieved. Practitioners were not always paying equal attention to all three domains of the triangle, and although they were aware of the need to take race and culture into account, were not always sure how to go about this. Horwath warned that the implementation of the Framework was becoming social services driven, and was not sensitive to the needs of other organisations. It was also becoming form led, with professionals focusing their efforts on information gathering in an attempt to complete the recording form within the set timescales, rather than effectively analysing the information. Horwath also concluded that the Assessment Framework was unlikely to further children's engagement in the assessment process because many practitioners lacked the knowledge and skills to elicit and act upon the views of children and young people.

Bunting (2004) reviewed the research evidence in relation to the Assessment Framework and concluded that findings had overall been reasonably positive, with parents, in particular, finding the new assessment process both inclusive and helpful. The professional view was, however, less straightforward. While many social workers reported that the Framework had improved the quality of assessments and multi-disciplinary working, there was an overall consensus that workloads had increased. Some practitioners were anxious about analysing the information and there were indications that information gathered through the records had not been used to inform decision making.

Rose (2009) points out that inspections of children's services are an additional source of information about how the Assessment Framework is working in practice and a number of joint Chief Inspectors' reports have expressed concerns about the variable quality of assessment practice (Department of Health 2002; Ofsted 2008b). On a more positive note she has also reminded us, however, of the considerable relevance that the Assessment Framework has had cross-nationally. Variations of the Framework have been incorporated into other countries' child welfare systems and the English framework has had considerable influence on the development of new assessment frameworks which have been introduced in Scotland and Northern Ireland as described below.

d. The Common Assessment Framework England

The Common Assessment Framework (CAF) was first introduced in England in 2004. An important part of the *Every Child Matters: Change for Children* (*ECM*) programme in England (Department for Education and Skills 2004), the government claimed it would:

- promote earlier intervention where additional needs were observed

- reduce the number and duration of different assessment processes that children and young people undergo

- improve the quality and consistency of referrals between agencies by making them more evidence-based

- help embed a common language about the needs of children

- enable information to follow the child

- promote appropriate sharing of information

- do so in the context of working in partnership with children, young people and their parents.

(HM Government 2006b)

'Trailblazing' local authorities began to pilot the CAF in 2005. All local authorities were required to begin implementation during 2006 with the programme fully implemented across England by the end of 2008. The CAF uses the same domains as the Assessment Framework and is similarly based on an ecological approach to assessment. It offers a national standardised approach to assist practitioners in conducting an assessment of the needs of a child or young person and deciding how best to meet additional needs which are identified. The CAF process is the subject of detailed government guidance (HM Government 2006b). It involves completion of a standard assessment form by a professional who identifies that a child has additional needs that cannot be met within their own agency. While the Framework for the Assessment of Children in Need and their Families had a specific focus on children in need under the Children Act 1989, the CAF focuses on a broader group of children who may have additional needs and require early intervention if a practitioner is concerned about their progress (Adamson and Deverell 2009; Horwath 2007; Luckock 2007; Seden 2007). It is not intended to be used for immediate and referable concerns about child protection, nor is it intended to replace specialist and statutory assessments; its focus is on universal and family support services:

> In essence, the CAF is a voluntary arrangement that seeks to promote practitioners, children, young people, parents and carers sharing information about actual or potential needs and co-operating to deliver solutions to meet them... Its use is thought to be particularly suitable for children's universal services in health, education, the voluntary and private sectors. (Pithouse *et al.* 2009, p.600)

e. The Common Assessment Framework Wales

The CAF has not been rolled out across Wales. In contrast to England there were no national policies and procedures issued to embed CAF in Wales but it was supported by the Welsh Assembly Government (WAG) who commissioned the Social Care Institute for Excellence (SCIE) to oversee its development (Cleaver *et al.* 2008). A WAG document issued in 2007 provided guidance to those developing the CAF in Wales; however, CAF Wales is evolving gradually with local partnerships responsible for developing their own arrangements for carrying out common assessments (Brandon *et al.* 2009). The CAF is a key part of the *Children and Young People: Rights to Action* programme (Welsh Assembly Government 2004). The early identification of need is a key objective of this programme and the introduction of a CAF to enhance multi-agency working, generate better information sharing and eliminate repeat assessments is seen as an important aspect of this (Brandon *et al.* 2009).

A computer based system was developed in order to record the outcome of a common assessment. These completed 'e-CAFs' were to be submitted and stored on a database which is accessible to all agencies working with children and families (Brandon *et al.* 2009). As in England, the Welsh CAF draws on the Framework for the Assessment of Children and their families to provide a holistic assessment of the child's or young person's needs. Its aims are to engage the wide range of practitioners involved with children and young people and their parents to undertake joint early problem solving, making best use of the potential of strengths within the family (Brandon *et al.* 2009). A number of features were incorporated into the design of the Welsh CAF:

- The CAF is completely voluntary and to be used with children showing low levels of need.

- It is a tool for multi-agency use – children's needs are everyone's business.

- All agencies involved in piloting the CAF are of equal status be they a large statutory or a small voluntary organisation.

- The strategic 'home' of CAF lies in the Children and Young People's Partnerships which operate across local authority areas (Brandon *et al.* 2009).

The WAG selected four areas (comprising five local authorities) to pilot the CAF and its database. A fifth area, which had established CAF independently, was included in the evaluation of the pilot which was

undertaken by the University of East Anglia (Brandon *et al.* 20
The ten month evaluation was intended to identify learning from
pilot sites to inform planning for implementation on an all Wales basis
(Brandon *et al.* 2009).

f. The implementation of CAF and its impact on practice

There have been a number of studies of the implementation of the CAF
and its impact in England. Prior to its implementation there were concerns
that the engagement of professionals in universal services in a common
assessment process would challenge their traditional roles. For example,
one author commented that this would necessitate a change from:

> 'reporters or detectors' of problems and concerns to the main players
> in facilitating families to find resolutions to their problems. (cited in
> Adamson and Deverell 2009, p.408)

Brandon, Howe and Dagley (2006) examined the implementation of
CAF and lead professional working in 12 areas chosen to trial these
processes ahead of the national roll-out. They found that the bulk of CAF
work was being undertaken by practitioners from education and health
and that assessing children holistically demanded a range of different
skills and a new way of thinking for many practitioners.

Gilligan and Manby's (2008) interviews with practitioners and
managers indicated commitment to, and enthusiasm for, many of the
principles underpinning the CAF. Many practitioners remained frustrated
that the services that they believed would benefit children were still not
provided to them after a CAF assessment. Despite high levels of need
very small numbers of children and young people were actually receiving
the service. Gilligan and Manby concluded that CAF assessments were
not equally available to all children with 'additional' needs. They also
found that assessments were most often recorded as being needed
because of concerns about a child or young person's behaviour and/or
parents' ability to cope with their behaviour; practitioners were more
likely to identify boys as having 'additional' needs than girls; the process
was not yet fully 'child centred'; and fathers had no involvement in the
overwhelming majority of assessments.

Professionals from a range of agencies who participated in a study
of implementation of CAF in a rural area (Adamson and Deverell 2009),
expressed concerns about the length of the CAF process and its time
costs. Practitioners varied in the extent to which they grasped the

purpose of the CAF with some tending to see and use it as a one-off referral mechanism or a request for help rather than an assessment linked to referral. In contrast to the findings of Gilligan and Manby (2008), Adamson and Deverell found that fathers or male carers were usually involved if they lived in the household.

Although CAF is now fully implemented across English local authorities, in a study of 280 completed CAFs in four local authorities White, Hall and Peckover (2009) found little evidence that a common language was emerging and revealed considerable variation in practice. For example, CAF was being used as a referral in 70 per cent of cases in trailblazer authorities, compared to 18 per cent in other sites.

Pithouse (2006) carried out an analysis of early common assessment work in Wales. He found that CAF facilitated better information sharing with social services and promoted a more focused service response to referrals. However, he also revealed a limited capacity among some occupational groups to engage with particular assessment fields in the CAF and noted that some practitioners were not seeking the views of children when conducting assessments.

Brandon *et al.*'s (2009) evaluation of CAF for the WAG highlighted limited CAF activity in most areas. Only 36 CAFs were completed in the pilot sites over the course of the evaluation. One of the five sites achieved a slow yet steady increase in the number of common assessments completed but the others did not achieve the same level of progress. An analysis of 13 completed CAF forms from two sites revealed that practitioners were able to provide good information from all three sides of the 'assessment triangle' and record children's and family's needs and strengths with sensitivity. Three families were interviewed and were enthusiastic about the help they received through CAF work. They valued the access to services the CAF gave them, the relationship with the worker and the fact that they did not have to retell their story. Brandon *et al.* (2009) found that the combination of minimal direction from the centre and local adaptation of the CAF process led to confusion in some areas about how to do the CAF and who should do it. The CAF was working most effectively in the area which had not been appointed as a WAG site. This area had adopted a clear structured model of working where CAF was part of a broader model of integrated working. The database was not being used in this area. In the other areas there was no clearly prescribed structure, no lead professional to drive the process, and inter-agency work was not built into the process with many practitioners having to do CAF work alone. There were also a number of problems with using the database, particularly associated with parents' reluctance to give consent for information to be stored and shared electronically (Brandon *et al.* 2009). Brandon *et al.* posed a number of questions for the WAG:

- Would they want to ensure compatibility of CAF systems across Wales so families who moved would understand how to get access to services?

- Could they ensure that sectors at central level agreed as far as possible to a single common assessment process?

- Would CAF work be monitored centrally, and if so how would success be gauged?

Writing in January 2009 Brandon *et al.* stated that 'CAF and its supporting database appear to be at a cross roads and decisions need to be made about future implementation' (p.168). At the time of writing CAF was being used in some local authorities in Wales but no decision has been made yet about how it would be implemented on an all Wales basis.

7.3 SCOTLAND

a. The *My World Triangle*

The My World Triangle, a new assessment framework in Scotland, is an important part of the Scottish Government's overarching policy for children's services – *Getting it Right for Every Child* (GIRFEC). Scotland's seven national indicators of well-being – healthy, achieving, nurtured, active, respected, responsible, and safe have been used for the purposes of identifying concerns, assessment and planning in the GIRFEC practice model (Aldgate and Rose 2008). The GIRFEC practice model has been piloted in one local authority in Scotland and is now being implemented across Scotland. Local authorities are at various stages of implementation. The *My World Triangle* has been developed to aid assessment of a child and family's circumstances and is an integral part of the GIRFEC practice model (Scottish Government 2008a). The domains within the *My World Triangle* draw on those in the English assessment triangle and enable practitioners to consider systematically the child's development needs, the parents' capacity to meet those needs and the impact of the child's wider family and environment. The three sides of the triangle – How I grow and develop; What I need from people who look after me; and My wider world – have, however, been deliberately framed from the point of view of a child to reinforce the GIRFEC principle that children are at the centre of all of the activities undertaken by practitioners (Aldgate and Rose 2008; Rose 2009).

The *My World Triangle* is designed to help practitioners gather further information about the needs of the child or young person. Scottish Government (2008) guidance states that practitioners working with children or young people can use the assessment triangle at every stage to think about the whole world of the child or young person. It promotes a model of practice that considers the child or young person's needs and risks, and therefore addresses some of the criticisms of the English assessment triangle in relation to the absence of risk factors. Practitioners are asked to use the practice model to assess both risks and need, to look at the connections and effects of risk in one area with what is going on in the rest of the child's life. The approach allows practitioners to consider the impact of risks on children's well-being in the long term as well as the short term (Aldgate and Rose 2008).

Information from the *My World Triangle* and other sources can be analysed using the new resilience matrix which is based on a model developed by Daniel, Wassell and Gilligan (1999) and Daniel and Wassell (2002). A detailed explanation of how to use the resilience matrix is available on the tools and resources pages of the GIRFEC website (Scottish Government 2008a). Where the concern raised about the child is routine, not particularly complex, and confirmed by analysis of the information around the triangle, it may not be necessary to use the resilience matrix (Scottish Government 2008a). Where needs and concerns are more complex, the resilience matrix helps practitioners to organise the information around the triangle and make sense of the strengths and pressures, in order to identify the scope for additional support to help the child and family build on the potential resources they already have (Stradling, MacNeil and Berry 2009). Information can be grouped around the four headings of resilience, vulnerability, protective environment and adversity so that the balance of strengths and needs can be judged. By grouping the information, the risks that are causing gaps in the child's well-being, and indications of what needs to change, will become clear. Practitioners are then asked to use professional judgement to weigh the balance of risks and positive factors and decide on the priorities for action (Aldgate and Rose 2008).

In common with the English Assessment Framework, the GIRFEC practice model is underpinned by a strong evidence base. Both the *My World Triangle* and the resilience matrix have been developed from an evidence base of research and contemporary theory about children's development (Aldgate and Rose 2008).

b. The impact of the GIRFEC assessment model on practice

The GIRFEC approach, including the practice model, was piloted and evaluated in Highland and the evaluation of the Highland pathfinder (Stradling *et al.* 2009) provides some evidence of the impact of the approach on practice. Stradling *et al.* found that lead professionals were using the *My World Triangle*, but not always using it effectively. Most practitioners were analysing the information relating to each side of the triangle:

> a sizeable and growing group of practitioners (mostly those who have been trained and get regular opportunities to apply the practice model) are learning how to use these processes to make professional judgements that are based on evidence which can be reviewed by others in terms of its soundness, the way in which it was interpreted and the validity of the conclusions that were drawn. (Stradling *et al.* 2009, p.135)

However, Stradling *et al.* (2009) commented that in a sizeable minority of cases practitioners were offering a description rather than an analysis. They tended to reiterate what had been found but did not necessarily identify how it was impacting on the child and family. Moreover, some practitioners were deciding what actions to take first and then retrospectively evidencing them using the triangle.

Social workers reported that the *My World Triangle* helped them organise a lot of disparate information about the child and his or her circumstances in order to identify the kind of intervention that would be most appropriate and proportionate to the level of need. There were also clear signs of a shared language of assessment emerging between health visitors, nursery nurses, early years' teachers and volunteers running childcare and parent toddler groups. Stradling *et al.* (2009) concluded, however, that this change of mindset was further advanced in the early years than in work with older children and adolescents. The resilience matrix was rarely being used and:

> Without it there was a tendency to focus on the pressures and to either exclude the strengths from the analysis or downplay their significance. (Stradling *et al.* 2009, p69)

Some professionals listed and described the strengths and pressures rather than using them to understand the impact they were having on the child and family and some specified outcomes purely in terms of the initial concern that was raised, rather than the summary of needs that had been identified through the assessment process. For example, a number of records and plans raised an initial concern about a child or young person's school attendance. The assessment around the triangle then revealed a complex picture where a number of factors in the child's life may have contributed to poor attendance, such as a mother's mental health problems, domestic abuse, and bullying. Sometimes the plan for the child then put in place a number of actions to address all these pressures and circumstances but the only specified outcome was improved school attendance (Stradling *et al.* 2009).

Stradling *et al.* (2009) concluded that practice was changing in the right direction but further professional development would be needed to bring all professionals' skills up to the same level in terms of analysing the information gathered around the *My World Triangle*; using the resilience matrix where appropriate; and ensuring this analysis informed the planning process in an appropriate and proportionate way. They also concluded that more needed to be done to facilitate the integration of specialist assessments into the overall assessment of the child's needs, and to relate specialist assessments to the *My World Triangle* in terms of their overall impact and implications for the child and family:

> At the beginning of the pathfinder phase there was a widespread tendency to see the information gathering and assessment process as a kind of jigsaw puzzle. Each agency would add its piece of the jigsaw into the picture... It was then assumed that this model would evolve into an electronic assessment which almost constructs the overall picture of the child for you. What has become apparent when looking at some of the more recent records and plans is that the jigsaw is a misleading heuristic device here. It leads to an assessment comprised of fragmented bits and pieces. A more appropriate heuristic device would be a Venn diagram which recognises that the information provided by each service can overlap and is not necessarily restricted to one side of the triangle or another. (Stradling *et al.* 2009, p.73)

7.4 NORTHERN IRELAND
a. Understanding the Needs of Children in Northern Ireland assessment framework

In Northern Ireland, the Department of Health and Social Services and Personal Safety (DHSSPS) has introduced a new standardised referral process for children in need to ensure greater standardisation of services and processes across the five Health and Social Care Trusts. This approach is based on the English Assessment Framework and followed a review of existing systems and practice (Bunting 2004). It is underpinned by similar policy intentions as in other parts of the UK, particularly earlier identification of needs (Rose 2009).

Gateway Teams, established in each trust, act as the front door to services for children and families (DHSSPS 2008b). Gateway staff undertake initial assessments prior to transferring cases to specialist teams or signposting to other services. The Gateway teams operate within agreed regional protocols to ensure consistent approaches and to facilitate transfer of cases within given timescales. The approach is underpinned by the introduction of Understanding the Needs of Children in Northern Ireland (UNOCINI), a common assessment framework for social work that is increasingly being adopted by other agencies (Devaney, McAndrew and Rodgers 2010; DHSSPS 2008c).

A number of principles underpin the new assessment framework in Northern Ireland:

- promoting the UN Convention on the Rights of the Child
- child-centred and rooted in child development
- building on the strengths of the family
- involving children and carers in the assessment of their needs
- being evidence and knowledge-based
- assessment being a continuing process and not just an event
- full inter-agency involvement
- facilitating more specialist assessments
- based on shared values
- allied to the Department of Health Framework
- deliverable in Northern Ireland and drawing on existing practice.

(DHSSPS 2006b)

The Assessment Framework consists of 12 domains which appear under three main headings: children's needs, parents' or carers' capacity to meet the child's needs, and family and environmental factors. The domains are similar to those in the English and Scottish models, but have been specifically designed for Northern Ireland's unique system of providing services to children and families. In contrast to the English and Scottish Frameworks the domains and dimensions in the Northern Ireland model are presented in a circle rather than a triangle.

The UNOCINI Framework sets out a number of assessment pathways:

- initial assessment

- family support pathway

- child protection pathway

- looked after children pathway

- leaving care pathway.

(Devaney *et al.* 2010)

These pathways reflect the continuum of interventions a child might experience, but the inclusion of the Family Support Pathway reflects a commitment to identify a family's needs at an earlier stage, rather than waiting for situations to worsen before intervening (Devaney *et al.* 2010). The Framework provides a format for a preliminary assessment that can be undertaken by any professional within any agency. The objective is to facilitate an accumulation of information known about a child or family with a view to assessing the need for referral to social services. The development of a framework of *thresholds of need* (DHSSPS 2008d) and *thresholds of intervention* (DHSSPS 2008e) allows professionals to consider what further supports and interventions they can offer, before they consider a referral to social services. These tools enable practitioners to complete a needs 'map' to assess children and articulate the needs and strengths of the child and the family and any risks and protection issues that may exist (DHSSPS 2006c). The issue of risk assessment runs as a theme throughout and is rooted in Gregg Kelly's work at the University of Queens (Kelly 2007).

On occasion other specialist assessments will be required and these should complement the UNOCINI assessment. A number of research based assessment models have been identified with a view to achieving endorsement of standardised assessment tools to be used across Northern Ireland in areas such as parental substance misuse, domestic violence and parental mental illness (Devaney *et al.* 2010).

To date there has been no formal evaluation of UNOCINI but anecdotal evidence suggests that UNOCINI assessments are increasingly being undertaken in schools, youth justice and probation as well as in health and social care (Devaney *et al.* 2010).

7.5 THE EFFECTIVENESS OF ASSESSMENT FRAMEWORKS

While all parts of the UK have developed frameworks for assessing children's needs, it is worth remembering that frameworks can only ever be used as memorandums for effective practice (Macdonald 2001). No assessment framework or tool will provide practitioners with the right answers in terms of identifying the needs of children (Horwath 2007) and the introduction of assessment frameworks will not, therefore, necessarily ensure good practice across the UK (Crisp 2007 *et al.*).

> The relative autonomy of the professional in the 1970s is now radically altered by the degree of managerial and statutory guidance, oversight and provision of tools to improve practice, e.g. the set of assessment forms in ICS and the detailed procedures set out in Working Together to Safeguard Children. Any such aids need to be seen not as passive objects but as active contributors to the overall quality of performance. There has, to date, been insufficient attention paid to whether these tools are having the intended beneficial effects on improving assessment and decision making, or creating adverse factors that make it harder for social workers to work to a high standard. (Munro 2011, p.55)

As outlined above, research studies on the impact of assessment frameworks have identified a number of barriers to their implementation in children's services and highlighted negative as well as positive effects on practice. Although the English Assessment Framework emphasised that a diversity of family styles should be recognised, Garrett (2003) maintained that the schedules developed for the Department of Health were intrinsically middle class in their assumptions about standards and behaviour. It will be interesting to see whether the tools developed in Scotland and Northern Ireland, which have similar theoretical underpinnings, can escape this kind of criticism. In Northern Ireland further work is being undertaken to consider the assessment of the needs of children with disabilities and their families, bearing in mind that these parents are not failing in their parenting capacity but often need support and assistance to continue to care for their children who have complex needs (Devaney *et al.* 2010).

One of the main reasons assessment frameworks were introduced was to address concerns that children and families were not receiving the services that were required to address their needs and prevent escalating difficulties. There is, however, evidence to suggest that while assessment frameworks may assist in identifying needs, they provide no further guarantee that children's needs will be met, because this is ultimately dependent on resources. Commentators point out that professionals have a responsibility to ration resources and a responsibility to identify need and these responsibilities conflict with one another. They have expressed concern that during times of severe financial constraint, the identification of needs areas will become very narrow, with services only provided to prevent serious deterioration or risk (Adamson and Deverell 2009; Gilligan and Manby 2008; Parry-Jones and Soulsby 2001; Seden 2007).

The models and frameworks for assessment that have been developed across the UK also reflect an underlying tension between assessment to meet needs and assessment of the risk of significant harm (Seden 2007). Prior to the introduction of the Assessment Framework in England there were concerns that a narrow focus on child abuse and child protection had caused the assessment process to be characterised by an assessment of the risk of abuse (Garrett 2003). The Assessment Framework therefore was designed to move the focus of assessment away from the assessment of risk of child abuse and significant harm towards assessment of the needs of vulnerable children and their families, and early identification of potential impairment to development. Safeguarding and promotion of a child's welfare were seen as connected aims for intervention and access to services was viewed as being via a common assessment route (Parton 2006; Rose 2009). The English Assessment Framework has, however, been criticised for focusing too heavily on the needs of children and marginalising concerns about risk. The term 'risk' was not used in the framework or guidance and practitioners struggled to incorporate risk into their assessment practice, reporting that the only way they were able to assess risk was to consider ways in which parenting capacity impacted on the developmental needs of the child (Brandon *et al.* 2006; Luckock 2007). Horwath (2002) expressed concern that 'the assessment triangle has the potential to become a Bermuda triangle as professionals and managers lose the focus on promoting and safeguarding the welfare of the child' (p.199).

The identification and management of risk is a key part of the assessment process and professionals need to feel confident they are able to assess both risk and needs. The development of assessment frameworks in Scotland and Northern Ireland has been informed by the experiences of the Assessment Framework in England and risk assessment and management have been incorporated into the new frameworks being implemented there. However, debate on this issue has continued in Scotland and the Scottish Government are developing a risk assessment 'tool', partly in relation to concerns from practitioners who are not confident they will be able to assess risk within the GIRFEC practice model. There is, therefore, a danger, that the original vision of GIRFEC as a unifying structure to encompass need, including need for protection, will be diluted and it is unclear how a new risk assessment tool will fit within the broad GIRFEC assessment framework. It is perhaps understandable that high levels of anxiety about 'risk' have led to a search for risk assessment tools, but there are dangers that such tools will offer false assurance, especially if they are used as an alternative to comprehensive assessment of all unmet needs (Vincent and Daniel 2010).

7.6 THE FUTURE OF ASSESSMENT FRAMEWORKS

Some of the frameworks to assess children's needs across the UK are stand-alone documents while others are incorporated into broader frameworks for services for children (Crisp *et al.* 2007). Scotland and Northern Ireland have recently developed co-ordinated frameworks for delivery of children's services and their new assessment frameworks constitute an integral part of these overarching frameworks. In contrast, the Framework for the Assessment of Children in Need and their Families (Department of Health 2000) in England and Wales was developed as a standalone assessment framework. It was, however, designed to support the implementation of Quality Protects (Department of Health 1998) and, in conjunction with the new CAF, plays an important role in the *ECM* programme in England and *Rights for Action* programme in Wales.

There are many similarities in the assessment frameworks being used in children's services across the UK, not least because the frameworks which have been developed in Scotland and Northern Ireland were heavily influenced by the English Assessment Framework. Assessment frameworks can be used as a vehicle for embedding research evidence into practice (Crisp *et al.* 2007) and the various frameworks share similar and explicit theoretical or conceptual underpinnings. Another commonality is that the involvement of children and carers is an integral part of the assessment process. All the frameworks which are used across the UK start from the assumption that assessment is about determining service users' needs, rather than a process that is 'done' to people (Crisp *et al.* 2007). The acknowledgement that assessment may require input from a range of agencies and should be multi-disciplinary to avoid children and carers having to provide the same information on multiple occasions is another common theme.

The Munro Review of child protection in England is examining assessment and considering whether, when a child is referred to children's social care, any existing assessment is continued by social workers, rather than the current system which starts a new bureaucratic process of initial and core assessments (Munro 2011). Munro (2011) is critical of current practice which is seen to be dominated by prescribed timescales and wants the review to result in a better balance between timeliness and quality: 'It should be possible to provide thoughtful assessment and timely decision making without the need for false assessment distinctions and timescales which seek to over standardise the many varied and complex needs of vulnerable children' (p.18).

The new Assessment Framework in Scotland is currently focused on the needs of the individual child. It was specifically designed to avoid some problems associated with the English Assessment Framework and as such, has avoided introducing prescribed timescales. The review of child protection in England is keen to learn from good practice models and there may be something to learn from Scotland's approach to assessment. However, as we have outlined above, the Scottish Government is developing a separate add-on risk assessment tool for professionals and it remains to be seen how well this will fit with the *My World Triangle* and its emphasis on meeting all the needs of a child, and not just their need for protection.

7.7 CONCLUSION

We have examined the frameworks that exist throughout the UK for assessing children's needs including their child protection needs. Each part of the UK has in place comprehensive tools or frameworks for assessing the needs of all children including those who may be in need of protection. Each part of the UK is at different stages in developing and taking forward frameworks nationally. In England, the Framework for Assessment of Children in Need was introduced by the Department of Health in 2000 to replace the *Orange Book*. It centred on an assessment triangle consisting of three domains representing key aspects of the child's world. The Assessment Framework was supported by proactive guidance, questionnaires, scales, assessment record forms and training. Research and review of the framework in England suggested that while the quality of assessments had improved this might have been at the price of having substantially increased work-loads.

The CAF was introduced in 2004 and was a key plank of *ECM* in England and was fully implemented in 2008. It uses the same domains as the assessment framework and is also subject to detailed guidance. In line with *ECM* it focuses on a broader group of children including those in need who may require early intervention but it is not intended for immediate and referable child protection concerns. Its use is voluntary and not governed by statute. Research in England has reviewed the impact and suggested that it is mainly being used by Health and Education professionals who reported feeling frustrated at the lack of services available following a CAF assessment. While the CAF has been rolled out in England, this is not the case in Wales where it is currently being piloted in four areas. Pithouse (forthcoming) analysed early use of it in Wales and suggested that while it did facilitate better communication and a more focused response, some practitioners showed limited capacity to engage with all parts of the CAF and at the time of writing it is not known if it will be rolled out across Wales.

In Scotland the *My World Triangle* was produced in 2010 in the context of GIRFEC. It drew heavily on the domains contained in the English Assessment Model and attempted to address concerns expressed that it focused on the 'needs' of the child rather than on both needs and risk. The Scottish Framework was also explicitly framed to take account of needs and risk. The Framework has not yet been rolled out across Scotland, rather it has been adapted for use and has been evaluated in one local authority area. The evaluation suggested that while practitioners were using it, it was not always being used effectively. Sometimes notes were descriptive rather than analytical and concluded that while practice was changing in the right direction, further policy development was required. While it is available for use in other local authorities, it is not yet known if it will be rolled out across Scotland.

Across the UK assessment frameworks seem to contain an unresolved, inherent tension between assessment to meet need and assessment for risk; and where there is assessment for need there is consistent criticism that where need is identified there is a lack of resources for support. The development of assessment frameworks in Scotland and Northern Ireland have been informed by the experience of the Assessment Framework in England and a risk assessment element has been added. Indeed, recently in Scotland, in the context of producing the new child protection guidance, work has begun to develop a separate risk assessment tool, but there is a danger that the vision of GIRFEC as a unifying structure to encompass child protection needs within the wider concept of meeting need may be diluted. It is unclear how a new risk assessment tool will fit within the broad GIRFEC assessment model.

While there are some differences between assessment frameworks in use across the UK, all have their origins in the model developed in England. They share theoretical underpinnings and their purpose is to outline domains for practitioners to consider in assessing children's needs, to guide practice towards analysis of these and to aid evidence based decision making.

In terms of our three types of system identified in Chapter 3, in relation to assessment frameworks across the UK it is possible to identify movement in the direction of the child focused orientation. Once again we see a process where a policy is first introduced in England, then following a process of review and information becoming available, is adapted and taken up in the devolved parts of the UK.

Chapter 8

Child Death Review Processes

8.1 INTRODUCTION

In this chapter we look at the most serious end of the child abuse continuum and at the arrangements that exist to review cases where a child has died as a result of child abuse and neglect.

Finding out what has happened when a child dies is a basic human right now enshrined in Articles 2 and 3 of the Human Rights Act 1998. All parts of the UK have processes for inquiring into or reviewing child deaths but there are some variations. All parts of the UK have well developed processes for reviewing deaths from abuse and neglect and other serious cases. In exceptional cases a public inquiry may be commissioned by government but most inquiries or reviews where abuse or neglect was known or expected to have played a part are commissioned at local level. In addition to processes for reviewing deaths from child abuse and neglect, some parts of the UK have introduced, or have plans to introduce, processes for wider review of child deaths; this is an attempt to expand child death review beyond the focus of child abuse and neglect to one of public health. This chapter outlines the processes and mechanisms currently operating across the UK to review both deaths from abuse and neglect as well as wider child death review processes. It concludes by considering some of the evidence in relation to the effectiveness of these review processes.

8.2 PROCESSES FOR INVESTIGATING DEATHS FROM ABUSE OR NEGLECT

a. Public inquiries

Any public body or government department in the UK may initiate an inquiry into issues which it considers to be of public concern. There are different types of inquiry with different legal powers and processes. Inquiries do not normally have a remit to examine the conduct of criminal investigations held in relation to a case. Rather their purpose is to examine the role of agencies who were involved in the case up to the point at which the death or serious abuse took place, to establish whether any lessons can be learned and to make recommendations to improve practice.

There appears to be little rationale behind the selection of cases to proceed to a public inquiry. It is often difficult to ascertain how a particular style of inquiry is determined for a particular case or how the decision was made to conduct an inquiry at all. Local issues sometimes determine whether the death or injury of a child results in a formal inquiry. In other cases inquiries may be instigated by media exposure. The media has played a key role in magnifying the profile of some inquiries. Other inquiries have come about as a result of pressure from a range of sources, including families and local communities. Formal inquiries are sometimes undertaken because a more informal review or inquiry has already been undertaken but has failed to satisfy all the parties involved (Corby 2003; Corby, Doig and Roberts 2001; Reder and Duncan 2004; Stanley and Manthorpe 2004).

Since the Children Act 1975 all public inquiries into child deaths or other serious cases of abuse ordered by central government have been statutory inquiries. There were public inquiries into child deaths and serious abuse cases before 1975 but these were not statutory inquiries. Statutory inquiries are normally conducted in public but parts of the inquiry may be held in private. They are usually held in a quasi-judicial way and are often chaired by lawyers. They have powers that other types of inquiry do not – they can compel witnesses, enforce the production of documents and pay legal and other costs to witnesses. Professionals are often not named in reports and are, therefore, given some degree of protection (Corby *et al.* 2001; Hallett 1989).

Until the 1980s most public inquiries in the UK were concerned with the deaths of children who had been physically abused while living with parents or carers in the community. In contrast, in the 1990s concern shifted to the abuse of children in residential homes and schools. This coincided with a reduction in the number of public inquiries into the abuse of children in their own homes and a considerable increase in the number of inquiries into the abuse of children in residential care. Only four out of 50 inquiries in the UK from 1945–1990 concerned residential care whereas from the 1990s inquiries into residential abuse took place in roughly equal numbers to those into abuse at home (Corby 2003; Corby *et al.* 2001).

Public inquiries commissioned by governments are rare in the UK. They figured most prominently in England and Wales in the 1970s and early 1980s and have generally been replaced by less formal types of inquiry.

8.3 LOCAL REVIEW PROCESSES

Inquiries or reviews commissioned by local authorities and health authorities using independent panels are most often used to investigate child deaths and significant abuse cases in the UK. Such inquiries or reviews do not have the power to compel witnesses or produce documents but some have been undertaken in the same adversarial manner as a statutory inquiry (Corby *et al.* 2001).

All parts of the UK have processes for reviewing serious cases. Case review processes vary in different parts of the UK but have the same overall purpose – to establish whether lessons can be learned from a case in terms of improving inter-agency working and better protecting children. Case reviews are not inquiries into how a child died or was seriously harmed, or into who is culpable. They are intended to be used as a learning tool, not as a means of attributing blame: 'It is intended that they should bring added value to judicial and other processes already in place and bring about improvements in practice' (Care and Social Services Inspectorate Wales (CSSIW) 2009, p.19).

8.4 SERIOUS CASE REVIEWS IN ENGLAND AND WALES

England and Wales were the first areas of the UK to introduce case review processes under the *Working Together Under the Children Act 1989* guidelines (HM Government 1989). The introduction of case review processes was a deliberate move away from the type of large scale inquisitorial style inquiries which characterised the 1980s. The government could still order a public inquiry after 1991, but only did so in exceptional circumstances, as they did following the death of Victoria Climbié (Corby 2003; Corby *et al.* 2001; Sinclair and Bullock 2002). The 1988 guidelines introduced a new process by which Area Child Protection Committees (ACPCs) would undertake Part 8 reviews (later known as Serious Case Reviews (SCRs)) in cases where children had been fatally abused, or abused with serious physical and psychological consequences. Local authorities were expected to inform the Department of Health of every case that was subject to a case review and could make their reports public if they considered there was sufficient public concern about the case. The guidelines were revised in England in the 1999 version of *Working Together to Safeguard Children* when the term 'Serious Case Review' was first introduced and in 2000 in Wales when the National Assembly produced its own version of *Working Together to Protect Children*.

The Children Act 2004 and its accompanying regulations placed SCRs on a statutory footing in England and Wales and it is now mandatory for Local Safeguarding Children Boards (LSCBs), which replaced ACPCs, to conduct a SCR if a child dies and abuse or neglect is suspected to be a factor in the death. Whereas ACPCs were responsible for *monitoring* the process of case review SCR has now become a *function* of LSCBs (Brandon *et al.* 2008; Rose and Barnes 2008). The criteria for determining when a SCR should be undertaken became broader. Until 2004 SCRs typically focused on deaths from severe physical assault or extreme neglect but now include suicide, deaths related to domestic violence incidents, deaths of children by a parent with a mental illness, and other deaths related to, but not directly caused by maltreatment (Brandon *et al.* 2008; Rose and Barnes 2008).

Lord Laming's report *The Protection of Children in England: A Progress Report* (2009) made a number of recommendations to strengthen and clarify the SCR process in England:

- The Department for Children, Schools and Families (DCSF) should revise *Working Together to Safeguard Children* so that it is explicit that the formal purpose of SCRs is to learn lessons for improving individual agencies as well as for improving multi-agency working.

- The DCSF should revise the framework for SCRs to ensure that the SCR panel chair has access to all of the relevant documents and staff they need to conduct a thorough and effective learning exercise.

- The DCSF should revise *Working Together to Protect Children* to ensure SCRs focus on the effective learning of lessons and implementation of recommendations and the timely introduction of changes to protect children.

- The DCSF should revise *Working Together to Protect Children* to underline the importance of a high quality, publicly available executive summary which accurately represents the full report, contains the action plan in full, and includes the names of the SCR panel members.

- LSCBs should ensure all SCR review panel chairs and overview authors are independent of the LSCB and all services involved in the case and that arrangements for the SCR offer sufficient scrutiny and challenge.

Lord Laming's recommendations were accepted by the Labour government and new statutory guidance to replace Chapter 8 of *Working Together* was introduced with immediate effect in December 2009. The only one of Lord Laming's recommendations that was not taken forward entirely was that executive summaries should include the names of SCR panel members. Following consultation, it was agreed that executive summaries should include the job titles of panel members but not their names.

In 2007 responsibility for evaluating the quality of SCRs in England transferred to Ofsted from the Commission for Social Care Inspection. LSCBs were required to send completed SCR reports to Ofsted who evaluated them against a set of grade descriptors and in accordance with an evaluation template. They assessed the extent to which the review fulfilled its purpose by reviewing the involvement of agencies, the rigour of analysis and the capacity for ensuring that the lessons identified were learned. Reports were graded as 'outstanding', 'good', 'adequate' or 'inadequate'. The outcome of the evaluation formed part of the evidence used for Ofsted's wider evaluation of the effectiveness of children's services in a local area. Ofsted's first evaluation report, published in 2008, was based on their analysis of 50 SCRs between 1 April 2007 and 31 March 2008. Their second report, published in 2009, covered evaluations of 173 SCRs undertaken between 1 April 2008 and 31 March 2009.

Ofsted's emphasis on the quality of the report was the subject of much criticism, for example:

> No attention, however, is being paid to what makes a good quality serious case review **process**. There is nothing in the grade descriptors used by Ofsted that would indicate any thinking has been done about either the methods by which a serious case review should be carried out, or the areas of academic research and discussion which might be relevant (Owen 2009a, p.267).

Lord Laming's report included a recommendation that Ofsted should in future 'focus its evaluation of serious case reviews on the depth of learning a review has provided and the quality of the recommendations it has made to protect children' (2009, p.66).

Lord Laming's report (2009) suggested that Ofsted evaluations should focus on:

- the quality of the process of the review
- the adequacy of learning and change

- professional practice

- the quality of the recommendations in protecting children to ensure that they are actively driving improved outcomes and better safeguarding systems.

Ofsted developed a revised evaluation framework for SCRs in response to Laming's recommendations but their evaluations continued to be criticised. Participants in the Sidebotham *et al.* (2010) study reported overwhelmingly that Ofsted evaluations had resulted in too much emphasis on getting the process right rather than on improving outcomes for children. While Sidebotham *et al.* (2010) concluded that Ofsted evaluations had led to an improvement in the overall quality of SCRs they recommended that reports should no longer be graded.

Since 2004 an independent author for the SCR overview report has been a requirement. Interestingly, however, Ofsted (2008b, 2009a) found there was no correlation between the quality of the overview report and the independence of its author. Their 2009 report concluded that the independence of the overview writer was important and increasingly more common (114 out of 173 reports were written by independent authors), but the quality of reports also depended on other factors such as the appropriateness of the terms of reference, the quality of the individual management reviews and the robustness of the recommendations and action plans. Lord Laming (2009) commented that there was a lack of clarity around independence in the 2006 Chapter 8 guidance and the updated Chapter 8 guidance offered more clarity around this.

Sinclair and Bullock's (2002) analysis of SCRs was critical of the fact that families were excluded from the SCR process. As a result the 2006 Chapter 8 guidance (HM Government 2006a) required agencies to consider not just whether, but how, family members should be involved. New Welsh guidance published in the same year (Welsh Assembly Government 2006) also stated that the review panel should consider how family members could contribute to the review and who should be responsible for facilitating their involvement. In their analysis of SCRs published in 2008 Rose and Barnes found that family members had contributed in a fifth of cases. They stated, however, that this may not have been the full picture since family members may have declined an invitation to contribute, the circumstances of the case may have made it inappropriate for them to contribute, or the report may not have recorded discussions or negotiations about family involvement. Families were involved in nine out of 47 of the cases Brandon *et al.* (2008) studied in depth and in a small number of cases the child also contributed. Ofsted (2008b) found little evidence that agencies were working with families when undertaking SCRs:

- Eight out of 50 of the case reviews they evaluated recorded that families made a contribution.

- A further eight reviews noted that families were invited to contribute but declined.

- In 19 case reviews the issue was not covered at all.

- In 11 reviews there was a statement that family members were not involved.

- A positive decision not to involve family members was noted in three reviews.

As part of their second evaluation of SCRs Ofsted (2009a) visited 10 LSCBs whose SCRs had been evaluated as good. They found there was a more concerted effort to involve families in these LSCBs. In some cases families were contacted at an early stage of the review process and there were offers to meet family members on more than one occasion. The updated version of the Chapter 8 guidance (DCSF 2010) states that as well as involving family members the SCR Panel should also make arrangements to provide feedback and debriefing to the child (if surviving) and family members/carers, following completion of the Executive summary. The Sidebotham *et al.* (2010) study found that family involvement remained problematic. Participants felt it was important for the family and community to be involved, but they were not clear about the purpose of engagement and felt there was no clear view as to whether families and communities could or should be holding agencies to account.

The 2006 Chapter 8 guidance (HM Government 2006a) and the Welsh guidance (Welsh Assembly Government 2006) included some guidelines on the format of the review report. Rose and Barnes (2008) found, however, that reports in England varied in length, style and presentation:

- Half the reports analysed were under 30 pages long but one-fifth were more than 75 pages.

- There was variation in the use of genograms and some reports omitted a genogram altogether.

- A quarter of reports highlighted lessons for national policy and practice as well as local lessons.

- Recommendations were generally relatively few in number (up to 20), focused, specific and capable of implementation. However, in 12 reviews there were up to 40 recommendations, one review had 40 to 60 recommendations, and one had 80.

The updated version of Chapter 8 (Department for Children, Schools and Families 2010) provided more guidance on how to structure the overview report and individual management reports. It acknowledged, however, that each case may give rise to specific questions or issues and the structure of a SCR would need to be considered in the light of the particular circumstances of the case. It also pointed out that the suggested outline was more applicable to abuse or neglect that had taken place in a family setting and that reviews where abuse had taken place in institutional settings were likely to be more complex.

The 2006 Chapter 8 guidance stated that reviews should be completed within four months of the LSCB chair's decision to initiate a review in England and the Welsh guidance stated that a review should normally be completed within six months. Twelve per cent of the reviews analysed by Rose and Barnes (2008) in England were completed within the timescales laid down, or nearly so, and a further third were completed within 12 months of the incident. Approaching half – 45 per cent – took over a year to complete and 17 per cent of reports were not dated. Ofsted (2008b) found that there were serious delays in most cases. It was not uncommon for SCRs to take more than a year to complete and some took as long as three years. Ofsted concluded that a large proportion of case reviews were inadequate because of the length of time it took to complete them. In their 2009 report Ofsted reported that SCRs were generally being carried out more speedily. They explored whether there was any link between the time taken and the quality of a review and concluded that:

> By itself the time taken did not automatically determine the quality of the review [however], in the most effective reviews clear expectations about timescales are set out at the beginning and the reasons for any subsequent delay are explained and addressed. (p.35)

The updated Chapter 8 guidance (Department for Children, Schools and Families 2010) increased the timeframe for undertaking a SCR from four to six months. It also stated that 'where lessons are able to be identified they should be acted upon as quickly as possible without necessarily waiting for the SCR to be completed' (p.9).

There have been attempts to learn from SCRs at national as well as local level through collation of findings in both England and Wales. In the 1990s three studies collated data from SCRs in England (Falkov 1996; Reder and Duncan 1999; Reder *et al.* 1993). More recently to try and bring clear standards and more consistent approaches to the case review process the findings of SCRs in England have been collated in biennial analyses which draw out key findings and assess their implications for policy and practice locally and nationally. The first of these biennial reviews by Sinclair and Bullock was published in 2002, and there have been further reviews by Rose and Barnes (2008) and Brandon *et al.* (2008, 2009). Sidebotham *et al.* (2010) undertook a scoping exercise to develop recommendations on how to improve national approaches to learning from SCRs. Participants who took part in the study were clear that the system of national collation of SCRs generated useful information and could influence policy and practice. Sidebotham *et al.* recommended a revised system of national analysis. They suggested a research team should be commissioned for at least five years to provide an observatory/reporting function on all SCRs. The team would report annually on the numbers, patterns and key learning from SCRs, compare the findings with data from other sources and have responsibility for reviewing any national implications of recommendations from SCRs. They also recommended the establishment of a national steering group whose role would include recommending specific themes for analysis.

A number of analyses of SCRs have also been commissioned to inform policy in Wales (Brandon *et al.* 2002; Morris, Williams and Beak 2007; Owers, Brandon and Black 1999). Depending upon the number of SCRs they receive, the Welsh Assembly Government have undertaken to commission overview reports every two years to draw out key findings and consider their implications for policy and practice. Marian Brandon and colleagues from the University of East Anglia have recently completed a fourth analysis of SCRs in Wales.

8.5 RECENT DEVELOPMENTS IN ENGLAND

There have been a number of recent changes in SCRs in England. In May 2010 the new Coalition Government announced that they were committed to publishing SCR de-identified overview reports as well as executive summaries. In June 2010 they sent a letter to LSCB Chairs and Directors of Children's Services informing them of a change to the statutory guidance set out in Chapter 8 of *Working Together* relating to publication of SCRs. From 10 June 2010 local authorities were to publish SCR overview reports 'unless there were compelling reasons relating to the welfare of any child directly concerned in the case for this not to happen' (Loughton 2010). The Government outlined that the aim of this policy change was to restore public confidence and improve transparency in the child protection system, and ensure the context in which the events occurred was properly understood so lessons could be learnt. The letter also announced that Eileen Munro had been appointed to undertake a review to improve child protection and that part of her remit would be to consider how SCRs could be strengthened.

Consistent with the move to reduce the burden of inspection referred to in Chapter 5, Eileen Munro's review of child protection in England (Munro 2011) is likely to recommend that Ofsted no longer evaluate SCRs but that the quality of learning more generally be given greater coverage within the overall inspection process. The review is considering:

- the establishment of a national training programme in the systems approach and research methods
- the creation of a central pool of reviewers to support local areas
- the benefits of a national arbiter for case review standards and methods
- the creation of a standardised typology for presentation of findings
- whether there is a basis to revise criteria for initiating SCRs.

It is also considering the establishment of a national body, similar to the National Patient Safety Agency, that will support national and local learning, train reviewers to conduct SCRs, provide quality assurance, and collate findings of reviews to enable national learning. The review appears to support the publication of overview reports. Munro (2011) admits the policy has caused concern in relation to identification but argues that by adopting systems methodology, with its focus on understanding why professionals acted as they did, it will be possible to write up and publish reviews with a focus on professional practice rather than on the detailed story of the child and family.

8.6 RECENT DEVELOPMENTS IN WALES

Until 2009 policy around SCRs in Wales was similar to that in England. There were some differences; for example, SCRs in Wales were not graded by inspection teams as they were in England, but it was not until 2009 that policy in Wales began to diverge markedly from that in England. In 2009 CSSIW commissioned a review of the arrangements for conducting SCRs in Wales and their effectiveness in improving practice and inter-agency working. As in England, there had been a significant increase in the number of SCRs being undertaken by LSCBs and the review suggested this provided evidence of the fact that current review arrangements were not working effectively:

> There are fundamental questions being asked, therefore, about the ability of serious case reviews, as currently constituted, to be the best vehicles for learning lessons when things have gone wrong and for improving safeguarding practice. There is a strange paradox that the greater the number of serious case reviews undertaken, the weaker their impact seems to become. (Care and Social Services Inspectorate Wales 2009, p.3)

The review found there was a high level of agreement across Wales about shortcomings in the present arrangements and the reasons for them, which limited the effectiveness and impact of SCRs: 'there needs to be a more coherent and comprehensive LSCB framework for reviewing, learning and improving safeguarding practice which does not rely solely on SCRs as the driver for achieving change in policy' (p.3).

The review recommended a continuum of reviewing, learning and improving policy and practice. The Deputy Minister for Social Services, in a statement to the National Assembly on 20 October 2009, welcomed the report and its recommendations and asked for specific proposals for implementing the ideas in the report and a second phase of work on next steps was commissioned in January 2010 with the purpose of developing proposals and guidance for implementation. A progress report by Wendy Rose – *Improving Practice to Protect Children in Wales: Developing a New National Framework for Learning and Reviewing* – was published in September 2010 and set out the broad direction of travel. It proposed that the new LSCB framework should consist of:

- *Multi-agency professional forums*: an LSCB programme of facilitated multi-professional learning events for practitioners or managers to examine cases for supervision, consultation and reflection, including cases that have been complex and gone well, cases currently on the register and cases causing concern.

- *Concise reviews:* case reviews held when a child has died as the result of abuse or neglect, or a child has been or was in danger of being seriously harmed and there are multi-agency concerns or high professional anxiety, involving practitioners and their managers in a fully planned and prepared facilitated event examining practice over the last 12 months, using a systemic approach, with a learning output report to the LSCB (and sent to WAG), completed within three months, learning disseminated as appropriate and recommendations and action plan taken forward and audited.

- *Comprehensive reviews:* case reviews held when a child has died as the result of abuse or neglect and was subject to a co-ordinated multi-agency child protection plan and on the child protection register, or was a looked after child, or had been subject to previous concise reviews, involving practitioners and managers throughout the process, using a systemic approach with a timeline normally of 12 months starting with individual management reviews and brought together in an overview report by an independent writer, and concluding with recommendations and an action plan, and a learning event held for the staff involved, a report to focus on agency action, and submitted to the LSCB and to WAG, and to be published. The review to be completed within six months and recommendations and action to be taken forward and audited.

In her progress report Wendy Rose pointed out that the new framework of learning and review would have a number of implications including the need to review the role of policy and the inspectorates in the new process, to seek compatibility with other related review systems, to amend existing regulations and guidance, to consider the resource consequences of the proposals and to ensure an effective quality assurance system is in place to test whether the intended benefits are being achieved.

> What is agreed is that this is not a technical exercise to replace one system, no longer fit for purpose, with another but that developing a national multi-agency approach for reviewing, learning and improving child protection practice will require wider and more far reaching changes in culture, systems and practice. (Rose 2010, p.3)

The progress report was endorsed by the Welsh Safeguarding Children Forum and in February 2011 the Welsh Assembly Government announced their plans to implement a new learning framework to replace SCRs by the end of 2011. They are currently working on developing new draft practice guidance to support implementation.

8.7 CASE MANAGEMENT REVIEW IN NORTHERN IRELAND

Since 2003 ACPCs in Northern Ireland have had responsibility to undertake Case Management Reviews (CMRs) (similar to SCRs in England and Wales) where a child dies, including death by suicide, and abuse or neglect is known, or suspected, to be a factor in the child's death. They are also asked to consider undertaking a CMR where a child has sustained a potentially life threatening injury through abuse (including sexual abuse) or neglect; has sustained serious and permanent impairment of health or development through abuse or neglect; or the case gives rise to concerns about the way in which local professionals and services worked together to safeguard children. Chapter 10 of *Co-operating to Safeguard Children* (DHSSPS 2003) provides guidance on when and how a CMR should be undertaken. The guidance is in the process of being updated following the replacement of ACPCs with a new safeguarding board and safeguarding panels in Northern Ireland.

The circumstances under which a CMR should take place are similar to those in England and Wales but the Northern Ireland guidance does not specifically state that a review should be undertaken where a parent has been murdered and a homicide review is being initiated, or where a child has been killed by a parent with a mental illness. The guidance states that reviews should normally be completed within five months. It says little about the involvement of families in the review process except that the ACPC chair should consider whether family members should be invited to contribute to the review.

ACPCs have to provide a copy of the review report to the Department of Health, Social Services and Public Safety (DHSSPS) which is responsible for identifying and disseminating common themes and trends. Co-operating to Protect Children (DHSSPS 2003) states that the Department will commission regional case management overview reports which will be published at intervals to maximise learning. Researchers from Queens University and the NSPCC have recently undertaken an analysis of CMRs. This is the first analysis of cases in Northern Ireland.

8.8 SIGNIFICANT CASE REVIEWS IN SCOTLAND

While ACPCs/LSCBs in England and Wales have undertaken case reviews when a child dies and abuse or neglect is known, or suspected, to be a factor in the child's death, for many years, until 2007, there was no equivalent procedure in Scotland. Prior to this there was no single system of notification, no agreed criteria for inclusion and no national system of review. The duty for local authorities to co-operate was, however, mandated in the Children (Scotland) Act 1995 and ministers could order an inquiry if they thought it necessary (Axford and Bullock 2005; Galilee 2005). There were a number of approaches for undertaking reviews into significant cases but no standard approach across Scotland. Some local areas, usually through Child Protection Committess (CPCs) did undertake reviews of professional practice following deaths of children known to agencies and where there were concerns about abuse or neglect reviews of significant cases were sometimes undertaken by agencies involved in child protection, whether singly or jointly. Local areas and individual agencies had their own processes and procedures in place and across Scotland there was a degree of inconsistency in how decisions were made about when to call for a review; what type of review to hold; the management of the process; the skills and expertise required to undertake the review; the reporting requirements of the review; and the implementation of the review's findings (Axford and Bullock 2005).

The report of the National Audit and Review of Child Protection in Scotland *Its Everyone's Job to Make Sure I'm Alright* (Scottish Executive 2002) recommended that the Scottish Executive consider the need for guidance on how reviews of child fatalities should be conducted. A Child Death and Significant Case Review Group was established as part of the Child Protection Reform Programme and extensive consultation took place during 2006 on draft guidance for conducting significant incident reviews. A study of international comparisons of child death review processes was commissioned to inform the review group (Axford and Bullock 2005).

Interim Guidance for Child Protection Committees (CPCs) for Conducting a Significant Case Review was published in 2007 to provide a systematic and transparent approach to the review process (Scottish Executive 2007a). The grounds for undertaking an SCR are similar to those for undertaking an SCR in England and Wales but do not include where a parent has been murdered and a homicide review is being initiated. Neither does the guidance specifically state that a review should be undertaken where a child has been killed by a parent with a mental illness though this is presumably covered by 'death by alleged murder or culpable homicide'.

There is a section in the guidance on the involvement of family or carers which states that the family or carers of the child should be kept informed at various stages of the review. It suggests that it may be useful to assign a member of staff as a liaison point for the family and their role could include making arrangements to interview the child, family, carers or significant adults involved. Until recently Scotland was the only part of the UK where guidance stated that the extent of family or carers' involvement should be documented as well as whether the child's views and wishes were sought and expressed. The new Chapter 8 guidance (HM Government 2009b) in England now states, however, that the overview report should include an integrated chronology of involvement with the child and family which should specifically note each occasion on which the child was seen, if the child was seen alone and whether the child's wishes and feelings were sought or expressed. The Scottish guidance has a useful section on supporting staff through the review process which again was not, until recently, found in the guidance in other parts of the UK. The new Chapter 8 guidance in England now states, however, that:

> On completion of each IMR report there should be a process of feedback and debriefing for the staff involved in the case, in advance of completion of the overview report. There should also be a follow-up feedback session with these staff once the SCR report has been completed and before the executive summary is published. It is important that the SCR process supports an open, just and learning culture and is not perceived as a disciplinary-type hearing which may intimidate and undermine the confidence of staff. (HM Government 2009b, p.13)

Timescales for completion of a review are not given in the Scottish guidance but it states that for every case the CPC should agree a deadline for when reports should be produced in the light of the circumstances and context of that particular case. It also states that there is an assumption that the CPC will proceed as speedily as is feasible through the various processes of review.

The guidance states that CPCs should produce a summary of cases sent to them over the course of the year and introduce these into the learning cycle, whether the decision was to undertake an SCR or not (Scottish Executive 2007b). CPCs are also asked to send summaries of cases to the government as some recommendations for reviews may be for consideration at national level. The guidance also states that the government will circulate reports to inspectorates and communicate with organisations such as universities and colleges, NHS Education, and regulatory bodies such as the Scottish Social Services Council if recommendations from reviews have implications for them. There have, however, been no analyses of the findings from SCRs across Scotland as there have been in England and Wales and inspectorates do not evaluate reviews as they do in England. As a result whether or not CPCs have involved families in the process and recorded the extent of their involvement and whether or not staff have been supported through the review process as the guidance suggests they should be, is not known. Neither is it known how many reviews have been undertaken in Scotland or how long reviews take to complete (Vincent 2010a).

The Scottish Government commissioned an independent short life working group of key multi-agency professionals in November 2009 to consider the SCR process. The key aims were to make recommendations to help improve consistency and practice, and to help Child Protection Committees build confidence and capacity in undertaking SCRs across Scotland. The group presented a report which made ten recommendations to the Scottish Government at the end of July 2010. The recommendations were signed off by the Minister for Children and Early Years as part of the Scottish Government's key priorities on child protection and the short life working group is continuing to take forward work emanating from the recommendations. One of the recommendations accepted by the Scottish Government was that they should commission an analysis of all SCRs undertaken since 2007 to provide a baseline and an understanding of the relevant issues for practice.

8.9 WIDER CHILD DEATH REVIEW PROCESSES
In addition to processes for reviewing deaths from child abuse and neglect, some parts of the UK have recently introduced, or plan to introduce, processes for wider review of child deaths in an attempt to expand child death review beyond the focus of child abuse and neglect to one of public health. Evidence presented in the Confidential Enquiry into Maternal and Child Health (CEMACH) child death review study (Pearson 2008) suggested that a public health approach might be a more effective way of learning. The CEMACH study was a pilot study to determine whether confidential enquiry methodology could be used to identify avoidable factors in child deaths. It concluded that half of the deaths which panels

considered might have been avoided would not have been identified as 'unexpected' under the *Working Together* definition, highlighting the need to review all child deaths rather than just unexpected ones.

The US, Canada, Australia and New Zealand have had wider child death review processes for some years. Child fatality review teams were first developed in the US because of concerns about the underreporting of child abuse deaths. The first documented multi-agency and systematic response to child deaths was initiated in 1978 by Los Angeles County. Since 1978 child death review processes have spread across the US and by 2007 all but one state had established a child death review team (Axford and Bullock 2005; Bunting and Reid 2005).

Until recently no parts of the UK had wider child death review processes equivalent to those in the US and some Canadian and Australian states. There have, however, always been health based approaches to infant and child mortality review in the UK and there is a long established history of hospital mortality reviews. Hospitals regularly carry out audits or internal reviews of some, but not all, child deaths.

a. England

As well as having a statutory responsibility to undertake SCRs, since 1 April 2008, LSCBs in England have had two new interrelated responsibilities in relation to review of child deaths:

- a duty to review all child deaths from 0 to 18 in a systematic way through a Child Death Overview Panel (CDOP)

- a duty to respond rapidly to individual unexpected deaths of all children, not just those in contact with organisations responsible for safeguarding their welfare, in the local authority area, through a rapid response team (RRT).

In addition, LSCBs have a statutory responsibility to use the aggregated findings from all child deaths, collected according to a nationally agreed data set, to inform local strategic planning on how best to safeguard and promote the welfare of children in their area. An unexpected death is defined as a death:

> Which was not anticipated as a significant possibility 24 hours before the death or where there was a similarly unexpected collapse leading to or precipitating the events which led to the death. (HM Government 2006a, p.129)

The overall purpose of these new child death review processes is to understand why children die and put in place interventions to protect other children and prevent future deaths.

Chapter 7 of *Working Together to Safeguard Children* (HM Government 2006a) set out the new processes for reviewing child deaths, setting the scene for England to become the first country in the world to have national standards and procedures for the investigation and management of unexpected child deaths and for reviewing all deaths (Sidebotham *et al.* 2008). The guidelines in *Working Together* were based on the findings of the Kennedy Report into the management of Sudden Unexpected Deaths in Infancy (SUDI) (Royal College of Pathologists and Royal College of Paediatrics and Child Health 2004) which was convened after three high profile infant death prosecutions failed. The government announced it would set up these new processes in its response to the Inquiry into the death of Victoria Climbié. Prior to these new processes it was likely that only a minority of child deaths received a post mortem and an even smaller number were accorded a public inquest but this information was not actually known since a breakdown of figures was not available by age from the Registrar General's office. Figures are available in Northern Ireland where only a fifth of child deaths receive a post mortem and just 13 per cent are subject to a public inquest (Bunting and Reid 2005).

In July 2008, in partnership with the Ministry of Justice, the DCSF amended the Coroners Rules 1984 to place a duty on coroners to notify LSCBs of all child deaths over which they have jurisdiction. A power for coroners to provide LSCBs with information relevant to children who die and for whom they have jurisdiction was also introduced. With the enactment of the Children and Young Persons Act 2008, from 1 April 2009 registrars have a duty to provide LSCBs with the information on the child's death certificate. In addition, the Registrar General has a duty to provide the Secretary of State with information on all child deaths including those abroad (Department for Children, Schools and Families 2010).

The public sector agreement to 'Improve children and young people's safety' (PSA 13) includes monitoring preventable child deaths as recorded through child death review panel processes (indicator 4) and LSCBs have to provide information to monitor the progress being made against this national indicator. From 1 April 2008 they had to collect information on the number of child deaths which had been reviewed by CDOPs, and the number of these cases which were assessed as being preventable child deaths. In July 2009 the DCSF published figures on child deaths for the first time which showed that LSCBs in England reviewed 2000 deaths between 1 April 2008 and 31 March 2009, of which 110 were considered to have been preventable (5%). Because this was the first year that child deaths had been reviewed and recorded the DCSF warned, however, that the figures should be interpreted with caution. Not all deaths in 2008–09 had been fully reviewed on 31 March 2009 by their CDOP due to the time lag between the death and the assessment of the available information about the child death. Panels also reported that they had encountered a number of process issues which had further reduced the number of deaths they were able to review. The DCSF (2009) concluded that the completeness of the data provided would have been compromised in the following ways:

- Not all LSCBs had been informed of every child death within their area and therefore had not been able to review all deaths.

- Where incomplete information about the child had been provided to panels, they were not able to identify the child, and therefore could not gather information to assess the death.

- Where panels experienced delays while waiting for post mortem results, coroners' reports, criminal investigation outcomes and SCRs outcomes they were unable to fully review some child deaths by 31 March 2009.

- Some LSCBs prioritised the order in which deaths were reviewed, due to the limited number of times the panels were able to meet before 31 March 2009. Some panels ensured that deaths where lessons needed to be learned were addressed first. This has resulted in a number of expected and probably unpreventable deaths yet to be reviewed by 31 March 2009.

- LSCBs reported difficulties in understanding and interpreting the definition of preventable child deaths resulting in a number of panels failing to reach a decision on preventability for some of the most complex deaths by 31 March 2009.

- There were inconsistencies in how panels interpreted the guidance around the reviewing of all child deaths, with some panels reporting that they had not reviewed neo-natal deaths or only reviewed unexpected deaths. Other panels felt that they were unable to review the deaths which occurred before the panels were set up and chairs and co-ordinators were recruited. In some LSCBs this has resulted in deaths for only a quarter of the year being considered by the panel.

Key changes in Chapter 7 of the updated *Working Together* (DCSF 2010) included revised definitions of preventable child deaths and unexpected deaths and clarity on the roles of coroners and registrars and on how to respond appropriately to the deaths of children with life limiting illnesses. There is also an additional section which clarifies the level of involvement of parents and other family members and the support they will need.

A total of 3450 child death reviews were completed by CDOPs in the year ending 31 March 2010 and 150 were assessed as preventable (Department of Education 2010a). In 2009–10 LSCBs were also asked to provide additional voluntary information about the child deaths they had reviewed, for example details about the child's age, gender, ethnicity and cause of death. These data were provided on behalf of 123 out of the 145 LSCBs and indicated that:

- The majority of deaths assessed as preventable were due to trauma and other external factors (54%); 27% were due to road traffic accidents; 15% to other events and 13% to other non-intentional injury, accidents or trauma.

- 27% of deaths which were assessed as preventable were for children aged 1–4 years; 26% for children aged 15–17 years; and 19% for children aged 10–14 years.

Since not all LSCBs provided data the Department for Education warned, however, that the figures did not accurately reflect national proportions and should be treated with caution. For 2010–11 LSCBs have been required to provide this information at aggregate level.

b. Wales

The Welsh Regulations under The Children Act 2004 do not require individual LSCBs in Wales to review all child deaths or to respond rapidly to individual unexpected deaths of all children. Because the population base of LSCBs in Wales was significantly less than the recommended 500,000 for child death review arrangements in England, the Welsh Assembly Government chose to investigate whether an all-Wales approach would be a more feasible way of administering child death reviews and they commissioned the National Public Health Service for Wales to undertake a pilot study of the practicality of this. The pilot began in July 2009 and was expected to run for a year resulting in a report for the WAG on how the child death review process should be taken forward in Wales. The pilot concentrated on three tasks:

1. Ascertaining all child deaths (0 to <18 years) from 1 October 2009 until the end of the Pilot

2. Establishing national reviews of deaths, initially focusing on suicides and apparent suicides since 1 October 2006

3. Testing the feasibility of establishing local reviews/case discussions and integrating completion of information requirements into current processes.

The pilot is expected to result in surveillance of all childhood deaths in Wales, underpinned by a child death database and by review of unexpected child deaths, as in England. Alongside their announcement of plans to replace the current SCR process in February 2011 the Welsh Assembly Government added that the child death review pilot would continue in 2011–12 and an independent evaluation would be commissioned to explore the structures and processes to ensure that they were the most effective.

c. Northern Ireland

New child death review processes are also being considered in Northern Ireland in response to a CMR following the death of David Briggs, a twin adopted in Romania, in 2003. The CMR report recommended a multi-agency approach be used in all cases of sudden unexpected child death in Northern Ireland. Regional child death review arrangements are now prescribed in the Safeguarding Board Act (Northern Ireland) 2011 but at the time of writing implementation was expected to be some way off.

d. Scotland

At the time of writing the Scottish Government had not announced any plans to introduce new processes for wider review of child deaths as in England and Wales.

8.10 THE EFFECTIVENESS OF CHILD DEATH REVIEW PROCESSES

As outlined above case review processes were intended to be used as a learning tool, not as a means of attributing blame, and all parts of the UK, apart from Scotland, have aggregated the findings from case reviews so that there can be national as well as local learning. The fact that SCRs continue to identify the same problems in front line practice and continue to make similar recommendations has, however, raised questions about their effectiveness as a learning tool for improving practice. Ofsted (2008b) concluded, for example, that SCRs were effective at identifying what happened to children but less effective at addressing why things happened. They were critical of the fact that recommendations tended to focus on policies and procedures as opposed to practice and what needed to change. Rose and Barnes (2008) also found that SCR recommendations focused predominantly on policies and procedures. Ofsted's 2009 report found there had been significant improvements in the quality of the case review process with more robust quality assurance, recommendations and action plans, but they concluded that more evidence was needed to ascertain whether the actions recommended and taken were actually improving the quality of the protection of children:

> improvements in the quality of the process – which are extremely important – cannot mask the fact that the rate of improvement in practice and in service delivery is as yet much slower. (p.6)

Sidebotham *et al.* (2010) concluded that SCRs were only partially achieving their aim of learning lessons, rather than apportioning blame, with front-line workers reporting that they felt anxious, unsupported and disempowered by the process.

Rose and Barnes (2008) have pointed out that it is important to bear in mind that SCRs are only one source of evidence about what is happening in work to safeguard children, while child deaths are comparatively rare, they have had an inordinate and inappropriate level of influence on safeguarding policy. The updated Chapter 8 guidance (Department for Children, Schools and Families 2010) pointed out that LSCBs should establish a culture of audit and review and 'make sure that tragedies are not the only reason inter-agency work is reviewed' (p.21).

Rose and Barnes (2008) argued that approaches which enable us to learn from effective safeguarding practice, rather than mistakes, would be a far better way to proceed and the Social Care Institute for Excellence (SCIE) has developed an alternative approach to case review (Fish,

Munro and Bairstow 2008) – a resource for undertaking a multi-agency systems approach for organisational learning across agencies involved in safeguarding children. The approach, which is widely used in engineering, health and other high risk industries, provides an opportunity to study the whole system so we can learn from what is working effectively as well as from what is not working well. The continuum approach to reviewing, learning and improving policy and practice outlined above, which is currently being taken forward in Wales, also recognises the need to learn from good practice and cases where things have gone well as well as from 'near misses' and cases where things have gone wrong.

While SCRs do provide useful information about child deaths from child abuse and neglect, 'the challenge is to expand child death reviews beyond the focus of child abuse and neglect to one of public health so as to identify preventable child deaths and achieve effective prevention' (Onwuachi-Saunders *et al.* 1999, p.278). New processes for wider child death review that are being introduced in various parts of the UK are an attempt to do just this. Sidebotham *et al.*'s (2008) pilot study provides some evidence of how new child death review processes are operating in England. Nine LSCBs who responded to an initial questionnaire were selected as sites for further research. CDOPs were at an early stage of development when the pilot study was undertaken but a number of outcomes were already being observed such as public awareness campaigns, community safety initiatives, training of professionals, development of protocols and lobbying of politicians. Further evidence of the effectiveness of wider child death review processes in the UK comes from the CEMACH child death review study (Pearson 2008). The CEMACH study concluded that confidential enquiry methodology could be effectively used to determine whether the deaths of children could have been avoided.

Although the Sidebotham *et al.* (2008) study provided some evidence of the effectiveness of new child death reviews processes it also identified a number of problems. One of the main problems was that none of the nine overview panels in the pilot had managed to set up a foolproof system of notification. Most sites commented that current systems for notification of deaths were inadequate and they reported that they had to rely on a combination of sources – Child Surveillance Teams or Decision Support Teams of the Primary Care Trusts; coroners; the police; children's social care; public health; hospital records departments; and registrars. Notification of deaths of children who lived in one area but who died outside this area was particularly problematic. One LSCB reported that they received notifications of all child deaths from a tertiary hospital in their area regardless of the child's place of residence. These concerns could prove to be significant since evidence suggests that 40 per cent of deaths of children under one and between one-quarter and one-third of deaths of older children occur outside the area in which the child resided, making local ascertainment of death problematic (Ward Platt 2007).

Participants in the Sidebotham *et al.* (2008) study cited various systems for review of children's deaths – local case discussions for SUDI; local case discussions for other unexpected child deaths; infant mortality reviews in hospital and by the perinatal unit; other hospital mortality reviews and domestic violence reviews; but reported that there was not a consistent process. The nine sites all had protocols for responding to unexpected childhood deaths, many of which had been operational for several years, but most covered only unexpected deaths of children under two. There were some concerns about reviewing all deaths from 0 to 18, particularly in relation to the neo-natal period and later adolescent period, since different professionals are involved with the older and younger age group. In many sites there was already some sort of hospital based neo-natal mortality review and the challenge was to try to include them in the CDOP process rather than replace an already well functioning system. Some teams were dividing deaths into categories and reviewing all deaths within one category at a time to enable appropriate expertise to be brought in to support the panel. While there was a general sense of enthusiasm for developing child death review processes there was some frustration at the perceived lack of central guidance other than that set out in *Working Together*. As a result in 2008 the DCSF made available a training resource to support LSCBs in implementing the Child Death Review Processes set out in Chapter 7 of *Working Together*.

Chapter 7 of *Working Together* (HM Government 2006a) required LSCBs to establish CDOPs for populations greater than 500,000 and stated that neighbouring LSCBs could form combined CDOPs to achieve this population size. Sidebotham *et al.* (2008) found that some panels were planning to develop a combined CDOP but others were not keen to do so even where population numbers were low. They found that teams could function with both smaller and larger populations and concluded that LSCBs should consider what configuration best met their needs. Ward Platt (2007) commented, however, that from his experience in the North of England (a participating region in the CEMACH child death project), it makes sense for adjacent LSCBs to pool expertise and cover larger populations than their own. He suggested populations of between

500,000 and one million would allow a reasonable number of deaths to be scrutinised each year without the process becoming too burdensome.

The *Working Together* guidance (HM Government 2006a) included a diagram to explain the interface between child death and SCR processes; however, Sidebotham *et al.* (2008) found there were problems around linkage of the two processes. There was a clear message from interviewees that SCRs were intensive, demanding and time consuming and that child death review processes could not, and should not, go into the same kind of depth. Participants were also unclear about the distinction between child death overview processes and rapid response processes. They talked about the differences between the multi-agency child death overview and other hospital based mortality reviews which were already being undertaken in many places and generally considered that the CDOP should consider cases only after the conclusion of any rapid response process, criminal investigation or SCR. The updated Chapter 8 guidance (Department for Children, Schools and Families 2010) provides more information on the interface between the separate processes for reviewing child deaths and in Wales CSSIW (2009) commented that its new continuum approach could fit well with the overall development of work on child death reviews in Wales.

The CEMACH study report (Pearson 2008) argued that there needs to be consistency and standardisation across LSCBs and aggregation at a regional and national level if major issues and trends in child mortality are to be identified. It also pointed out that enquiry staff who were involved in the CEMACH study found the emotional content of their work demanding and stressful at times. This is likely to apply to staff involved in reviews in LSCBs as well and the report states that it will be important to ensure they are appropriately supported. Accountability is a further issue which the report suggests requires further clarification. It asks to whom CDOP decisions on contributory factors are accountable and who is responsible if recommendations for prevention are made but not carried through (if, for example, children continue to die from preventable road accidents)?

It appears that the new child death review procedures in England are beginning to lead to positive prevention initiatives. The 2010 Department of Education statistical release included a list of actions that LSCBs have taken following reviews of child deaths:

- awareness campaigns around safe sleeping to reduce the number of sudden infant deaths and deaths related to sleeping in parents beds or on the sofa with parents

- making improvements to local roads, including traffic calming measures, cycle lanes and barriers, parking restrictions, warning signs and reducing foliage, as well as introducing additional road safety training for school children to reduce the number of deaths due to traffic accidents

- running community road shows to share a range of findings from child death reviews

- making sure leaflets are available in more languages, especially around safe sleeping for babies

- reviewing how children who present at A&E departments because of apparent self-harm are assessed and monitored

- reviewing procedures following non-attendance at health appointments, including vaccinations

- raising awareness of the dangers of leaving children unattended in the bath whether in a bath seat or not

- reviewing services available to children, ranging from advice on pregnancy and sexual health to accessibility of services for re-housed families with disabled children or children with life limiting illnesses

- contacting GPs to ensure that databases are up to date so that end of life plans are accurate and can be shared with other services, such as ambulance services

- reviewing the bereavement support offered to families

- offering feedback to services including recognising good practice and sharing with others

- awareness raising campaigns around securing disabled children's wheelchairs in vehicles

- reviewing psychological support for children with chronic conditions, namely epilepsy and diabetes

- obtaining information on research and work being conducted across the UK where children from consanguineous parents die

- producing leaflets warning of the dangers of air weapons and displaying these in hospitals, police stations and schools.

There is a growing body of evidence on the effectiveness of child death review processes in other countries; however, much of it relates to activity stemming from the process rather than specific outcomes for children. Bunting and Reid (2005) identified a number of benefits including improved multi-agency working and communication; more effective identification of suspicious cases and a decrease in inadequate death certificates; a more complete and accountable process; and a more in-depth understanding of the causes of child death from a narrow and stigmatising focus on child abuse towards a public health model which focuses on the prevention of all deaths.

In the US, Canada and Australia comprehensive child death review programmes have contributed significantly to knowledge about child abuse and neglect, and knowledge from child death review has led to policies and initiatives which have made major contributions to keeping children safe for a number of years now. Child Death Review has been particularly successful in documenting the risk factors to help steer prevention efforts regarding sudden unexpected deaths of infants in the US and has provided evidence that infants in an unsafe sleep environment have an increased risk of death (Brixey, Kopp and Schlotthauer 2011). Box 8.1 highlights a number of successful initiatives in the US and Canada. Evidence from child death reviews can also be used to identify special population groups that need targeted prevention programmes. For example, the Arizona Child Death Review Team found that unintentional injury deaths and suicide were more common in Native American communities, whereas deaths attributable to gunshot wounds occurred more frequently in Hispanic communities (Rimsza *et al.* 2002). In Washington State, Quan and colleagues used CDR data to document the disproportionate risk of drowning among Asian immigrant youth in open water and at unguarded public parks. Their data were used to inform policy development and carefully focused drowning prevention campaigns (Quan *et al.* 2011).

Child death review teams in the US have, however, faced a number of difficulties. One of the main challenges has been the difficulty of obtaining and sustaining adequate resources and many teams have reported an inability to put prevention programmes into place (Durfee, Durfee and West 2002). Recent budget cuts have meant that most CDR teams do not have adequate resources to conduct public health campaigns in support of prevention objectives (Johnston and Covington 2011). Lack of national leadership and co-ordination has meant there is wide variation in child death review team organisation and processes across the US and there

BOX 8.1 SUCCESSFUL CHILD DEATH REVIEW INITIATIVES IN
THE US AND CANADA

In Alabama the Child Death Review Team identified several newborn
infants who had been abandoned or left to die. The chairperson of the
review team partnered with local media and developed a programme
called *Safe Place* which allowed mothers to leave newborns, who were
less than 72 hours old, at hospital emergency departments with no
questions asked. This programme was passed into Alabama law in May
2000 and the model has been replicated across many other US states
(Wirtz, Foster and Lenart 2011).

In British Colombia the Child Death Review Unit is the only
agency that systematically collects data on adult supervision among
fatal childhood injuries. Results of a review of child pedestrian fatalities
showed that only one-third of children below 10 years of age were
under active supervision of an adult at the time of the fatal incident.
This finding supported the need to raise awareness of child pedestrian
injury and improve supervision practices among parents and caregivers
(Despriya *et al.* 2011).

The work of the Sacramento, California Child Death Review
Team contributed to the introduction of home visitation services in
the county. Wirtz *et al.* (2011) document how the team worked with
local leaders to assess the current resources and political context and
recommended the formation of a high level task force to create and
sustain evidence based home visitation services. The result was the
multi-million dollar *Birth and Beyond* programme targeting eight high
risk neighbourhoods. Following the programme's implementation, the
team documented a significant decline in child maltreatment homicides.

are no national criteria by which programme structure and impact might
be judged (Webster *et al.* 2003). A lack of standardised methods of data
collection across teams has made comparability of child deaths between
states and the identification of national trends impossible (Bunting and
Reid 2005). The National Center for Child Death Review (NCCDR)
was funded by the US government in 2002 to explore the feasibility
of building a standardised reporting tool for local and state child death
review teams. NCCDR found that 44 of 50 states had a case reporting
tool for child death review; however, there was little consistency in the

type of information that was collected and analysed (Covington 2011). It developed a National Child Death Review Case Reporting System (NCDR-CRS) to provide child death review teams with a method for capturing, analysing, and reporting on the full set of information shared at a child death or serious injury review. The system is currently being used by 35 out of 50 US states and more than 84,000 reviewed child deaths have now been entered into the system (Covington 2011). States are able to download their data on an annual basis and generate annual reports on all deaths reviewed as well as specialised reports on specific types of deaths such as suicides or drownings. Covington (2011) admits, however, that there are still a number of limitations. Most important, the data still cannot be compared state to state, and sometimes not even team to team within a state, because of variation in the types and timing of death reviews. There are also differences in the quality of data between teams and states, and some of the data elements are subjective and can be interpreted differently by each team, for example whether the death was preventable and whether an act of omission contributed to the death.

Despite these limitations there is no doubt that child death review 'generates an ecological understanding of preventable child mortality and is a powerful tool for advancing evidence based, multi-level strategies to promote and protect child health and safety' (Desapriya *et al.* 2011, p.i8).

8.11 CONCLUSION

In this chapter we looked at the most serious end of the child abuse continuum, at the arrangements that exist to review cases where a child has died as a result of abuse and neglect. All parts of the UK now have processes in place for inquiring into or reviewing child deaths. While there are similarities between these processes, there are also variations.

Across the UK, prior to 2000, elaborate public inquiries used to be a relatively frequent response to high profile child death and abuse cases. Since then, across the UK, the trend has been to conduct far fewer of these, and to rely on local review mechanisms. Processes for this vary and are at different stages of development. England and Wales were the first countries in the UK to introduce formalised systems and mechanisms for local review of child deaths. The 2004 Children Act and accompanying regulations placed SCRs on a statutory footing in England and Wales and it became mandatory for LSCBs to conduct an SCR if a child died under certain conditions. In 2009, Lord Laming's report made further recommendations to strengthen SCRs in England. In 2007 responsibility for evaluating the process of conducting and the quality of SCR in England was transferred to Ofsted.

In Wales, policy surrounding SCRs was similar to England but since 2009 has begun to change with the Welsh Assembly Government announcing plans to implement a new learning framework to replace SCRs by the end of 2011.

While local authorities in Scotland did conduct local review of child deaths, a national approach was not in place until 2007 when national guidance was issued. Currently in Scotland SCRs are not inspected, no reviews or analysis have been conducted and as yet there are no requirements to submit reviews to a central point. In 2010 a Short Life Working Group was set up under the Multi-agency Response Service who made recommendations to government which are under consideration.

In Northern Ireland, ACPCs have had responsibility for undertaking CMRs since 2003. The circumstances under which a review is undertaken are similar to England with slight differences. ACPCs have to provide a copy of reports to DHSSPS and recently there has been a first national analysis of CMRs.

Since 2008 in an attempt to create a wider public health approach to understanding all child deaths, England now has a duty to review all deaths through child death overview panels and to produce aggregated findings; Wales has introduced an all Wales child death review pilot project. No similar processes are yet planned for Northern Ireland and Scotland, although interest in doing this has been expressed by officials in Northern Ireland.

In relation to serious and significant child death processes as a whole across the UK, once again we see a process where a policy is first introduced in England, then following a process of review and information becoming available, it is adapted and taken up in the devolved parts of the UK.

Chapter 9

Child Protection and
Offender Management
Systems across the UK

9.1 INTRODUCTION

Most of this book has been concerned with comparing and contrasting systems across the UK relating to the direct protection of children. In this chapter we examine arrangements and mechanisms in place across the UK to keep children safe from adults who may pose a risk to them. This is also a useful area of child protection from which to 'test' our assertion that the devolution process in the UK contains within it simultaneous processes for both convergent and divergent policy. Offender management systems and Vetting and Barring systems are areas of policy devolved to Scotland and Northern Ireland and there is therefore the opportunity for divergent policy making. However, given that it is also important that all parts of the UK are seen to be equally vigilant in protecting children from sex offenders, it could also be argued that pressures for convergent policy are more likely. Indeed, as we shall see, the systems across the UK are broadly the same with some differences in detail.

Policy aimed at reducing the opportunities for unsuitable adults to harm children have expanded considerably over the past 20 years. This chapter considers three elements related to this area of policy; multi-agency management of serious offenders; criminal records checks for adults working with children; and arrangements for barring unsuitable individuals from working with children. Such policies aim to reduce the risk to children through 'pre-emptive' action (Matravers 2003; Parton 2006). All of these systems across the UK use an individual's previous behaviour as an indicator of potential future risk; and this necessitates the exchange of information between agencies. This mirrors developments in other aspects of child protection policy where there has been an increasing emphasis on inter-agency co-operation (Parton 2006). The structure and networks created to support these systems are the focus of this chapter.

The expansion of policy in this area emerged mainly as a reaction to increased concern about the risks to children from sex offenders, influenced in particular by: publicity surrounding various high profile child murders and abductions; increasing knowledge and information about the dangers faced by children in the community from adults working or volunteering to work with them; and the growing understanding of the risks to children cared for away from home in public and institutional care. Over the past 20 years, in keeping with the increasingly punitive criminal justice agenda, the response to this by public authorities has included longer sentences, increased surveillance and greater restrictions on sex offenders in the community; and a corresponding expansion of state power to apply restrictions on those deemed to pose a risk to children (McAlinden 2010).

In practice, policy in this area has expanded from a narrower focus on sex offences to include serious violent offences; and in some cases drawing into the system those deemed to pose a risk but where there may not be a criminal conviction.

This policy agenda has been subject to the criticism that it is overly focused on known offenders and on risk to children from strangers. The policy direction is consistent with successive Governments' pursuit of more punitive criminal justice and penal policy and risk based crime control policy (McAlinden 2010). These are powerful elements which potentially bind policy together across the UK. As this chapter will show, there is much that is similar in offender management and vetting and barring policy across constituent parts of the UK.

9.2 OFFENDER MANAGEMENT SYSTEMS

a. Multi-agency Public Protection Arrangements

The past decade has brought an expansion of policy, legislation and guidance intended to more stringently manage those who have committed serious offences, including sex offences (McAlinden 2007). Criminal justice agencies have a duty to work with offenders to reduce the risk of future offending through identification, risk assessment and risk management. Agencies are increasingly expected to work together with statutory requirements to do so set out in the Multi-agency Public Protection Arrangements (MAPPA) (Bryan and Doyle 2003).

MAPPA arrangements were first established in England and Wales in 2001, with MAPPA guidance setting out the functions (National MAPPA Team 2009). Public Protection Arrangements for Northern Ireland (PPANI) and MAPPA arrangements for Scotland were established later (Scottish Government 2008c). Arrangements in Northern Ireland and Scotland are autonomous but have closely borrowed from those in England and Wales.

All three sets of public protection arrangements have the same broad objective, that of managing the risk from those deemed to be a potential danger (Parton 2006). Everyone identified as a risk through MAPPA requires a risk assessment, and a risk assessment plan which is then monitored, reviewed and adapted to meet any changes in circumstances. The practicalities of this are described in the section below.

b. Structures

MAPPA arrangements were set up to operate through existing agencies rather than through the setting up of a new agency (Bryan and Doyle 2003; National MAPPA Team 2009). In England and Wales the agencies (Responsible Authorities) with the duty to deliver are the police, probation and the prison service. These are supported by a wider range of specified public, private and voluntary bodies with legal requirements to co-operate including: youth offending teams; local authority social care services; NHS bodies; Jobcentre Plus; and other bodies such as Registered Social Landlords (National MAPPA Team 2009).

In Scotland, the Responsible Authorities are: the police, the Scottish prison service; health forensic services and the local authorities (primarily criminal justice social work) (Scottish Government 2008b). Voluntary organisations working with offenders, housing providers, the Principal Reporter for Scotland's Children's Hearing System, electronic monitoring providers and health services have a duty to co-operate (Scottish Government 2008b).

Statutory public protection arrangements for Northern Ireland are delivered through Local Area Public Protection Panels (LAPPAs). These are chaired by Probation Board Managers and involve criminal justice and other relevant agencies.

Across all of the public protection systems, the responsibility for serious offender management lies mainly with the police, the prison service and criminal justice social work/probation, in conjunction with a range of other agencies.

c. Coverage

The MAPPA/PANNI arrangements exist primarily to deal with serious sexual or violent offenders (see Table 9.1). In England and Wales there are three categories of eligible MAPPA offenders. Category 1 are registered sex offenders, Category 2 are people convicted of a serious violent offence who have received a minimum 12 month custodial sentence, and Category 3 are those dangerous offenders, not in category one or two, where 'the circumstances surrounding the offence indicate that the offender has a capacity for serious harm…[and]…that was not reflected in the charge on which the offender was ultimately convicted' (National MAPPA Team 2009, p.56).

The MAPPA arrangements in Scotland also set out three categories: Category 1 is registered sex offenders; Category 2 is for violent offenders (not yet in operation); and Category 3 is for other offenders not in category one or two 'who have been convicted of an offence and if by reason of that conviction they are considered by the responsible authorities to be a person who may cause serious harm to the public at large' (Scottish Government 2008c, p.10). Also managed under MAPPA in Scotland are 'mentally disordered restricted patients who are also sexual or violent offenders' under MAPPA[1] (Scottish Government 2008b; Weaver 2010).

Northern Ireland also has three categories for PPANI assessment; Category 1 includes those with a conviction for a sexual offence, those who are subject to notification requirements or about whom there are significant concerns. Category 2 concerns those with a conviction for a relevant violent offence against a child or vulnerable adult, in domestic circumstances. Since 2011 in Northern Ireland this category has also included those convicted of a violent crime motivated by hate. Category 3 is relevant for other potentially dangerous people; a criminal conviction is not a requirement for this category. It covers people who have been interviewed by police and are in the process of being prosecuted for an alleged: 'sexual offence against a child; or serious sexual assault against an adult; an alleged or suspected violent offence against a child or vulnerable adult; or an alleged or suspected violent offence…motivated by hate' (Northern Ireland Office undated).

Across the four parts of the UK there are distinct arrangements for managing young offenders. In England and Wales young offenders

---

1   'that is, patients who are subject to the special restrictions under the Mental Health (Care and Treatment) (Scotland) Act 2003. Such patients cannot be granted suspensions of detention from hospital, transferred between hospitals or returned to prison without the consent of Scottish Minister' (Risk Management Authority 2007).

are managed under MAPPA arrangements, although special provisions require youth offending teams to lead such cases using a tailored risk assessment tool. In Scotland young offender cases are mainly managed within the Children's Hearing System; although children convicted of sex offences are managed through MAPPA (Scottish Government 2008c). In Northern Ireland only in exceptional cases are young people managed through PPANI in the belief that most of them can be adequately managed through existing arrangements.

Thus across the UK, categories of people to whom public protection measures apply are broadly consistent (see Table 9.1). The Northern Ireland arrangements include the broadest categories and may include people without a conviction for a sexual or violent offence.

TABLE 9.1 PERSONS FOR INCLUSION IN MAPPA/PPNI

England and Wales	
Category 1	registered sexual offenders (RSOs)
Category 2	violent offenders with over 12 months' custody and over and some sex offenders not qualifying for registration
Category 3	other dangerous offenders who are 'not in either Category 1 or 2 but who are considered by the RA to pose a risk of serious harm to the public which required active interagency management' (National MAPPA Team 2009, p.55)
Scotland	
Category 1	registered sex offenders those subject to the notification requirements under Part 2 of the Sexual Offences Act 2003
Category 2	violent offenders defined as 'convicted on indictment of an offence inferring personal violence who are subject to a probation order, or who are or will be on release from prison, subject to statutory supervision in the community' 'person acquitted on grounds of insanity or found to be insane following proceedings…' (Scottish Government 2008c, p.9)
Category 3	those not in 'Category 1 or 2 who have been convicted of an offence <u>and</u> if by reason of that conviction they are considered by the responsible authorities to be a person who may cause serious harm to the public at large' (Scottish Government 2008c, p.10)

TABLE 9.1 PERSONS FOR INCLUSION IN MAPPA/PPNI *cont.*

Northern Ireland	
Relevant sexual offender	'a person is a relevant sexual offender if he/she: is subject to the notification requirements of Part 2 of the Sexual Offences Act 2003 has been convicted of a sexual offence or sexually motivated offence, is not subject to the notification requirements of Part 2 of the Sexual Offences Act 2003, but about whom an agency has current significant concerns
Relevant violent offenders	a person is a relevant violent offender if he/she: has from 6 October 2008 been convicted of a violent offence (including homicide) against a child or vulnerable adult; or who has a previous conviction for a violent offence against a child or vulnerable adult and about whom an agency has current significant concerns has from 1 April 2010 been convicted of a violent offence (including homicide) in domestic or family circumstances; or who has a previous conviction for a violent offence in domestic or family circumstances and about whom an agency has current significant concerns has from 1 April 2011 been convicted of a violent offence (including homicide) where the offence has been motivated by hate
Relevant other potentially dangerous person	a person is a relevant other potentially dangerous person if he/she: is subject to a Risk of Sexual Harm Order (RSHO) has been interviewed by police for an alleged or suspected sexual offence against a child or a serious sexual assault on an adult and is in the process of being reported with a view to prosecution from 6 October 2008 has been interviewed by police for an alleged or suspected violent offence (including homicide) against a child or vulnerable adult and is in the process of being reported with a view to prosecution from 1 April 2011 has been interviewed by police for an alleged or suspected violent offence (including homicide) in domestic or family circumstances and is in the process of being reported with a view to prosecution from 1 April 2011 has been interviewed by police for an alleged or suspected violent offence (including homicide) where the offence has been motivated by hate and is in the process of being reported with a view to prosecution' (Northern Ireland Office undated, p.11)

d. Activities

Public bodies are required to have knowledge of all individuals to be managed through MAPPA/PPANI arrangements in their area, and of those due to be released from prison. All MAPPA/PPANI monitored individuals are required to be allocated a risk level upon which a management plan is formulated. The purpose of the plan is to reduce the risk of re-offending. The risk level allocated is the main basis for decision making about resources to be allocated to offender management (see Table 9.2 for a summary of risk level categories). The use of risk levels is intended to bring consistency to the definitions of risk. The risk plan should be monitored and altered where circumstances deem it.

There are four risk levels used in MAPPA in England and Wales (National MAPPA Team 2009) and Scotland (Scottish Government 2008c). These are:

- Low: evidence does not suggest a risk of serious harm

- Medium: some risk of serious harm but it is unlikely to happen unless there are changes in the situation

- High: indicates there is a serious risk of harm and that it could happen at any time

- Very high: indicates imminent risk of serious harm.

In Northern Ireland there are three levels of risk:

- Category 1: little evidence someone will cause serious harm

- Categories 2 and 3: risk of serious harm. Where it is highest there is compelling evidence that someone is likely to cause serious harm.

Although a range of cases fall under the responsibility of MAPPA, it is only the highest risk cases and those subject to notification requirements which are actually managed through the multi-agency process. This is based on the principle that cases should be managed at 'the lowest level... which provides a defensible management plan' (Scottish Government 2008c). Defensible decision making draws on the work of Kemshall *et al.* (Kemshall 2003; Kemshall *et al.* 2005; Scottish Government 2008b). This requires: the use of risk management tools; that decisions can be seen to be 'grounded in evidence'; that policy and procedures have been followed; and that clear accountability for decisions are documented (National MAPPA Team 2009; Scottish Government 2008b). Cases

TABLE 9.2 PUBLIC PROTECTION ARRANGEMENTS IN THE UK: RISK LEVELS

England and Wales	Low: does not indicate likelihood of causing serious harm	Medium: identifiable indicators of serious harm but unlikely unless change in circumstances	High: identifiable indicators of serious harm. Potential event could happen at any time and with serious impact	Very high: imminent risk of serious harm (National MAPPA Team 2009)
Scotland	Low: 'current evidence does not indicate likelihood of causing serious harm' (Scottish Government 2008c, p.6)	Medium: identifiable indicators of risk of serious harm. Has the potential to cause harm, but is unlikely to do so unless there is a change in circumstances	High: identifiable indicators of risk of serious harm. The potential event could happen at any time and the impact could be serious	Very high: imminent risk of serious harm. The potential event is more likely than not to happen immediately, and the impact could be serious (Scottish Government 2008c)
Northern Ireland	Category 1: 'Someone whose previous offending (or current alleged offending in the case of potentially dangerous persons), current behaviour and current circumstances present little evidence that they will cause serious harm through carrying out a contact sexual or violent offence'	Category 2: 'Someone whose previous offending (or current alleged offending in the case of potentially dangerous persons), current behaviour and current circumstances present clear and identifiable evidence that they could cause serious harm through carrying out a contact sexual or violent offence'	Category 3: 'Someone whose previous offending (or current alleged offending in the case of potentially dangerous persons), current behaviour and current circumstances present compelling evidence that they are highly likely to cause serious harm through carrying out a contact sexual or violent offence' (Northern Ireland Office undated, p.10)	

TABLE 9.3 LEVELS OF MANAGEMENT IN MULTI-AGENCY

England and Wales		
Level 1: ordinary Risk Management Cases where the risk posed by the offender can be managed by the agency responsible for supervision/case management of the offender	Level 2: MAPPA Risk Management Plan and Offenders management dealt with by Multi-Agency Public Protection Panels (MAPPPs)	Level 3: (critical few) as with Level 2 with involvement of Senior Management to authorise additional resources that may be required in such cases
Scotland		
Level 1: ordinary Risk Management The risk presented can be managed by a single agency (mainly criminal justice social work; police or prison services) without significant involvement of others but communicate and work with as required	Level 2: require active involvement of more than one agency and MAPPA agencies to be actively involved in the risk management	Level 3: as Level 2 but case is unusual and may require additional resources so involvement of senior staff from a RA agency required to authorise additional resources
Northern Ireland		
Category 1: managed by one agency and not subject to PPANI	Category 2: responsibility of LAPPP to manage and individuals subject to agreed PPANI multi-agency risk management plan	Category 3: requires a range of inter-agency support and substantial levels of resourcing; 'rather than discharge this responsibility at a local level, agencies may choose to do so through the establishment of a central co-located public protection team whose actions in delivering risk management plans will also fall within the oversight of the relevant LAPPP' (Northern Ireland Office undated, p.31)

classified at the lowest risk level are primarily supervised by one agency: the police for registered sex offenders and probation/criminal justice social work for those on licence. Other agencies are to be involved as per the requirements of the specific case. Level two cases are managed through Multi-agency Public Protection Panels (MAPPPs) (or Local Area Public Protection Panels (LAPPPs) in the case of Northern Ireland) which consider and formulate a risk management plan for each managed case. Cases assessed as high or very high risk or that are exceptional are managed through MAPPPs/LAPPPs with involvement of senior staff so significant additional resources can be authorised as required (see Table 9.3). The agency with the statutory responsibility for managing the offender has the job of co-ordinating the Risk Management Plan.

Across the UK there are arrangements within MAPPAs/PPANIs to enable the sharing of information with relevant people in the community, although there are a raft of legal requirements that apply to disclosure decisions. Discretionary powers enable the agency with responsibility to inform a third party of a conviction for a sexual offence including a voluntary organisation or in some cases a partner. Arrangements for disclosure are dealt with in the risk management plan. Information can also be released as a result of specific intelligence received by police (National MAPPA Team 2009; Weaver 2009).

The disclosures discussed here complement the Community Notification Schemes introduced in England and Wales which allow members of the public to request information about another person. The public can ask the police to provide the criminal records of someone they may have concerns about who may have regular unsupervised access to a child. This was originally restricted to parents and carers and continues to be so in Scotland, but has now been widened in England and Wales. Enquirers are required to keep information disclosed confidential and they are offered support and guidance in relation to keeping a child safe.

In addition to multi-agency information sharing in relation to the management of individual offenders, MAPPA/PPANI also have responsibility for making links with other relevant fora and bodies to further public protection. Thus in England and Wales, MAPPA link with Local Safeguarding Children's Boards (LSCBs) and should also link with agencies dealing with high risk victims of domestic abuse – Multi-agency Risk Assessment Conferences (MARACs) – given the possibility of offenders being known to multiple agencies. Links should also be made with other relevant inter-agency crime bodies such as the Local Criminal Justice Boards. The Strategic Management Board of PPANI has a duty to forge links with Area Child Protection Committees (ACPCs), domestic abuse fora and Community Safety Partnerships.

Inter-agency contact and information sharing is also required to deal with individuals subject to MAPPA arrangements when they move between jurisdictions. This is complex due to the slightly different arrangements in place and differences in broader legal requirements for offender management in each part of the UK. Guidance currently deals with transfers between England, Wales and Scotland; but not with Northern Ireland.

e. Conclusion

The MAPPA/PPANI arrangements encompass those who have committed a serious violent or sexual crime (or those alleged to have done so) in England, Wales and Northern Ireland, or sex offenders and restricted patients in Scotland, and uses past behaviour as a basis for assessing future potential risk. Techniques are used to allocate a risk level to each individual; this is the basis for putting in place arrangements to deal with the risk. It can draw on the resources of a number of agencies and private individuals. For most, the arrangements are minimal and consist of monitoring by a single agency. The MAPPI/PPANI systems are focused on reducing future risk. They go beyond management of those who have committed sexual offences. England also includes serious violent offenders. Northern Ireland has shifted to draw into the system those considered a danger but who do not yet have a criminal conviction.

9.3 VETTING AND BARRING ARRANGEMENTS ACROSS THE UK

In this section we examine the systems across the UK for 'vetting' individuals using criminal records to check suitability to work with children, and for 'barring' those individuals deemed to be unsuitable to work with them. As with the MAPPA/PPANI arrangements, the principle behind 'vetting and barring' is that someone's past behaviour is an indication of future risk.

Across the UK there have long been avenues for certain agencies working with children to conduct police checks on their staff and potential recruits. It was in the early 1990s and 2000s that we first saw the rise of the large-scale centralised, formalised systems for vetting and barring and its emergence from being a system in the background to one which had a high profile and a central role in child protection systems across the UK. Much of the recent change to vetting and barring policy across the UK has occurred since devolution and this has had an impact on how these policies have developed.

a. The purpose of vetting and barring

Vetting in this context is the use of third party information, specifically criminal history information by employers as part of the process of recruiting staff to posts with children. In the UK, posts involving certain types of work with children qualify for the highest level of check, providing information about criminal convictions, police cautions and relevant police intelligence (i.e. non-conviction data). Information is also made available where a person is on the 'list' of people 'barred' from working with children. For those listed, it is a criminal offence to take up, remain in, or attempt to take up a post working with children; it is an offence also for an organisation to employ someone who is on the list of people barred from working with children. This applies equally to paid and voluntary posts.

The 'vetting' system, at the moment, leaves responsibility with the employer for making an employment decision about an individual following receipt of criminal history information.

b. The expansion of the vetting and barring arrangements in the UK

The expansion of these arrangements to protect children in organisations was fuelled by a number of factors. The final catalysts for significant reform were high profile child murder cases, particularly the murders in Dunblane Primary School of 16 pupils and their teacher in 1996, and in 2002 of Holly Wells and Jessica Chapman in Soham (McAlinden 2007).

Underpinning this were the revelations in the late 1980s and 1990s of maltreatment of children by those working with them (Corby 2000; Marshall, Jamieson and Finlayson 1999; Utting *et al.* 1997). A number of proposals were made in the resulting inquiries and reviews (Marshall *et al.* 1999; Warner 1992; Waterhouse 2000). Resulting recommendations included the need for more rigorous practice in recruiting staff, greater use of criminal history information and 'soft intelligence' for vetting adults for posts with children (Corby 2000). Parallel plans were underway to introduce a statutory system for barring unsuitable people from work with children (Gillie, Roll and Baber 1999).

Much of the policy activity in this area has been concerned with ensuring that employers receive the information they need to ensure children are safe, while at the same time protecting the rights of the individual to privacy and confidentiality. The expanding systems have been accompanied by complex legislation, policy and guidance and new agencies and public bodies have been set up across the UK to manage the arrangements.

There are some functional differences between the systems. However, they are broadly similar in structure, purpose and in the way they operate across the UK. They have developed in broadly similar ways in four main phases. These are:

- Phase 1: the extension and centralisation of provision of criminal history information for posts with children

- Phase 2: introduction of statutory arrangements for the identification of 'unsuitable' people from working with children

- Phase 3: reform of barring arrangements

- Phase 4: development of registration schemes for staff in posts with children: the linking of vetting and barring arrangements.

Not all of the four phases have been introduced in each part of the UK. Phase 4 was introduced in Scotland in 2011. Plans to do so were halted by the then incoming government and important changes were proposed to the vetting and barring arrangements. These are under consideration, and this section covers the development and operation of the systems currently operating in England, Wales, Scotland and Northern Ireland.

9.4 VETTING AND BARRING ARRANGEMENTS IN ENGLAND, WALES AND NORTHERN IRELAND

a. Vetting

Since the 1990s vetting and barring systems across the UK have become more centralised and formalised. New legislation, policy and guidance have been introduced which set out complex arrangements as the system has expanded to include voluntary organisations and cover an expanding number of posts. The new arrangements have clarified the types of posts to be checked and the type of check to be conducted. The Enhanced Disclosure has been until relatively recently the highest level of check conducted.

While some of the legislation introduced applied across the UK, new, separate bodies were set up to conduct checks and provide information: the Criminal Records Bureau (CRB) is responsible for arrangements in

England and Wales; AccessNI is for arrangements in Northern Ireland and Disclosure Scotland is the agency in Scotland. These new bodies have been set up since devolution.

The systems and processes involved in vetting and barring across the UK are partly concerned with ensuring that information from criminal records checks is seen only by those people who have a legitimate right to do so. It is the responsibility of an authorised person within an organisation to apply for an Enhanced Disclosure. Where an organisation cannot meet requirements to maintain information securely and confidentially, checks can be initiated on its behalf by an intermediate organisation. Currently a new Disclosure is required each time an individual moves post.

b. Barring

A separate complementary process for barring unsuitable people from work with children has also become statutory and high profile. Lists of individuals deemed to be unsuitable to work with children were introduced across the UK: the Protection of Children Act (POCA) list in England and Wales and the Disqualified from Working with Children (Northern Ireland) List. The systems also placed responsibility on employers for referring individuals for possible inclusion on the 'list'. This was compulsory for certain specified agencies, primarily statutory organisations, but optional for others. These lists sat alongside other arrangements including 'List 99' which was a list of those disqualified from working in education, and the Disqualification Orders of those convicted of offences (Smith 2010).

These were all replaced by alterations to barring arrangements in England, Wales and Northern Ireland as a result of the Safeguarding Vulnerable Groups Act 2006 (SVG). At this time Northern Ireland made an active decision to join the scheme in England and Wales. The Independent Safeguarding Authority (ISA) was set up as a Home Office sponsored non-departmental public body. It was given responsibility for the vetting and barring scheme as a whole for England, Wales and Northern Ireland. The new scheme retained elements of the previous scheme with some reforms, including the following elements:

- a new single Children's List with details of individuals banned from working with children; and with new powers to enforce the ban

- definitions of the posts and organisations covered by the barring scheme

- the duties for referring individuals to the scheme, and circumstances in which individuals can be referred to the List

- arrangements for making barring decisions and establishing whether or not an individual should be Listed.

c. The Children's List

The Children's List of those prohibited from working with children is the central component of the barring system. For anyone named on the Children's List it is a serious criminal offence to work or attempt to work in a regulated activity with children in either a paid or voluntary capacity. It is also a criminal offence if someone in an organisation knowingly allows someone on the Children's List to work with children (HM Government 2010). Enhanced Disclosures show employers if an individual is Listed.

Inclusion on the Children's List is not time limited and individuals are Listed for a minimum specified period before they obtain the right to request a review of their inclusion on the List. Review is allowed one year after registration for under 18s; after five years for 18–25 year olds; and after ten years for those 25 and over. Removal from the list depends on sufficient changes to circumstances since Listing. An individual has the right to appeal against inclusion on the Children's List on the basis of error of fact or law but not against the barring decision (HM Government 2010).

d. Definitions of posts and organisations covered by the barring requirements

All posts meeting the definition of 'regulated activity relating to children' are covered by its requirements (DCSF, Home Office and Department of Health 2007). Regulated activity relating to children posts include: paid and unpaid work; providing services to children including education, care, treatment and advice. It covers specified posts in institutions for children (see Box 9.1 for further information about specified posts). Registered child minders and foster-carers are also included. The 2006 Act also makes clear that family life and activities arranged on a personal non-commercial basis are not included. Definitions of posts apply to public, private and voluntary organisations.

BOX 9.1 SVG: REGULATED ACTIVITY RELATING TO CHILDREN

2.6 Regulated activity is the statutory term used to describe specific activities which involve working or volunteering with children or vulnerable adults and certain situations where individuals have the opportunity to have contact with children or vulnerable adults. It covers any such work, either paid or unpaid, which is carried out on a frequent, intensive or overnight basis... but does not include family or personal arrangements.

2.7 Regulated activity includes:
- specified activities...such as teaching, instructing, supervising, caring for or providing children/vulnerable adults with guidance or treatment
- fostering and childcare services
- specified positions...such as school governor or director of children's or adult social services
- all activity undertaken within specified settings...where there is the opportunity for contact with children or vulnerable adults. Activities include teaching, training and instruction, as well as catering, cleaning, administrative and maintenance workers or contractors
- roles that involve managing or supervising, on a regular basis, the day-to-day work of those carrying out specified activities or working in specified settings.

THE FREQUENCY AND INTENSIVENESS TESTS

Most work in any of the specified activities...is regulated activity if it is done frequently (once a week or more), intensively (on four days or more in a single month) or overnight. In health and personal care services, frequent is once a month or more. Work in any of the specified settings is regulated activity if it is done frequently or intensively. However, maintenance contractors who visit different care homes or children's hospitals will not meet the frequent or intensive tests if they visit several different care homes but do not work frequently in the same one...

2.26 **Registered childminders** and foster carers are engaging in
regulated activity and will be subject to all the requirements
of the Scheme, regardless of how frequently they engage in
registered childminding activities or fostering.

Source: HM Government 2010, pp.13–16

e. Referring to the Children's List

A key purpose of the barring arrangements is to identify those unsuitable
to work with children. Conviction for a serious offence is not the only
reason for Listing. Individuals can also be referred where behaviour may
not be criminal or for which they have not been successfully prosecuted.
Referrals can only be made by organisations, not by individuals who
should use the usual process of reporting concerns to social work/services
or the police. A wide range of bodies have a duty to refer, including
employers, those responsible for volunteers, professional bodies, education
institutions and inspection agencies. The circumstances under which
organisations must refer an individual are prescribed, but vary according
to the relationship with the referred individual. An employer must refer
to the ISA, if they 'withdraw permission' for someone to perform as
a Regulated or Controlled Activity Relating to Children because they
believe the individual:

- engaged in *relevant conduct*; specifically where an individual harmed
  or put a child at risk of harm; used or possessed sexual material
  relating to children for sexual gratification; used violent sexual
  material the ISA would judge as inappropriate

- satisfied the *harm test*; that is circumstances where the referrer
  believes an individual may harm a child based on his attitudes but
  does not require any actual harmful behaviour

- received a caution or conviction for a *relevant offence* or the
  individual is subject to a particular court order.

(Independent Safeguarding Authority undated)

This duty to refer applies even if the relevant conduct, harm test or
relevant offence was committed outside of work. It also applies if the
individual leaves the post for any reason. In a similar way, employment

businesses and agencies have a duty to refer an individual (when they will no longer supply that person for a regulated activity) if they meet the relevant conduct, harm test or received a caution or conviction for a relevant offence. The position is similar for education institutions, who have a duty to refer when, for example, they decide not to send a student on placement in a regulated activity because of relevant conduct, the harm test or because of a caution or conviction.

Keepers of the Registers of a range of professional bodies, supervisory authorities, and inspection and auditing bodies all have a duty to refer individuals to the ISA when they think an individual who is engaged in or may engage in a regulated or controlled activity has engaged in relevant conduct, satisfied the harm test or received a caution or conviction for a relevant offence (HM Government 2010). These arrangements exceed the reach of the previous barring system, with more organisations required to report, and the activities generating a referral broadened to include possible or intended actions in addition to actual actions.

f. Decisions about referring to the Children's List

Referrals for Listing received by the ISA are dealt with in one of two ways: they are either subject to assessment, or subject to automatic barring. In the latter an individual is Listed without further action. Two circumstances can result in automatic barring. First, in cases of convictions or cautions for very serious offences against a child or other vulnerable person, there is no right of representation or for removal. Second, when there has been a conviction or caution for other specified serious offences, there is the right of representation to the ISA against Listing.

The second group of 'non-autobar' cases arises from referrals from organisations on the grounds of 'relevant conduct' or the 'harm test'. At the outset the ISA establishes whether or not the case is legitimately the responsibility of the ISA. Where this is the case it is then examined, using information from the referral and previous referrals and any criminal records data. Where it is judged 'on the balance of probabilities, whether the event (or events) happened, and whether or not relevant conduct or risk of harm occurred' (Independent Safeguarding Authority 2009, p.15) the case proceeds to the next stage. These cases are then subject to risk assessment by the ISA 'to assess if there is "a future risk of harm"' (Independent Safeguarding Authority 2009, p.15). At this stage the person is contacted and provided with an opportunity to respond to the details of the referral. Other relevant people and organisations can be approached and are required to provide the information they hold. The case is considered with regard to any other information received and a final decision regarding Listing is taken.

g. The current situation

Organisations can establish where someone is on a barred list through an Enhanced Disclosure check. These should only be seen by relevant personnel in permitted organisations. New proposals developed intended that these existing proposals would be superseded by a compulsory registration scheme for those in regulated activities relating to children. Registration would be refused to those barred from such posts.

The proposals to implement the registration scheme were halted in 2010 by the new Coalition Government pending review of the entire vetting and barring system. Although details are not yet finalised it seems likely that some form of central barring system will continue; that criminal records checks will continue to be available to relevant employers. However, the posts covered will be subject to a narrower definition of 'only those who may have regular or close context with vulnerable groups' (Department for Education *et al.* 2011, p.4). The ISA and CRB will be merged into a single agency.

9.5 PROTECTION OF VULNERABLE GROUPS IN SCOTLAND

The barring system in Scotland, while separate, is similar to the system in England, Wales and Northern Ireland. The Protection of Children (Scotland) Act 2003 (POCSA) established a single list of those barred from working with children called the 'Disqualified from Working with Children List'. The original bill introduced into the Scottish Parliament mainly duplicated the POCA legislation in England and Wales. However, some elements were amended during its passage through the Scottish Parliament. For example, its provisions applied to all posts defined as child care positions, not just statutory organisations as was the case in England and Wales. Under this system, employers were given new duties to refer unsuitable people to the List. The system in Scotland was further reformed as a result of the Protection of Vulnerable Groups (PVG) (Scotland) Act 2007 which was implemented in 2011. Here, Disclosure Scotland became an executive agency which brought the hitherto separate functions of vetting and barring together in one agency (Smith 2009).

The PVG Act introduced a new Children's List which replaced the existing Disqualified from Working with Children List. The structure of the existing system was retained. It remains a criminal offence for anyone on the PVG Children's List to work with or attempt to work with children; or for organisations to offer work to someone on the Children's List. An individual is listed indefinitely. After ten years, the individual may apply to Disclosure Scotland for removal from the List; the minimum period is five years for those under 18 at the time of listing.

Application for removal can be made earlier where the person believes their circumstances have changed. Lists held in England, Wales and Northern Ireland are recognised in Scotland and vice versa; Listing in one jurisdiction means being barred in all four jurisdictions.

Posts covered by the legislation in Scotland were based on those already specified but with some changes (see Box 9.2), including the inclusion of new types of post, for example chat room moderators. The legislation clarified that 'Regulated Work with Children' covered those posts where there was unsupervised contact with children; also that contact with a child was part of 'normal duties' of the post and not incidental to them. Particular posts with responsibility for children, even where there may be no direct contact with children as part of 'normal duties' were also included, for example Chief Social Work Officers and the Office of Commissioner for Children.

BOX 9.2 PVG: REGULATED WORK WITH CHILDREN (SCOTLAND)

The PVG Guidance sets out 'five steps to assess if an individual is doing regulated work' (Scottish Government 2010c, p.56) in summary:

1. The post falls under the broad meaning of 'work' in the PVG including paid and unpaid posts and other roles such as foster carer.

2. The work must be with children, i.e. aged up to 18 years old.

3. Regulated activities are posts where certain activities with children are carried out; teaching, providing advice and guidance, being in sole charge or having unsupervised contact. Or are positions in particular establishments such as school, detention centre mainly for children, a children's home or a further education college are also covered. There are also specific positions included i.e. member of a children's panel or a chief social work officer.

4. These all must form part of the 'normal duties' of the post.

5. Finally 'some but not all, activities with children or protected adults are excluded from being regulated work if the activity is occurring incidentally to working with individuals who are not children or protected adults'. This is termed the 'incidental test'.

(Scottish Government 2010c)

---

a. Duties and circumstances of referrals to the Children's List

Courts have a duty to refer anyone to the Children's List who has been convicted of a 'relevant offence' as listed in Schedule 1 of the PVG Act. Courts retain discretion to refer to the List those convicted of any offence where they are 'satisfied it may be appropriate for the individual to be included in the Children's List (Scottish Government 2010c, p.89). Organisations have a duty to refer to the Children's List any individual in 'regulated work with children' (p.123) who has:

- harmed a child

- placed a child at risk of harm

- engaged in inappropriate conduct involving pornography

- engaged in inappropriate conduct of a sexual nature involving a child

- given inappropriate medical treatment to a child.

As a result the organisation must have removed the individual from regulated work with children or would have done if the individual had not already vacated the position.

The duty to refer exists regardless of whether the inappropriate activity took place during the course of regulated work with children or in another setting. Agencies that provide individuals for regulated work with children also have a duty to refer an individual on the same grounds. Regulatory bodies can refer individuals when they know information has not been provided from elsewhere.

b. Decision about whether a referred person should be Listed

The process for dealing with a referral to the Children's List in Scotland differs according to the referral. An individual referred on conviction of a specified serious criminal office is automatically added to the Children's List with no right of appeal or to make representation (Automatic Listing). Referrals from the courts on conviction of other offences would be subject to consideration by Disclosure Scotland. This is also the case for referrals from employers. A referral is considered where Disclosure Scotland is satisfied there is suitable information and that the referral is not 'vexatious' or 'frivolous'. Other information is then gathered and individuals involved have the opportunity to comment. Once sufficient information is gathered, Disclosure Scotland embark on a 'structured decision-making process' to identify and assess the risk factors to come to a decision as to whether the individual should be Listed (Scottish Government 2010c). In a few particularly complex cases the barring decisions are decided by an Expert Panel (Scottish Government 2010c). The guidance highlighted that decisions on whether to List or not are based on past behaviour and 'no individual can be listed solely on the basis of anticipation of future conduct' (Scottish Government 2010c, p.97).

In the Scottish system the possibility of Listing exists where a requested vetting check reveals criminal history information. In these cases, where criminal history information indicates that an individual is unsuitable to work with children, they will be added to the Children's List. In practice, most criminal records information concerns minor offences and it is envisaged that only in a minority of cases will vetting information prove to be the basis for Listing.

c. Establishing if an individual is on a Barred List

The system for vetting individuals underwent major reform in Scotland with the introduction of a new Membership Scheme to cover all personnel in regulated work with children. An application for Scheme Membership activates a vetting process of checking criminal history information. It is undertaken by Disclosure Scotland (Scottish Government 2007c). Those barred from working with children are refused membership and Scheme Membership is verification that the person is not barred from working with children. For members, a Scheme Record is issued; this contains criminal history information i.e. if the individual is on the Sex Offenders' Register, convictions, cautions and relevant police intelligence, and it is sent to the individual and the employer.

Whilst it is not mandatory for an individual in regulated work with children to be a Scheme Member, this is the method by which an employer can establish whether an individual is not on any Children's List. Thus, in practice the workforce and volunteers in regulated work with children are expected to be Scheme Members. That the legal requirement sits with the recruiting organisation rather than the individual is an important distinction between the system in Scotland and those proposed for elsewhere in the UK. The SVG scheme made it the responsibility of the individual to be a member.

The new arrangements in Scotland are intended to be more pro-active in the provision of information to employers. Scheme Records are maintained and updated. Where new vetting information arises and is serious enough to constitute consideration for Listing, both the person and their relevant employers will be notified. Where the vetting information does not result in Listing, it will still be included in the Scheme Record and will be part of any future release. This new process removes the need for repeat disclosure checks.

Thus unlike the rest of the UK, Scotland has moved ahead with its proposals to introduce a more integrated vetting and barring scheme which has at its core a membership scheme. If followed to its conclusion, this could leave England, Wales and Northern Ireland with elements of difference in the arrangements from Scotland for protecting children from adults who pose a risk to them. It will be interesting to keep this under close review in future to see if forces for convergence once again push the systems closer together.

9.6 CONCLUSION

Policy to protect children through targeting those identified as a potential danger to them, particularly in public space, has been subject to significant development and change across the UK over the past ten years. While differences in policy and practice in this area have emerged from devolved control, the fundamentals of the policy intent are identical; using previous behaviour as a key indicator of future actions, and focusing on risk and exchange of information. All of this depends on passing sensitive information between agencies, and sometimes the public, and raises issues about the impact on individuals' rights to confidentiality, risk management and on whom such policies are focused.

From a UK policy perspective, these are matters over which the Scottish Parliament and Northern Ireland Assembly have powers to legislate. There are three separate systems of multi-agency management of violent and sexual offenders: England and Wales, Scotland and Northern Ireland. There are three separate systems and bodies for criminal records checks for posts with children and there are two systems for prohibiting unsuitable individuals from working with children. Even with separate systems the policy content is essentially homogenous. This is in large part because the UK has been subject to identical drivers to develop them and ensure they are reasonably consistent. As has been seen elsewhere in this book, it is in the policy detail and practice that differences emerge between the jurisdictions rather than the broad policy.

Chapter 10

Summary and Conclusion
Child Protection across the UK

10.1 INTRODUCTION

In this concluding section, we set out ideas and findings from earlier chapters and draw conclusions about the current state of child protection across the UK.

Earlier we explained that the purpose of writing this book was at the same time the purpose for setting up our research centre at the University of Edinburgh in 2007. There was growing recognition that one consequence of devolution in the UK might be for child protection systems and processes to diverge from each other, and for the devolved parts of the UK to seek more local solutions to long standing child protection problems. Part of the work of the Centre has involved examining developments in child protection across the UK in the context of devolution. In writing this book we have distilled and synthesised much of the work and thinking that has gone on in the Centre in the first few years of its life.

Preceding chapters took both as wide a view as possible of child protection in the UK, by comparing the UK system with other systems world-wide; and as deep a view as possible, by scrutinising and comparing the inner-workings of child protection across the UK.

10.2 CONTEXTS AND DRIVERS OF POLICY CHANGE IN CHILD PROTECTION

We began by focusing on the factors that seemed to us to have been most influential in driving reform of child protection across the UK. These were complex; what drives policy change is multi-layered, convoluted and difficult to unravel. We used the framework for policy analysis developed by Hudson and Lowe (2009) who tried to build understanding of the policy making world at three levels: the macro level, the micro level and the meso level. We suggested that at the macro level, globalisation had loosened certain state structures leading to new organisational forms and ways of working. One effect of this has been to underpin and accelerate the break-up of Britain as a unitary state into a fragmented and differentiated polity, with devolution central to this. For us, it is the space now available for policy and practice variation across the UK that has been the stuff of this book. We were interested in how global forces, in the context of devolution, are taken up at the meso level, mediated by local networks and institutions, which then impact on child protection in each part of the UK. At micro level we claim that policy cannot be read from official documents. We have tried to understand how policy impacts at the point of implementation; at how policy is mediated and translated by practitioners.

We have also argued that it is not possible to understand reform of child protection across the UK without an understanding of the unique role the UK media plays in reporting high profile child death and child abuse cases. We concluded that the media has been and remains one of the main drivers of system change and the effect of this has increased greatly over the past 15 years.

10.3 CHILD PROTECTION ACROSS THE UK IN AN INTERNATIONAL CONTEXT

As part of our quest to understand the unfolding story of child protection across the UK, we tried to step back from our own system to consider where the UK sits in relation to other systems. We reviewed the international comparative research conducted over the past 15 years in this area. We described how interest in this as a research activity grew in the 1990s out of perceived problems with child protection systems in most of the Anglophone countries. The focus was the burgeoning levels of child protection referrals. The international studies were an explicit search for how other countries were more successful than the UK, and they had the clear objective of trying to improve the child protection system in the UK.

Across these studies two broad approaches or orientations to protecting children were identified. On the one hand there were the more investigative, procedurally focused systems of North America, the UK, Australia and New Zealand. On the other, the systems of the Nordic countries and Continental Europe with their broader focus on family support, attempting to address child protection in the context of wider child welfare systems.

For the Anglophone systems, it was the work of Kempe *et al.* in the 1960s and the discovery of the 'battered baby syndrome' that contributed greatly to the development of systems which were focused on identifying, monitoring, investigating and prosecuting cases of child abuse (Kempe *et al.* 1962). We argued that this approach contained within it a number of inherent flaws: it underestimated the complexity of child abuse as a phenomenon, and the numbers of children who were affected. By the 1990s, reports increasingly highlighted that these systems were at best out of balance, and at worst were in crisis. The twin problems of over-identification of children at risk, and that of under-identification were highlighted. Where cases were reported and investigated, children and families were not necessarily receiving the help they needed. Those who did receive support did not always experience it as helpful. Rather, it could be stigmatising and unhelpful.

Information from this body of comparative research also highlighted that this 'crisis' in the systems of the Anglophone countries was not necessarily being replicated in parts of the world with other types of system. Cooper *et al.* (1995) reported the results of their comparative research: unlike the system in England, the system in France was described as being infused with 'optimism' and 'trust'. In England, child protection at the time was characterised by 'pessimism' and 'distrust'. Morale was lower in England and social workers did not feel supported. There was a more managerialist culture of 'defensive accountability' sitting alongside a system based on checking whether procedures had been followed along with a culture of 'pervasive anxiety' (Cooper *et al.* 1992).

While most of the international comparative research was focused on the system in England, similar debate about child protection was also occurring elsewhere in the UK. In Scotland, for example, in the context of the Audit and Review of Child Protection in 2000, an international seminar was organised with speakers representing both types of systems.

Since then, further work has updated our understanding of what has occurred in child protection. In their 2011 study, Gilbert *et al.* (2011a) highlighted that across the countries and systems originally studied, approaches to child protection seemed to have become more complex and sophisticated than they were in the 1990s. There was information to suggest that in the context of globalisation and 'policy transfer', countries which had previously operated a family service model had made more effort to respond to concerns about harm and family violence and child sexual abuse; and that countries previously identified with a child protection orientation had moved towards a family service orientation.

In addition, the researchers noticed something new. Across all of the systems, whether originally displaying a child protection or a family service orientation, there seemed to be a new orientation – a child focused orientation – where the focus is on the child, who has an increasingly independent relationship to the state. This seemed to go beyond the more traditional role of the state in protecting children from harm and abuse to one of promoting children's overall well-being and welfare. The researchers suggested that this is shaped by two contrasting ideological perceptions of the child. The first is the notion of the 'social investment state' which sees children as future citizens whose development and well-being need to be nurtured and protected; second, the very different ideological perception of children as rights holders, taking account of the UN Convention on the Rights of the Child (Gilbert *et al.* 2011b). They concluded that it might be that countries are no longer on a continuum line between child protection and family support but rather lie somewhere within a three dimensional framework, closer to some planes than others.

Our interest then, is focused on the detail of how each of the systems of the UK have shifted over the past 15 years, and where they might now sit on this three dimensional plane whose three elements comprise: a narrow child protection orientation; a family support orientation; and the more recently identified child focused orientation.

10.4 LEARNING BY COMPARING

We described the conceptual and methodological challenges of conducting this kind of intra-country comparative work. We identified how at the heart of our work lie the twin concepts of 'learning' and 'comparing'. Central to our approach is our belief that making comparison between one thing and another is an important way of learning, and a commitment to the notion that comparison in public policy rests on its ability to be a source of explanation. However, from our examination of the extensive literature that now exists on comparative social policy and associated methodologies we were also aware that inter- or intra-country comparative analysis can be fraught with difficulty. A central problem is that in making comparison, there is a difficulty in establishing whether two things that might appear to be the same, are; or whether two things that might appear to be different really are different. Because of this, many such studies have often tended to use formalised and highly sophisticated methods, inter-country standards and outcome measures. Even here results are highly caveated.

For our purposes, we used a different methodological approach. We used a qualitative case study approach, where the researcher is immersed in each case/country allowing issues and themes to emerge. This has allowed us to tell a country-specific 'story' which we have argued provides richer data than when using formal methods alone.

We have highlighted that to date most comparative social policy has been concerned with inter-country comparison looking at countries with clear and distinct national boundaries, histories and cultures. The methodology for our book involved 'a methodological twist', where we used methods mainly developed to conduct inter-country comparison to look at the constituent parts of the UK in the context of devolution. We argued that debates and methodological approaches associated with comparative analysis of nation states can be usefully applied to intra-country comparison in the context of devolution; where constituent parts of the UK are potentially more similar than different, and have less autonomy than full nation states. In this context, learning means comparing using more nuanced differences.

We have argued that devolution is itself a complex and diverse concept, and that it has manifested itself differently in various parts of the world. We suggested that it is impossible to understand developments in child protection across the UK without some insight into the way devolution is unfolding. We examined how child protection policy change in the context of devolution is partly driven by political aims and objectives, introduced in part to demonstrate difference, to delineate one part of the UK from another and to assert distinct national identities. We also argued that real policy difference in this context is tricky to unpick and is partly a task of decoupling policy from its rhetoric. This 'unpicking' process partly justifies our case study approach and we have tried to understand policy change from a number of angles to gain as much understanding as possible.

Early aspirations for devolution were that it would bring divergence of policy; opportunities for the constituent parts of the UK to find distinct policy solutions to local problems. As yet this has been a slower process than anticipated. Academics have proposed several explanations for this. Not least is that there are pressures and forces which both predispose the constituent parts of the UK towards developing policy that is similar; and counter forces which tend towards creating policy that is divergent. Thus while there are opportunities for divergence there are also opportunities for constraint.

We suggest that it is not possible to understand devolution in the UK without understanding the unique position England occupies. England is by far the biggest player with five times the population of the three devolved parts of the UK put together. England is unique too in that the Westminster parliament also operates as the parliament of England.

Because of its size, and because it has the bulk of the policy capacity and resources, England is often able to set the context within which the devolved nations operate. This means there is a tendency towards bi-lateral links between England and the devolved countries, rather than between the devolved countries with each other. There is, then, more 'policy borrowing' from England than between the devolved parts of the UK. It could be argued that this has merely been a feature of the early stages of devolution where, particularly in the case of Wales and Northern Ireland, lack of divergence might be explained by the 'weak policy capacity of the devolved governments' (Keating *et al.* forthcoming). Jeffrey has asserted that there has been more territorial policy innovation in England than in the other three devolved administrations together (Jeffrey *et al.* 2010). However, this may change as policy capacity in the devolved parts of the UK continues to develop. It is also likely that the majority of policy resources are likely to remain in London. This lack of policy capacity will continue to have implications for autonomous policy making in other parts of the UK, with continuing pressures for 'policy borrowing' and adapting. There may also be a change in direction in the context of the Coalition Government who may be likely to have a less active approach to generating new policy than New Labour. The way these processes have played out in relation to developments in child protection policy across the UK was the focus of the second part of this book.

We shifted our analysis to a different conceptual level to deepen our understanding of child protection systems in each part of the UK. By applying our intra-country comparative approach to the main features making up child protection, our purpose was to hold a mirror to the inner workings of each system to gain a better understanding of each one and a better understanding of the whole.

10.5 POLICIES AND PROCEDURES FOR SAFEGUARDING AND PROTECTING CHILDREN ACROSS THE UK

We looked at the broad legislative and policy frameworks underpinning the child protection systems of the UK. Across the UK, services to safeguard and protect children are underpinned by complex systems of legislation, guidance, regulations and procedures. These are different in each part of the UK and we examined the extent of these differences. Our analysis has suggested that while each part of the UK has undergone significant reform of child protection *policy* over the past ten years, *legislative* change in the context of devolution has been relatively minor.

The key legislation underpinning the child protection system in each part of the UK remains the different Children Acts of the late 1980s and 1990s; and these preceded devolution. In England and Wales this is the Children Act 1989, although the Children Act 2004 amended some of its provisions. There are differences between the application of the Children Act in England and Wales. Since 2006, Wales has had new powers to pass its own primary legislation, so further legislative divergence from London is possible in the future; this is illustrated by the recently passed Vulnerable Child Measures and Children and Family (Wales) Measure 2009.

In Northern Ireland the Children (Northern Ireland) Order 1995 remains the primary Order relating to the protection of children, but the Safeguarding Board Act (Northern Ireland) 2011 now allows for a single Safeguarding Board for Northern Ireland to replace Area Child Protection Committees (ACPCs). In Scotland the Children (Scotland) Act 1995 remains the key legislation. However, the new Children's Hearings (Scotland) Act 2011 has introduced the first legislative change to the system since it was set up in the 1960s. England has had most legislative change over the time period, and Scotland has had the least.

There are broad similarities between the Acts. All of them define the thresholds for intervention in family life to protect children. In each part of the UK the threshold for intervention is 'significant harm': nowhere is the concept of 'significant harm' well defined. The concept 'children in need' also exists in each part of the UK.

Turning to the broad policy frameworks underpinning child protection across the UK, we have highlighted that a major similarity between parts of the UK is that it is now no longer possible to separate policy and practice to safeguard and protect children from the wider policy context surrounding children's welfare as a whole. In each case child protection is embedded in wider systems of welfare.

Each part of the UK has its own overarching policy framework for children's services. The first of these was developed in England following the Laming inquiry into the death of Victoria Climbié. Similar strategy documents were developed in Wales, Northern Ireland and Scotland. All of them borrowed heavily from *Every Child Matters* in England (HM Government 2004). They are similar in broad aims, scope, structures and aspirations for children and all are underpinned by broad national outcomes, with some differences in the national outcomes specified. All aim to provide a strategy to support the integration of children's services and improve outcomes. They stress the importance of early intervention and providing continuity of services from early intervention through to child protection and risk.

A central plank of child protection in each part of the UK is the multi-agency guidance for professionals working together to support children. Once again, each part of the UK has such guidance: *Working Together to Safeguard Children in England* 2010; *Safeguarding Children: Working Together Under the Children Act in Northern Ireland* 2006; *Co-operating to Safeguard Children in Northern Ireland* 2003; and the *National Child Protection Guidance in Scotland* 2010. England and Wales updated their guidance following the Children Act in 2004, and it was further updated in England in 2010. Scotland updated the 1998 guidance in 2010; Northern Ireland has not updated the guidance since 2003 but is now in the process of doing so. All of the guidance contains definitions of abuse. These definitions are broadly similar with some differences in detail.

Common to all, inter-agency guidance has tended to become longer and more complex (Parton 2011). While this is more pronounced in England, it has been a feature of the guidance throughout the UK: the 2006 version of *Working Together* in England (HM Government 2006a) is 231 pages long; the 2010 guidance (DCSF 2010) has grown to 390 pages; the Scottish guidance is 170 pages long; and in Wales the guidance is 334 pages.

Thus while each part of the UK has separate inter-agency guidance and while there are differences, their content covers the same broad areas.

All parts of the UK have Local Safeguarding Children's Boards (LSCBs) or Child Protection Committees (CPCs), but Child Protection Committees (CPCs) are not statutory in Scotland, and Northern Ireland has a single statutory Safeguarding Board. In contrast to England, Wales does not have Children's Trusts; instead, it has retained social services and each Local Authority must have a lead Director responsible for children's services. In Northern Ireland, Local Authorities do not have responsibility for children's services; rather, it is the function of Integrated Health and Social Services Boards. In Scotland, there is no national requirement for integrated children's departments.

Arrangements for inspecting child protection services differ throughout the UK, but all four parts look to inspection to provide the same end results in terms of improvement in services and public assurances of quality. Within each part of the UK, inspection is an important component of measuring outcomes for children against national standards.

Thus in terms of the wider legislation, structures and processes which underpin the child protection systems in the UK, each part has its own clear and separate vision for what it wants to achieve for children and its own distinctive policy for achieving it. While there are some differences in structures and polices to safeguard and protect children, there are many parallels. All parts of the UK approach the protection of children in broadly similar ways. While there is legislative difference, much of this was in place before devolution. The purpose of much of the legislative and policy reform across the UK has been to increase levels of accountability as a result of high profile child death and child abuse cases and this has been a major theme. To date, the devolved parts of the UK have looked to and borrowed heavily from England when developing their overarching framework documents and local guidance.

10.6 MANAGING INDIVIDUAL CASES WHERE THERE ARE CHILD PROTECTION CONCERNS

We then shifted away from our comparison of the wider structures and mechanisms for managing child protection to examine arrangements to protect individual children at risk of abuse and neglect, including: responding to referrals; investigating child protection concerns; protecting children in an emergency; registering, reviewing and de-registering children at risk of abuse.

We argued that there are similar arrangements in place for initiating investigations into child protection concerns in each of the four parts of the UK. However, the child protection system in Scotland adds another dimension to this in cases where a decision needs to be made about whether or not a child might be in need of compulsory measures of care and a referral to the Reporter to the Children's Hearing System is required.

All of the guidance across the UK stipulates timescales for initial assessment and these vary somewhat. Slightly different statistical data is published in the four parts of the UK about referrals and this makes UK-wide comparison problematic.

Measures to protect children in emergency child protection situations exist across the UK and have in common: Emergency Protection Orders (Child Protection Orders in Scotland); Police Protection Powers; and Exclusion Orders. Data on numbers of protection orders or exclusion orders are not published in any part of the UK. Although there is no official data, exclusion orders do exist in each part of the UK; however, they are rarely used.

Multi-agency case conferences are convened to consider individual child protection cases in each part of the UK. While there are differences in detail and timescales, processes are similar and their role is consistent across the UK. All parts of the UK have procedures in place for providing written reports and minute taking, although these differ in detail. While differences in arrangements for case conferences are relatively small across the UK, and despite data on case conferences being published, information gathered is different and again there are difficulties in making UK-wide comparison.

All parts of the UK have arrangements in place for registration, review and de-registration and arrangements for this have remained relatively unchanged over time and are broadly similar in each part of the UK. A decision to register is taken by the child protection case conference. If a child is registered, it is specified that a clear plan is necessary for how professionals will work together to protect the child. The aims and aspirations of holding case conferences as a means of case planning have been in existence since the system was set up. The processes for arranging them are similar throughout the UK; differences mainly concern planning arrangements and timescales. Again, despite the similarity of systems, there are differences in the way statistical information is gathered and published and this makes UK comparison in this area difficult.

With regard to arrangements for registration, while Scotland, Wales and Northern Ireland have retained the Child Protection Register, England has not. In England registration was replaced with the Integrated Children's System (ICS). However, this does record children who have a child protection plan. Across the UK, Registration is still the central point of inquiry for professionals where there are concerns about a child's safety. All four parts of the UK publish data on Registration, but once again, this is not directly comparable.

Each part of the UK has its own code governing arrangements for information sharing between professionals and agencies when there are concerns about a child. All share as the norm that children and families have the right to confidentiality, and they specify the conditions for sharing with or without consent. These circumstances are broadly the same across the UK, with differences in specific wording.

All parts of the UK have guidance for managing cases where children may be particularly vulnerable. It has been argued by Parton (2011) that the guidance produced to take account of new understandings of specific harm to children and widening definitions of abuse, has resulted in the tendency for the guidance to increase greatly in size and complexity; mainly explained by the development of lengthy supplementary guidance to the main guidance. While this tendency towards longer and more complex guidance is evident throughout the UK, it has perhaps been more evident in England and less so in the devolved countries. New national guidance in Scotland has developed some Scotland-specific supplementary guidance; in others cases it refers readers directly to the equivalent English guidance.

Thus while there are distinctive features between different parts of the UK in relation to arrangements to protect individual children, the broad stages of the system are similar and have remained relatively unchanged since the system was set up. Included in Figure 6.1 earlier in the book (see p.110) is a diagram reproduced from the *National Guidance for Child Protection in Scotland 2010* entitled 'Responding to child protection concerns' (Scottish Government 2010a) outlining the referral stages in a child protection investigation. While there are some differences in, for example, timescales for responding to a referral and in what constitutes a referral, the broad stages correspond and the diagram could equally apply to any part of the UK. However, while the processes are very similar, and differences between them small, there are subtle differences in definitions of abuse used. This means that data collected about child abuse differs and makes UK-wide comparison problematic.

Despite significant reform of child protection policy over the past ten years being towards prevention and early intervention and in line with a shift towards a family support orientation, there remains a clear point in all four parts of the UK where more traditional child protection processes come into play. Policy and guidance governing these processes have remained relatively unchanged since the system was set up; there has been remarkably little change in the procedures for managing individual cases where there are child protection concerns. The numbers of children entering the system at this point have also remained remarkably static. Whatever changes professionals have experienced as a result of burgeoning levels of policy and guidance issuing from central government and more bureaucratic demands, the experience of children and families caught up in a child protection investigation is unlikely to have changed significantly.

10.7 ASSESSMENT FRAMEWORKS

We examined the frameworks that exist throughout the UK for assessing children's needs including their child protection needs. Each part of the UK has in place comprehensive tools or frameworks for assessing the needs of all children including those who may be in need of protection. Each part of the UK is at different stages in developing and taking forward frameworks nationally. In England, the Framework for Assessment of Children in Need was introduced by the Department of Health in 2000 to replace the *Orange Book*. It centred on an assessment triangle consisting of three domains representing key aspects of the child's world. The Assessment Framework was supported by proactive guidance, questionnaires, scales, assessment record forms and training. Research and review of the Framework in England suggested that while the quality of assessments had improved this might have been at the price of having substantially increased work-loads.

The Common Assessment Framework (CAF) was introduced in 2004 and was a key plank of *ECM* in England and was fully implemented in 2008. It uses the same domains as the assessment framework and is also subject to detailed guidance. In line with *ECM*, it focuses on a broader group of children including those in need who may require early intervention, and because of this, is not intended for immediate and referable child protection concerns. Its use is voluntary and not governed by statute. Research in England has reviewed its impact and suggested that it is mainly being used by Health and Education professionals and they reported feeling frustrated at the lack of services available following a CAF assessment. While the CAF has been rolled out in England, this is not the case in Wales where it is currently being piloted in four areas. Pithouse (forthcoming) analysed its early use in Wales and suggested that while it did facilitate better communication and a more focused response, some practitioners showed limited capacity to engage with all parts of the CAF and at the time of writing it is not known if it will be rolled out across Wales.

In Scotland *My World Triangle* was produced in 2010 in the context of *Getting it Right for Every Child* (Scottish Government 2008a). It drew heavily on the domains contained in the English Assessment Model and attempted to address concerns expressed that it focused on the 'needs' of the child rather than on both needs and risk. The Scottish Framework was explicitly framed to take account of needs and risk. The Framework has not yet been rolled out across Scotland, rather it has been adapted for use and has been evaluated in one local authority area. The evaluation suggested that while practitioners were using it, it was not always being used effectively. Sometimes notes were descriptive rather than analytical and it was concluded that while practice was changing in the right direction, further policy development was required. While it is available for use in other local authorities, it is not yet known if it will be rolled out across Scotland.

The development of assessment frameworks in Scotland and Northern Ireland have been informed by the experience of the Assessment Framework in England and a risk assessment element had been added. Indeed, recently in Scotland, in the context of producing the new child protection guidance, work has also begun to develop a separate risk assessment tool. With this there may be a danger that the vision of *Getting it Right for Every Child* (GIRFEC) as a unifying structure to encompass child protection needs within the wider concept of meeting need is diluted.

Across the UK, assessment frameworks all seem to contain an unresolved, inherent tension between assessment to meet need and assessment for risk; and where there is assessment for need there is consistent criticism that where need is identified there is a lack of resources for support. While there are some differences between assessment frameworks in use across the UK, all have their origins in the model developed in England. They share theoretical underpinnings and their purpose is to outline domains for practitioners to consider in assessing children's needs, to guide practice towards analysis of these and to aid evidence based decision making. Once again we see a process where a policy is first introduced in England, then following a process of review and information becoming available, is adapted and taken up in the devolved parts of the UK.

10.8 CHILD DEATH REVIEW PROCESSES

In Chapter 8 we looked at the most serious end of the child abuse continuum and arrangements that exist to review cases where a child has died as a result of abuse and neglect. All parts of the UK now have processes in place for inquiring into or reviewing child deaths. While there are similarities between these processes, there are also variations.

Across the UK, prior to 2000, elaborate public inquiries used to be a relatively frequent response to high profile child death and abuse cases. Since then, across the UK, the trend has been to conduct far fewer of these, and to rely on local review mechanisms. Processes for this vary and are at different stages of development. England and Wales were the first part of the UK to introduce formalised systems and mechanisms for local review of child deaths. The 2004 Children Act and accompanying regulations placed SCRs on a statutory footing in England and Wales and it became mandatory for LSCBs to conduct an SCR if a child died under certain conditions. In 2009, Lord Laming's report made further recommendations to strengthen SCRs in England. In 2007 responsibility for evaluating the process of conducting and the quality of SCR in England was transferred to Ofsted. In Wales, policy around SCRs was similar to England but since 2009 has begun to change with the Welsh Assembly Government announcing plans to implement a new learning framework to replace SCRs by the end of 2011.

While Local authorities in Scotland did conduct local review of child deaths, a national approach was not in place until 2007 when national guidance was issued. Currently, SCRs are not inspected in Scotland, no reviews or analyses have been conducted, and as yet there are no requirements to submit reviews to a central point. In 2010 a Short Life Working Group was set up under the Multi-agency Response Service (MARS) who made recommendations to Government and these are currently under consideration. In Northern Ireland, ACPCs have had responsibility for undertaking CMRs since 2003. This is also underpinned by guidance. The circumstances under which a review is undertaken are similar to England, with slight differences. ACPCs have to provide a copy of reports to the Department of Health, Social Services and Public Safety (DHSSPS) and recently there has been first analysis of CMRs.

Since 2008, in an attempt to create a wider public health approach to understanding all child deaths, England now has a duty to review all deaths through Child Death Overview Panels and to produce aggregated findings. No similar processes are yet planned for Wales, Northern Ireland and Scotland, although a pilot scheme of this is being tested in Wales.

Once again, we see a process where a policy is first introduced in England, then, following a process of review and information becoming available, is adapted and taken up in the devolved parts of the UK.

10.9 OFFENDER MANAGEMENT SYSTEMS

Most of the book has been concerned with comparing and contrasting systems across the UK related to the direct protection of children. In Chapter 9 we examined the arrangements and mechanisms in place to keep children safe from adults who may pose a risk to them. This included consideration of arrangements for the management of violent and sexual offenders; systems for 'vetting' individuals and checking their suitability to work with children; and for 'barring' those already deemed to be a risk to children.

Across the UK there have always been avenues for agencies working with children to conduct police checks on their staff; albeit for most of the 1960s, 1970s and 1980s, these have not been statutory. It was not until the 1980s and 1990s that we saw the rise of large scale systems for vetting and barring. This is an area of child protection that makes an interesting case study to test our assertion that the devolution process contains within it simultaneous pressures for policy to both converge and diverge. Vetting and barring is a devolved area of policy which means it has had the potential to develop divergently. However, because of cross-border issues and the need to ensure that no part of the UK is seen to be a safer haven for sex offenders than others, it could be argued that pressures for convergent policy are more likely. Indeed, at present all three systems of the UK operate in virtually the same way, with, for example, Scotland pursuing an almost replica of the broad framework that exists in England, Wales and Northern Ireland. While there is some difference in detail, the policy intentions and broad aims are the same.

For the future, and in the context of the UK Coalition Government's Review of the proposed system in England, Wales and Northern Ireland, proposals already in the pipe-line have been put on hold. What the outcome of this Review will be for England is as yet unclear but may result in a winding back of some aspects of it. However, at the time of writing, the Scottish Government has introduced reform of the system as planned. This, if followed to its logical conclusion could leave England and Scotland with different arrangements for protecting children from adults who may pose a risk to them.

10.10 THE FUTURE OF CHILD PROTECTION IN THE UK

Finally, we have argued that while each part of the UK has its own clear and separate vision for what it wants to achieve in relation to protecting children, and while there are significant differences between England and the devolved parts of the UK in terms of mechanisms and structures for achieving it, there are many parallels. All parts of the UK approach the protection of children in broadly similar ways.

We have argued that the process of reform of child protection policy across the UK is partly driven by political aims to demonstrate difference and delineate one part of the UK from another. 'Unpicking' real policy difference from rhetoric in this context has been complex. We highlighted that England, as the biggest player, has the bulk of the policy making capacity and often sets the agenda and policy framework. To date England has often been the originator of new child protection policy development, which is then taken up at a later date and adapted for use by the devolved countries. Much of the policy borrowing, spillage and transfer is currently one way from England to one of the devolved countries, with the devolved countries not yet looking to each other to any great extent.

While many of the main child protection policy documents appear different and are often titled differently, their origins sit mainly in England. The content often varies very little. Where it does differ, this is often to take account of challenges identified as a result of inspection or review. It will be interesting in the context of the devolution project maturing to monitor how child protection develops across the UK. Will the earlier bi-lateral arrangements with England continue to be the norm or will the devolved parts of the UK begin to look more to each other for policy borrowing and sharing.

In the context of the Coalition Government and the Munro Review of child protection set up in its wake in 2010/11, the child protection system in England is once again in the spotlight. The future of child protection in England is uncertain and the impact on its near neighbours who are unlikely to remain unaffected is also unknown. The Coalition Government's response to the Review's recommendations will be at least as important as the Review itself; and this is also unclear. There are, however, a few pointers.

Even before the review is complete many of the newer features of *Safeguarding in England* that grew up under New Labour and were closely associated with the *ECM* agenda have already been dismantled, are in the process of being dismantled or are under review. These include the ContactPoint Data Base; Children's Trusts; the role of LSCBs; the vetting and barring systems. Notably, the adoption of some of these specific measures were either not adopted or adopted with rather less alacrity in other parts of the UK.

The Munro Review is a review of child protection in England, rather than of the wider safeguarding system that has been set up there. It is unclear at this stage what the final outcome will be. It could result in a pulling back from this wider safeguarding system to one where state interest is once again more narrowly focused on children deemed to be at most significant risk. It will be interesting to note whether or not the devolved countries follow suit.

It seems likely that the basic structure of the child protection system will remain intact. The report has been critical of the fact that the child protection system had become a top-down, compliance-driven system and that professionals no longer had space to exercise professional judgement. Her stated aim in conducting the Review included wanting to reduce the amount and size of procedural guidance which has been introduced in England in recent years, the need to build more flexibility into the system, reduce the burden of inspection, and remove many of the rigid procedures and timescales. These measures may make it easier for professionals to operate in a less bureaucratically specified, more flexible way, and to enable staff to apply more of their own professional judgement. While the end result may ensure that the narrow child protection end of the safeguarding system does work better in England, it is perhaps unlikely to radically change the nature of our child protection system as we know it. In this context, it is unclear what will happen to the wider safeguarding system.

In terms of the broad orientations identified earlier, Stafford and Vincent (2008) have argued, that at the time of the Audit and Review of Child Protection in Scotland in 2000, while the Scottish system with its welfare based Children's Hearing System was more hybrid, all the systems of the UK could be seen to fit within the Child Protection orientation which was adversarial, and predominantly focused on investigation and prosecution. During the 2000s it seems that all countries of the UK began to develop in ways which were closer to the systems of Continental and northern Europe. They have been moving away from being more narrowly child protection focused towards a system where children's protection needs are met in the context of their wider support needs. In terms of the third orientation, like other international child protection systems, the systems of the UK have increasingly moved to one where the focus of attention is the child (as opposed to the family) who has their own independent relationship with the state.

With regard to the Munro Review of child protection in England, what remains unclear is the impact it will have on the direction of travel. For the future, there are several options. The Review may bring minor system change, leaving the main features of the child protection and safeguarding systems intact and travelling in the same direction. Or perhaps the implementation of the Review will lead to changes of a more profound kind; altering the direction of travel back to being a system more narrowly focused on child protection, with the wider safeguarding agenda, developed under New Labour and *Every Child Matters* being left to dwindle away in the context of the cuts and 'The Big Society'. The spill-over effect on the other devolved nations is also still to be determined.

The period since May 2010 is the first time that the four administrations of the UK have been so different in terms of political make-up. It will be interesting see how these different political contexts impact on devolution and child protection. Will the devolved countries continue to follow in England's footsteps or will they more confidently assert their differences? As the story of child protection unfolds across the UK in the context of devolution, it will be useful to keep it under review and continue to scrutinise it from the broadest vantage point.

Appendix

Legislation Regarding Child Protection and Emergency Orders

Child Protection Legislation

England, Northern Ireland and Wales

Protection and Emergency Orders

1) An Emergency Protection Order (EPO) is used to remove a child from where he is kept, in emergency situations. It is an order that requires 'exceptional justification' and can only be granted for 'extraordinarily compelling reasons'.[1]

2) Under legislation, a court may only grant an EPO[2] if it is satisfied that:

a) there is reasonable cause to believe that the child is likely to suffer significant harm if he is not removed to accommodation provided by the application or he does not remain in the accommodation he is currently being kept in; or

b) in the case of a local authority, the authority has made enquiries under section 47 to establish risk and those enquiries have been frustrated through the denial of access to the child and the authority has reasonable cause to believe that access is required as a matter of urgency; or

c) in the case of an authorised person, the authorised person has reasonable cause to suspect that a child is suffering or likely to suffer significant harm and has attempted to make enquiries that have been frustrated through denial of access and the authority believes access is required as a matter of urgency.[3]

Scotland

Protection and Emergency Orders

1) A Child Protection Order (CPO) is for emergency cases and lasts for eight days until a children's hearing is commenced. In order for a CPO to be granted the sheriff must be satisfied that there are reasonable grounds to believe that the child:

a) is being so treated (or neglected) that he is suffering significant harm; or

b) will suffer such harm if he is not removed to and kept in a place of safety, or if he does not remain in the place where he is presently being kept; and

c) An order under this section is necessary to protect the child from harm (or further harm).[4]

2) Any person can apply[5] to the sheriff for a CPO but has to convince the sheriff that all of the criteria apply.

3) The local authority can apply for a CPO and the sheriff will grant such an application if he is satisfied that:

a) The authority has reasonable grounds to suspect that a child is being or will be so treated (or neglected) that he is suffering or will suffer significant harm;

b) That the authority are making or causing to make enquiries to allow them to decide whether they should take any action to safeguard the welfare of the child; and

3) An EPO[6] will have the following effects:

a) it ensures any person shall produce the child to the applicant,[7]

b) it authorises the removal of the child to accommodation provided by the applicant;

c) it authorises the prevention of a child being removed from any hospital or other place in which he is being accommodated; and

d) it gives the applicant parental responsibility for the child.[8]

4) Where an applicant believes a child is no longer in danger, he must return a child to the place of residence before the EPO was granted.[9]

5) The applicant is also under a duty to allow reasonable contact between the child and his parents (or other persons such as those with parental responsibility for the child).[10]

6) An EPO shall last no longer than eight days in total,[11] and may be extended by application from any person who has parental responsibility for the child as a result of the EPO or is entitled to apply for a care order, to a maximum of 15 days.[12]

7) There is no right of appeal against an EPO during the making of or refusal of an EPO, the extension or refusal to give any direction in connection with such an order.[13]

8) Under Section 47,[14] a police constable can remove a child to suitable accommodation and keep him there or prevent him from removal of safe accommodation, where he believes that a child would otherwise suffer significant harm.[15]

9) No child shall be kept for longer than 72 hours in police protection.[16] It is important to note that the police do not obtain parental responsibility for the child as a result of an order[17] but they can, on behalf of the relevant authority, apply for an EPO.[18]

c) That those enquiries are being frustrated by access to the child being unreasonably denied, the authority having reasonable cause to believe that such access is required as a matter of urgency.[19]

4) If the criteria for making a CPO are discovered by the sheriff he must make a CPO.[20]

5) A CPO may do any of the following:

a) Require any person to produce the child;

b) Authorise the removal of the child by the applicant[21] to a place of safety and keep the child at that place;

c) Prevent the removal of a child from a place he is being accommodated;

d) Prevent the disclosure of a child's location to any person classified in the order.[22]

6) The sheriff may consider it necessary to make directions[23] as to what should happen to a child with regards to contact between the child and any parent, or any person with parental rights and responsibilities or any other person or class of persons.[24]

7) When a CPO has been made and the child has been taken to a place of safety or prevention from being removed from any place, the reporter shall arrange an initial[25] children's hearing (on the second day after implementation of the order[26]) to decide whether it is in the best interest of the child to continue the CPO.[27]

8) Where the initial children's hearing are satisfied that the conditions for the making of a CPO[28] are established they may continue the CPO (with or without variation of the order) until the commencement of the children's hearing which would be six days from this initial hearing.[29]

9) The CPO is served at the same time the child is removed.

	10) After the CPO has been made, the child, parents, other relevant persons and the applicant of the order all have the right to ask[30] a sheriff to set aside or vary[31] an order.[32]
	11) The CPO ceases to exist when the children's hearing commences.[33]
	12) Where, on the application of any person,[34] a Justice of the Peace is satisfied that both the conditions laid down for the making of a CPO to be made to a sheriff or for the sheriff to consider the application, then he may grant an authorisation[35] of an emergency order.[36]
	13) The authorisation shall cease to have effect if nothing is done within the first 12 hours of the application having been made, or if 24 hours have passed since authorisation or if the application is disposed of before the 24 hours have passed.[37]
	14) A police constable may also remove the child[38] if the conditions for making a CPO are satisfied, that it is not practicable for an application to a sheriff to occur and that in order to protect the child from significant harm, it is necessary for the constable to remove the child to a place of safety.[39]
	15) Under legislation, a justice of the peace may use any of the above CPO powers where application to a sheriff is not possible.[40]

1. Re X: Emergency Protection Orders [2006] EWHC501 (Fam).
2. Such an order shall not be made unless the court is satisfied that it is both necessary and proportionate and that no other option will suffice. Additionally, separation of the child from the parents should only be allowed if immediate separation is essential to secure the child's safety and an 'imminent danger' must be 'actually established'. Further, any order must provide for the least interventionist solution and notice of the EPO must be given to the parents regarding the notice of the date, time and place of the application, along with the evidence the local authority is relying upon (Re X: Emergency Protection Orders [2006]EWHC 501 (Fam) 64).
3. CA Act 1989 s.44(1).
4. CA Act 1995 s.57(1).
5. Where an application has been made the reporter may request a hearing, the purpose of which being that the hearing may provide any advice they consider appropriate to assist the sheriff in his determination of the application (CA Act 1995 s.60(10)).

6. A court may also give directions with regards to contact between a child and any named person and with regards to any medical or psychiatric examination or other assessment of the child (CA Act 1989 s.6). The child may refuse to consent to such examinations, however, and any direction may be varied at any time by any person falling under the rules of the court (CA Act 1989 ss.7 & 9).

7. Where it appears to the court making an EPO that adequate information as to the child's whereabouts is not available to the applicant for the order but is available to another person, it may order the other person to disclose any information they may have (CA Act 1989 s.48(1)). An EPO may also authorise the applicant to enter premises specified by the order and search for the child (CA Act 1989 s.48 (3)). Where there is reasonable cause to believe that an EPO ought to be made against another child on the premises an order can be made to search for that child (CA Act 1989 s.48(4)) and if the child is found and the criteria for the making of an EPO is present, then the 'search order' shall have the same effect as an EPO (CA Act 1989 s.48(4)). A fine may be issued to a person who obstructs entry onto the premises (CA Act 1989 s.48(8)) and where a person has been prevented from exercising their powers under an EPO by being refused entry to premises, warrants may be issued by a court authorising a constable to assist a person to enter the premises (CA Act 1989 s.48(9)). The police may, in exceptional circumstances and where they believe a life or limb situation has arisen, enter and search the premises under the Police and Criminal Evidence Act 1984.

8. CA Act 1989 s.44(4).

9. CA Act 1989 s.10.

10. CA Act 1989 s.13.

11. CA Act 1989 s.45(1).

12. CA Act 1989 s.45(4) & (5).

13. CA Act 1989 s.45(10). In a nutshell, there is no right to appeal whatsoever. However, a child, parent, any person who has parental responsibility for the child and any person whom the child was living with immediately before the order can apply to the court to have the order discharged (CA Act 1989 s.45(8)). Note, however, that no application can be made where that person had been notified about the hearing at which the order was made and that person attended the hearing, and the same applies for the case of an extension of an EPO (CA Act 1989 s.45(10) & (11)). Thus, the opportunity to discharge is limited to only those who did not receive notice and were not present at the hearing. Further, no application to discharge can be made before the expiry of 72 hours beginning with the making of the order (CA Act 1989 s.45(9)). A court may also vary or discharge an exclusion requirement and/or power of arrest part of the EPO by application from a person to whom the exclusion requirement applies (CA Act 1989 s.45(8A) & (8B)).

14. As soon as this occurs, the constable shall inform the local authority, inform the child of the steps that have been taken and are about to be taken with regards to his safety, take steps to discover the child's feelings, secure that the case is enquired into by a police officer and move the child to accommodation that is either a refuge or accommodation provided by the local authority (CA Act 1989 s.46(3)). The constable shall also inform the parents or any person who has parental responsibility for the child or any person who was living with the child (CA Act 1989 s.46(4)).

15. CA Act 1989 s.46(1).

16. Contact shall be allowed between the child and the parents, any person who has parental responsibility for the child, any person who was living with the child, any person in whose favour has a contact order in force with respect to the child, any person who is allowed contact and any person acting on behalf of those persons, if it is both reasonable and in the best interests of the child (CA Act 1989 s.46(10)).

17. CA Act 1989 s.46(9)(a).

18. CA Act 1989 s.46(7).

19. CA Act 1995 s.57(2).

20. CA Act 1995 s.55(2).

21. The applicant shall hand notice to the local authority and to the report (CA Act 1995 s.57(5)). The applicant shall only act where he reasonably believes that to do so would be necessary to safeguard or promote the welfare of the child (CA Act 1995 s.57(6)).

22. CA Act 1995 s.57(4).

23. The direction may prohibit contact between the child and the above mentioned parties or, it may make contact between the parties (CA Act 1995 s.58(2)). A direction may also deal with the exercise of parental rights and responsibilities, and in doing so, such directions may allow for any physical or mental examination, assessment or interview, or treatment of the child (CA Act 1995 s.58(4)). It is important to note that the consideration of family life, under Article 8 of the European Convention on Human Rights is in the mind of the sheriff at all times as he must consider the issue of contact between a child and his family when making a CPO.

24. CA Act 1995 s.58(1).

25. This is not the children's hearing that will take place on the eighth working day after the CPO was implemented, instead this is an initial hearing with the sole purpose of assessing whether the CPO should continue (CA Act 1995 s.65(2)). This initial hearing must take place on the second working day after the CPO has been implemented (CA Act 1995 s.59(3)).

26. CA Act 1995 s.59(2) & (3).

27. CA Act 1995 s.59(2).

28. The reporter may also 'drop' the CPO if he believes the conditions for the making of a CPO are no longer satisfied whether as a result of a change in the circumstances or the case of further information having been discovered (CA Act 1995 s.59(3)).

29. CA Act 1995 s.59(4).

30. The request can be made immediately, or before the initial hearing takes place, or if the initial hearing takes place and the order is continued, within two days after the initial hearing (CA Act 1995 s.60(8)).

31. After consideration of the application to vary or set aside the CPO, the sheriff shall do one of the following: a) he can confirm or vary the order, or any term or condition on which it is granted; b) he can confirm or vary any direction given; c) he can give a new direction; d) continue the CPO until the children's hearing; and/or e) he can recall the order and cancel any direction if he believes the conditions for making a CPO are not satisfied (CA Act 1995 s.60(12) & (13)).

32. CA Act 1995 s.60(7).

33. CA Act 1995 s.60(6).

34. Likewise, if a local authority applied under the second application rule (i.e. the CPO application that is utilised solely by local authorities) then the same applies (CA Act 1995 s.61(2)).

35. An authorisation by the justice of the peace may require any person in a position to do so to produce the child to the applicant, may prevent any person from removing the child from a place where he is being accommodated and may authorise the applicant to remove the child to a place of safety and keep him there until the expiration of the authorisation (CA Act 1995 s.61(3)).

36. CA Act 1995 s.61(1).

37. CA Act 1995 s.61(4).

38. The authorisation shall cease on disposal of the application and it shall not last longer than 24 hours (CA Act 1995 s.61(7) and s.61(6)).

39. CA Act 1995 s.61(5).

40. CA Act 1995 s.61(3).

References

Adamson, S. and Deverell, C. (2009) 'CAF in the country: Implementing the Common Assessment Framework in a rural area.' *Child and Family Social Work 14*, 4, 400–409.

Ainsworth, F. (2002) 'Mandatory reporting of child abuse and neglect: Does it really make a difference?' *Child and Family Social Work 11*, 1, 31–41.

Aldgate, J. and Rose, W. (2008) *Assessing and Managing Risk in Getting It Right for Every Child.* Edinburgh: Scottish Government.

Arts, W. and Gelissen, J. (2002) 'Three worlds of welfare capitalism or more? A state-of-art report.' *Journal of European Social Policy 12*, 2, 137–158.

Ashenden, S. (1996) 'Reflective governance and child sexual abuse: Liberal welfare rationality and the Cleveland Inquiry.' *Economy and Society 24*, 1, 64–88.

Ashenden, S. (2004) *Governing Child Sexual Abuse: Negotiating the Boundaries of Public and Private, Law and Science.* London: Routledge.

Aspalter, C. (2006) 'New developments in the theory of comparative social policy.' *Journal of Comparative Social Welfare 22*, 1, 3–22.

Audit Commission (1994) *Seen But Not Heard: Coordinating Community Health and Social Services for Children in Need.* London: HMSO.

Axford, N. and Bullock, R. (2005) *Child Death and Significant Case Reviews: International Approaches.* Edinburgh: Scottish Executive.

Bateson, G. (1972) 'The Logical Categories of Learning and Communication.' In G. Bateson (ed.) *Steps to an Ecology of Mind.* New York: Ballantine.

Bauman, Z. (1998) *Globalization: The Human Consequences.* Cambridge: Polity Press.

Beck, U. (1992) *Risk Society: Towards a New Modernity.* London: Sage.

Bell, S. (1988) *When Salem Came to the Boro: The True Story of the Cleveland Child Abuse Crisis.* London: Pan Books.

Birrell, D. (2009) *The Impact of Devolution on Social Policy.* Bristol: Polity Press.

Birrell, D. (2010) 'Devolution and Approaches to Social Policy.' In G. Lodge, K. Schmuecker and C. Jeffrey (eds) *Devolution in Practice 2010.* London: IPPR.

Bradshaw, J., Hoelscher, P. and Richardson, D. (2007) 'An index of child well-being in the European Union.' *Social Indicators Research 80*, 1, 133–177.

Brand, J. (1978) *The National Movement in Scotland.* London: Routledge and Kegan Paul.

Brandon, M., Anthony, R., Colquhonn, F. and Connolly, S. (2009) *Evaluating the Common Assessment Framework and Database in 2008.* Cardiff: Welsh Assembly Government.

Brandon, M., Belderson, P., Warren, C., Howe, D. *et al.* (2008) *Analysing Child Deaths and Serious Injury Through Abuse and Neglect: What Can We Learn?* London: Department for Children, Schools and Families.

Brandon, M., Howe, D., Black, J. and Dodsworth, J. (2002) *Learning How to Make Children Safer Part 2: An Analysis for the Welsh Office of Serious Child Abuse Cases in Wales.* Norwich: University of East Anglia/Welsh Assembly Government.

Brandon, M., Howe, A. and Dagley, V. (2006) 'What appears to be helping or hindering practitioners in implementing the Common Assessment Framework and Lead Professional Working?' *Child Abuse Review 15*, 6, 396–413.

Brixey, S.N., Kopp, B.C. and Schlotthauer, A.E. (2011) 'Use of child death review to inform sudden unexplained infant deaths occurring in a large urban setting.' *Injury Prevention 17*, 1, i23–i27.

Bromfield, L. and Holzer, P. (2007) *A National Approach for Child Protection Project Report.* Melbourne: National Child Protection Clearinghouse; Australian Institute of Family Studies.

Bryan, T. and Doyle, P. (2003) 'Developing Multi-Agency Public Protection Arrangements.' In A. Matravers (ed.) *Sex Offenders in the Community.* Cambridge: Willan Publishing.

Buckingham, D. (2000) *After the Death of Childhood: Growing Up in the Age of Electronic Media.* Cambridge: Polity Press.

Bunting, L. (2004) *Assessment of Children in Need in Northern Ireland.* Belfast: NSPCC.

Bunting, L. and Reid, C. (2005) 'Reviewing child deaths: Learning from the American experience.' *Child Abuse Review 14,* 2, 82–96.

Cameron, G., Coady, N. and Adams, G.R. (eds) (2007) *Moving Towards Positive Systems of Child and Family Welfare: Current Issues and Future Directions.* Waterloo, Canada: Wilfrid Laurier University Press.

Cameron, G., Freymond, N., Cornfield, D. and Palmer, S. (2007) 'Positive Possibilities for Child and Family Welfare: Expanding the Anglo-American Child Protection Paradigm.' In G. Cameron, N. Coady and R. Adams (eds) *Moving Toward Positive Systems of Child and Family Welfare: Current Issues and Future Directions.* Waterloo, Canada: Wilfrid Laurier University Press.

Canavan, J., Dolan, P. and Pinkerton, J. (eds) (2000) *Family Support: Direction from Diversity.* London: Jessica Kingsley Publishers.

Care and Social Services Inspectorate Wales (2009) *Improving Practice to Protect Children in Wales: An Examination of the Role of Serious Case Reviews.* Cardiff: CSSIW.

Castells, M. (2000a) *The Rise of the Network Society.* Second edition. Oxford: Blackwell.

Castells, M. (2000b) 'Materials for an exploratory theory of the network society.' *British Journal of Sociology 51,* 1, 5–24.

Castles, F.G. (1998) *Comparative Public Policy: Patterns of Post-War Transformation.* Cheltenham: Edward Elgar.

Castles, F.G. (2001) *Do Institutions Matter? One Question, Two Approaches.* Inaugural lecture. Edinburgh: University of Edinburgh.

Cerny, P. and Evans, M. (1999) *Working Paper No.70: New Labour, Globalization and the Competition State.* Cambridge, MA: Center for European Studies, Harvard University.

Clark, C. and McGhee, J. (eds) (2008) *Private and Confidential? Handling Personal Information in the Social and Health Services.* Bristol: Policy Press.

Clarke, J. (2005) 'Welfare states as nation states: Some conceptual reflections.' *Social Policy and Society 4,* 4, 407–415.

Clasen, J. (ed.) (1999) *Comparative Social Policy: Concepts, Theories and Methods.* Oxford: Blackwell.

Cleaver, D., Cleaver, H., Parry, O., Pithouse, A. *et al.* (2008) *Development of an Electronic Common Assessment Framework for Wales.* Wrexham: North East Wales Institute of Higher Education.

Cleaver, H. and Walker, S. (2004) 'From policy to practice: The implementation of a new framework for social work assessments of children and families.' *Child and Family Social Work 9,* 1, 81–90.

Cooper, A. (1992a) 'Anxiety and child protection work in two national systems.' *Journal of Social Work Practice 6,* 2, 117–128.

Cooper, A. (1992b) *Methodological and Epistemological Considerations in Cross-National Comparative Research.* London: CCSWS.

Cooper, A., Freund, V., Grevot, A., Hetherington, R. and Pitts, J. (1992) *The Social Work Role in Child Protection: An Anglo-French Comparison.* London: CCSWS.

Cooper, A., Hetherington, R., Bairstow, K., Pitts, J. and Spriggs, A. (1995) *Positive Child Protection: A View from Abroad.* Lyme Regis: Russell House Publishing.

Cooper, A., Hetherington, R. and Katz, I. (2003) *The Risk Factor: Making the Child Protection System Work.* London: Demos.

Corbett, J. and Rose, W. (2010) 'Children and Young People: Rights to Action in Wales.' In A. Stafford, S. Vincent and N. Parton (eds) *Child Protection Reform Across the UK.* Edinburgh: Dunedin University Press.

Corby, B. (2000) *Child Abuse.* Buckingham: Open University Press.

Corby, B. (2003) 'Towards a new means of inquiry into child abuse cases.' *Journal of Social Welfare and Family Law 25,* 3, 229–41.

Corby, B., Doig, A. and Roberts, V. (1998) 'Inquiries into child abuse.' *Journal of Social Welfare and Family Law 20,* 4, 377–395.

Corby, B., Doig, A. and Roberts, V. (2001) *Public Inquiries into Abuse of Children in Residential Care.* London: Jessica Kingsley Publishers.

Corby, B., Millar, M. and Pope, A. (2002) 'Assessing children in need assessments – a parental perspective.' *Practice 14,* 4, 5–15.

Covington, T.M. (2011) 'The US National Child Death Review Case Reporting System.' *Injury Prevention 17*, 1, i34–i37.

Crisp, B.R., Anderson, M.R., Orme, J. and Lister, P.G. (2007) 'Assessment frameworks: A critical reflection.' *British Journal of Social Work 37*, 6, 1059–1077.

Curtice, J. (2010) 'Policy Divergence: Recognising Difference or Generating Resentment?' In G. Lodge and K. Schmuecker (eds) *Devolution in Practice 2010*. London: IPPR.

Daniel, B., Vincent, S. and Ogilvie-Whyte, S. (2007) *A Process Review of the Child Protection Reform Programme*. Edinburgh: Scottish Executive.

Daniel, B. and Wassell, S. (2002) *Assessing and Promoting Resilience in Vulnerable Children*. London: Jessica Kingsley Publishers.

Daniel, B., Wassell, S. and Gilligan, R. (1999) *Child Development for Child Care and Protection Workers*. London: Jessica Kingsley Publishers.

Department for Children, Schools and Families (2010) *Working Together to Safeguard Children: A Guide to Inter-Agency Working to Safeguard and Promote the Welfare of Children*. London: DCSF.

Department for Children, Schools and Families, Home Office and Department of Health (2007) *Safeguarding Vulnerable Groups Act 2006: ISA Scheme Consultation Document*. London: DCSF; Home Office; Department of Health.

Department for Education (2010a) *Preventable Child Deaths in England: Year Ending 31 March 2010*. London: Department for Education.

Department for Education (2010b) *Children in Need in England, Including their Characteristics and Further Information on Children who were the Subject of a Child Protection Plan (Children in Need Census – Final) Year Ending 31 March 2010*. London: Department for Education.

Department for Education, Department of Health and Home Office (2011) *Vetting and Barring Scheme Remodelling Review – Report and Recommendations*. London: Department for Education, Department of Health, Home Office.

Department for Education and Skills (2004) *Every Child Matters: Change for Children*. London: DfES.

Department of Health (1988) *Protecting Children: A Guide for Social Workers Undertaking a Comprehensive Assessment*. London: The Stationery Office.

Department of Health (1995) *Child Protection: Messages From Research*. London: HMSO.

Department of Health (1998) *Quality Protects: A Framework for Action*. London: The Stationery Office.

Department of Health (2000) *Assessing Children in Need and their Families: Practice Guidance*. London: The Stationery Office.

Department of Health (2002) *Safeguarding Children: A Joint Chief Inspectors' Report on Arrangements to Safeguard Children*. London: DoH.

Department of Health, Home Office, and Department of Education and Employment (1999) *Working Together to Safeguard Children: A Guide to Inter-Agency Working to Safeguard and Promote the Welfare of Children*. London: The Stationery Office.

Department of Health and Social Security (1974) *Non-Accidental Injury to Children*. Local Authority Social Services Letters (74) (13).

Department of Health, Social Services and Public Safety (2003) *Co-operating to Safeguard Children*. Belfast: DHSSPS.

Department of Health, Social Services and Public Safety (2006a) *Our Children and Young People – Our Shared Responsibility: Inspection of Child Protection Services in Northern Ireland*. Belfast: DHSSPS.

Department of Health, Social Services and Public Safety (2006b) *UNOCINI and the Comprehensive Assessment of Children in Need*. Belfast: DHSSPS.

Department of Health, Social Services and Public Safety (2006c) *Children and Young People – Our Pledge*. Belfast: DHSSPS.

Department of Health, Social Services and Public Safety (2008a) *Standards for Child Protection Services*. Belfast: DHSSPS.

Department of Health, Social Services and Public Safety (2008b) *Gateway Services – Processes*. Belfast: DHSSPS.

Department of Health, Social Services and Public Safety (2008c) *UNOCINI Guidance*. Belfast: DHSSPS.

Department of Health, Social Services and Public Safety (2008d) *UNOCINI Thresholds of Need Model*. Belfast: DHSSPS.

Department of Health, Social Services and Public Safety (2008e) *UNOCINI Family & Child Care Thresholds of Intervention*. Belfast: DHSSPS.

Department of Health, Social Services and Public Safety (2009) *Code of Practice on Protecting the Confidentiality of Service User Information*. Belfast: DHSSPS.

Department of Health, Social Services and Public Safety (2010a) *Children Order Child Protection and Referral Statistics for Quarter Ending 30 September 2010*. Belfast: DHSSPS.

Department of Health, Social Services and Public Safety (2010b) *Children Order Child Protection and Referral Statistics for Quarter Ending 31 March 2010*. Belfast: DHSSPS.

Department of Health, Social Services and Public Safety (2010c) *Children Order Statistical Tables for Northern Ireland 2008/09*. Belfast: DHSSPS.

Desapriya, E., Sones, M., Ramanzin, T., Weinstein, S., Scime, G. and Pike, I. (2011) 'Injury prevention in child death review: Child pedestrian fatalities.' *Injury Prevention* 17, 1, i4–i9.

Devaney, J., McAndrew, F. and Rodgers, T. (2010) 'Our Children and Young People – Our Shared Responsibility: The Reform Implementation Process in Child Protection Services in Northern Ireland.' In A. Stafford, S. Vincent and N. Parton (eds) *Child Protection Reform Across the UK*. Edinburgh: Dunedin University Press.

Dingwall, R. (1989) 'Some Problems About Predicting Child Abuse and Neglect.' In O. Stevenson (ed.) *Child Abuse: Public Policy and Professional Practice*. Hemel Hempstead: Harvester Wheatsheaf.

Dolowitz, D. and Marsh, D. (1996) 'Who learns what from whom? A review of the policy transfer literature.' *Political Studies 44*, 2, 343–57.

Donahue, J.D. (1997) *Disunited States*. New York: Harper Collins.

Durfee, M., Durfee, D.T. and West, M.P. (2002) 'Child fatality review: An international movement.' *Child Abuse and Neglect 26*, 6–7, 619–36.

Eley, G. and Suny, R. (eds) (1996) *Becoming National: A Reader*. Oxford: Oxford University Press.

Ermisch, J. and Francesconi, M. (1999) *Cohabitation in Great Britain: Not For Long But Here To Stay*. Colchester: Institute for Social and Economic Research.

Esping-Anderson, G. (1990) *The Three Worlds of Welfare Capitalism*. Princeton, NJ: Princeton University Press.

Esping-Anderson, G. (1999) *Social Foundations of Postindustrial Economies*. Oxford: Oxford University Press.

Evans, M. and Cerny, P. (2003) 'Globalization and Social Policy.' In N. Ellison and C. Pierson (eds) *Developments in British Social Policy*. Basingstoke: Palgrave.

Fairclough, N. (2000) *New Labour, New Language?* London: Routledge.

Falkov, A. (1996) *A Study of Working Together Part 8 Reports: Fatal Child Abuse and Parental Psychiatric Disorder*. London: Department of Health.

Ferri, G., Bynner, J. and Wadsworth, M. (eds) (2003) *Changing Britain, Changing Lives: Three Generations at the Turn of the Century*. London: Institute of Education, University of London.

Fish, S., Munro, E. and Bairstow, S. (2008) *Learning Together to Safeguard Children: Developing a Multi-Agency Approach for Case Reviews*. London: Social Care Institute for Excellence.

Flora, P. and Heidenheimer, A. (eds) (1981) *The Development of Western States in Europe and America*. New Brunswick, NJ: Transaction Books.

Franklin, B. (1989) 'Wimps and Bullies: Press Reporting of Child Abuse.' In P. Carter, T. Jeffs and M. Smith (eds) *Social Work and Social Welfare Yearbook One*. Buckingham: Open University Press.

Franklin, B. (1994) *Packaging Politics: Political Communication in Britain's Media Democracy*. London: Arnold.

Franklin, B. (1997) *Newzak and News Media*. London: Arnold.

Franklin, B. (2003) 'The Hand of History: New Labour, News Management and Governance.' In A. Chadwick and R. Heffernan (eds) *The New Labour Reader*. Cambridge: Polity Press.

Fraser, D. (1984) *The Evolution of the British Welfare State*. Second edition. Basingstoke: Macmillan.

Freeman, R. (2006) 'Learning in Public Policy.' In M. Moran, M. Rein and R.E. Gordin (eds) *The Oxford Handbook of Public Policy*. Oxford: Oxford University Press.

Freeman, R. (2007) 'Epistemological bricolage: How practitioners make sense of learning.' *Administration and Society 39*, 4, 476–496.

Freeman, R. (2008) 'A national health service: By comparison.' *Social History of Medicine 21*, 3, 503–520.

Freeman, R. (2009) 'Comparing Health Systems.' In R. Mullner (ed.) *Encyclopaedia of Health Services Research*. Thousand Oaks, CA: Sage.

Freymond, N. and Cameron, G. (eds) (2006) *Towards Positive Systems of Child and Family Welfare: International Comparisons of Child Protection, Family Service and Community Caring Systems*. Toronto: University of Toronto Press.

Frost, N. and Parton, N. (2009) *Understanding Children's Social Care: Politics, Policy and Practice*. London: Sage.

Gabel, S.G. and Kamerman, S.B. (2006, June) 'Investing in children: Public commitment in twenty-one industrialized countries.' *Social Services Review 80*, 2, 239–263.

Galilee, J. (2005) *Learning From Failure: A Review of Major Social Care/Health Inquiry Recommendations*. Edinburgh: Scottish Executive.

Garrett, P.M. (2003) 'Swimming with dolphins: The Assessment Framework, New Labour and new tools for social work with children and families.' *British Journal of Social Work 33*, 4, 441–463.

Gibbons, J., Conroy, S. and Bell, C. (1995) *Operating the Child Protection System*. London: HMSO.

Giddens, A. (1990) *The Consequences of Modernity*. Cambridge: Polity Press.

Giddens, A. (1991) *Modernity and Self-Identity: Self and Society in the Late Modern Age*. Cambridge: Polity Press.

Gilbert, N. (ed.) (1997) *Combating Child Abuse: International Perspectives and Trends*. New York: Oxford University Press.

Gilbert, N., Parton, N. and Skivenes, M. (eds) (2011a) *Child Protection Systems: International Trends and Orientations*. New York: Oxford University Press.

Gilbert, N., Parton, N. and Skivenes, M. (2011b) 'Changing Patterns of Response and Emerging Orientations.' In N. Gilbert, N. Parton and M. Skivenes (eds) *Child Protection Systems: International Trends and Orientations*. New York: Oxford University Press.

Gillie, C., Roll, J. and Baber, M. (1999) *Protection of Children Bill*. London: House of Commons Library.

Gilligan, P. and Manby, M. (2008) 'The Common Assessment Framework: Does the reality match the rhetoric?' *Child and Family Social Work 13*, 2, 177–187.

Greer, S. (2010) 'Devolution and Health: Structure, Process and Outcomes Since 1998.' In G. Lodge and K. Schmuecker (eds) *Devolution in Practice*. London: IPPR.

Greer, S.L. (ed.) (2009) *Devolution and Social Citizenship in the UK*. Bristol: Policy Press.

Hacking, I. (1988) 'The sociology of knowledge about child abuse.' *Nous 2*, 1, 53–63.

Hacking, I. (1991, Winter) 'The making and moulding of child abuse.' *Critical Inquiry 17*, 2, 253–88.

Hacking, I. (1992) 'World-Making by Kind-Making: Child Abuse for Example.' In M. Douglas and D. Hull (eds) *How Classification Works: Nelson Goldman Among the Social Sciences*. Edinburgh: Edinburgh University Press.

Hall, P. and Taylor, R. (1996) 'Political Science and the Three New Institutionalisms.' *Political Studies 44*, 5, 936–57.

Hallett, C. (1989) 'Child Abuse Inquiries and Public Policy.' In O. Stevenson (ed.) *Child Abuse: Professional Practice and Public Policy*. London: Harvester Wheatsheaf.

Hammond, H. (2001) *Child Protection Inquiry into the Circumstances Surrounding the Death of Kennedy McFarlane, D.O.B. 17 April 1997*. Dumfries: Dumfries and Galloway Child Protection Committee.

Harder, M. and Pringle, K. (eds) (1997) *Protecting Children in Europe: Towards a New Millennium*. Aalborg: Aalborg University Press.

Healthcare Inspectorate Wales (2009) *Safeguarding and Protecting Children in Wales: A Review of the Arrangements in Place Across the Welsh National Health Service*. Cardiff: HIW.

Held, D. and McGrew, A. (eds) (2000) *The Global Transformations Reader*. Cambridge: Polity Press.

Hellinckx, W., Colton, M. and Williams, M. (eds) (1997) *International Perspectives on Family Support*. Aldershot: Arena.

Hendrick, H. (2003) *Child Welfare: Historical Dimensions, Contemporary Debate*. Bristol: Policy Press.

Hetherington, R. (1996) 'The educational opportunities of cross-national comparison.' *Social Work in Europe 3*, 1, 26–30.

Hetherington, R. (2006) 'Learning From Difference: Comparing Child Welfare Systems.' In N. Freymond and G. Cameron (eds) *Towards Positive Systems of Child and Family Welfare: International Comparisons of Child Protection, Family Service and Community Caring Systems*. Toronto: University of Toronto Press.

Hetherington, R., Bairstow, K., Katz, I., Mesie, J. and Trowell, J. (2002) *The Welfare of Children with Mentally Ill Parents: Learning from Inter-Country Comparison.* Chichester: Wiley.

Hetherington, R., Cooper, A., Smith, P. and Wilford, G. (1997) *Protecting Children: Messages From Europe.* Lyme Regis: Russell House Publishing.

Hetherington, R. and Piquardt, R. (2001) 'Strategies for Survival: Users' Experience of Child Welfare in Three Welfare Regimes.' *Child and Family Social Work 6*, 3, 239–49.

Hill, M., Stafford, A. and Lister-Green, P. (2002) International Perspectives on Child Protection. Appendix B of the Scottish Executive *'It's Everyone's Job to Make Sure I'm Alright': Report of the Child Protection Audit and Review.* Edinburgh: Scottish Executive.

Hills, A. (1980) 'How the press sees you.' *Social Work Today 11*, 36, 19–20.

HM Government (1989) *Working Together Under the Children Act.* London: HMSO.

HM Government (2004) *Every Child Matters: Change for Children.* London: The Stationery Office.

HM Government (2006a) *Working Together to Safeguard Children: A Guide to Inter-Agency Working to Safeguard and Promote the Welfare of Children.* London: The Stationery Office.

HM Government (2006b) *The Common Assessment Framework for Children and Young People: Practitioners' Guide.* London: Department for Education and Skills.

HM Government (2009a) *Information Sharing: Guidance for Practitioners and Managers.* Nottingham: Department for Children, Schools, Families, Communities and Local Government.

HM Government (2009b) *Information Sharing: Further Guidance on Legal Issues.* London: Department for Children, Schools and Families, Communities and Local Government.

HM Government (2010) *The Vetting and Barring Scheme Guidance.* London: HM Government.

HM Inspectorate of Education (2009a) *How Well Do We Protect Scotland's Children? A Report on the Findings of the Joint Inspections of Services to Protect Children 2005–2009.* Edinburgh: HMIE.

HM Inspectorate of Education (2009b) *How Well Do We Protect Children and Meet Their Needs?* Edinburgh: HMIE.

HM Inspectorate of Education (2009c) *A Common Approach to Inspecting Services for Children and Young People: Consultation Report.* Edinburgh: HMIE.

Hobsbawm, E. (1994) *The Age of Extremes: The Short Twentieth Century, 1914–1991.* London: Michael Joseph.

Horwath, J. (2002) 'Maintaining a focus on the child?' *Child Abuse Review 11*, 4, 195–213.

Horwath, J. (2007) 'The missing assessment domain: Personal, professional and organisational factors influencing professional judgements when identifying and referring child neglect.' *British Journal of Social Work 37*, 8, 1285–1303.

Hudson, J. and Lowe, S. (2009) *Understanding the Policy Process: Analysing Welfare Policy and Practice.* Second edition. Bristol: Policy Press.

Hutchison, E. (1993) 'Mandatory reporting laws: Child protection case findings gone awry.' *Social Work 38*, 1, 56–62.

Hutton, W.E. and Giddens, A. (2001) *On the Edge: Living with Global Capitalism.* London: Vintage.

Independent Safeguarding Authority (2009) *Guidance Notes for the Barring Decision Making Process.* Darlington: ISA.

Independent Safeguarding Authority (undated) *ISA Decision-Making Process.* Darlington: ISA.

Jeffrey, C. (2006) *ESRC Devolution and Constitutional Change Programme Final Report: Devolution and Public Policy.* Edinburgh: ESRC Devolution Programme.

Jeffrey, C., Lodge, G. and Schmuecker, K. (2010) 'The Devolution Paradox.' In G. Lodge and K. Schmuecker (eds) *Devolution in Practice 2010.* London: IPPR.

Johnston, B.D. and Covington, T.M. (2011) 'Injury prevention in child death review.' *Injury Prevention 17*, 1, i1–i3.

Jordan, B. (2006) *Social Policy for the Twenty-First Century: New Perspectives, Big Issues.* Cambridge: Polity.

Katz, I. (1997) *Current Issues in Comprehensive Assessment.* London: NSPCC.

Katz, I. and Hetherington, R. (2006) 'Co-operating and communicating: A European perspective on integrating services for children.' *Child Abuse Review 15*, 4, 429–439.

Katz, I. and Pinkerton, J. (eds) (2003) *Evaluating Family Support: Thinking Internationally, Thinking Critically.* Chichester: John Wiley.

Keating, M. (2005) 'Policy convergence and divergences in Scotland under devolution.' *Regional Studies 39*, 4, 453–463.

Keating, M. (2009) 'Social Citizenship, Devolution and Policy Divergence.' In S. Greer (ed.) *Devolution and Social Citizenship in the UK.* Bristol: Polity Press.

Keating, M. (2010) *The Government of Scotland.* Edinburgh: Edinburgh University Press.

Keating, M., Cairney, P. and Hepburn, E. (forthcoming) 'Policy convergence, transfer and learning in the UK under devolution.' *Regional and Federal Studies.*

Keating, M., Stevenson, L., Cairney, P. and Taylor, K. (2003) 'Does devolution make a difference? Legislative output and policy divergence in Scotland.' *Journal of Legislative Studies 9*, 3, 110–139.

Kelly, G. (2007) 'Competence in Risk Analysis.' In K. O'Hagen (ed.) *Competence in Social Work Practice.* London: Jessica Kingsley Publishers.

Kempe, H., Silverman, F., Steele, B., Droegemueller, W. and Wilver, H. (1962) 'The battered child syndrome.' *Journal of the American Medical Association 181*, 1, 17–24.

Kemshall, H. (2003, March) 'The community management of high-risk offenders.' *Prison Service Journal.*

Kemshall, H., Mackenzie, G., Wood, J., Bailey, R. and Yates, J. (2005) *Strengthening Multi-Agency Public Protection Panels (MAPPAs).* London: Home Office.

Kennett, P. (2001) *Comparative Social Policy: Theory and Research.* Buckingham: Open University Press.

Khoo, E.G., Hyvönen, U. and Nygren, L. (2002) 'Child welfare protection: Uncovering Swedish and Canadian orientations to social intervention in child maltreatment.' *Qualitative Social Work 1*, 4, 451–71.

Kiernan, K. and Estaugh, V. (1993) *Cohabitation, Extra-Marital Childbearing and Social Policy.* London: Family Policy Studies Centre.

Klein, R. and Marmor, T.R. (2007) 'Reflections on Policy Analysis: Putting It Together Again.' In M. Moran, M. Rein and R.E. Goodin (eds) *The Oxford Handbook of Public Policy.* Oxford: Oxford University Press.

Laming, Lord (2003) *The Victoria Climbié Inquiry: Report of an Inquiry by Lord Laming, Cm 5730.* London: The Stationery Office.

Laming, Lord (2009) *The Protection of Children in England: A Progress Report.* London: The Stationery Office.

Leeke, M., Sear, C. and Gay, O. (2003) *An Introduction to Devolution in the UK.* London: House of Commons Library.

Lewis, G. (ed.) (1998) *Forming Nation, Framing Welfare.* London: Routledge.

Lindblom, C.E. (1959) 'The science of 'muddling through'.' *Public Administration Review 19*, 2, 79–88.

Lindblom, C.E. (1979) 'Still muddling through.' *Public Administration Review 39*, 6, 517–25.

Lindon, J. (2008) *Safeguarding Children and Young People: Child Protection 0–18 Years.* London: Hodder Education.

London Borough of Brent (1985) *A Child in Trust: Report of the Panel of Inquiry Investigating the Circumstances Surrounding the Death of Jasmine Beckford.* London: London Borough of Brent.

London Borough of Greenwich (1987) *A Child in Mind: Protection in a Responsible Society. Report of the Commission of Inquiry into the Circumstances Surrounding the Death of Kimberley Carlile.* London: London Borough of Greenwich.

London Borough of Lambeth (1987) *Whose Child? The Report of the Panel Appointed to Inquire into the Death of Tyra Henry.* London: London Borough of Lambeth.

Lonne, B., Parton, N., Thomson, J. and Harries, M. (2009) *Reforming Child Protection.* London: Routledge.

Loughlin, J. (2004) 'The 'transformation' of governance: New directions in policy and politics.' *Australian Journal of Politics and History 50*, 1, 8–22.

Loughlin, J. (2007) 'Reconfiguring the state: Trends in territorial governance in European states.' *Regional and Federal Studies 17*, 4, 385–403.

Loughton, T. (2010) Private communication to LSCB chairs and Directors of Children's Services.

Luckock, B. (2007) 'Safeguarding Children and Integrated Children's Services.' In K. Wilson and A. James (eds) *The Child Protection Handbook.* 3rd edition. London: Baillière Tindall.

Mabbett, D. and Bolderson, H. (1999) 'Theories and Methods in Comparative Social Policy.' In J. Clasen (ed.) *Comparative Social Policy: Concepts, Theories and Methods.* Oxford; Blackwell.

MacDonald, G. (2001) *Effective Interventions for Child Abuse and Neglect.* Chichester: Wiley.

Marshall, K., Jamieson, C. and Finlayson, A.F. (1999) *Edinburgh's Children: The Report of the Edinburgh Inquiry into Abuse and Protection of Children in Care*. Edinburgh: Edinburgh Inquiry.

Mathiesen, T. (1997) 'The viewer society: Michel Foucault's 'Panopticon'.' *Theoretical Criminology* 1, 2, 215–234.

Matravers, A. (ed.) (2003) *Sex Offenders in the Community: Managing and Reducing the Risks*. Cambridge: Willan Publishing.

May-Chahal, C. and Herczog, M. (eds) (2003) *Child Sexual Abuse in Europe*. Strasbourg: Council of Europe Publishing.

McAlinden, A.-M. (2007) *The Shaming of Sexual Offenders: Risk, Retribution and Reintegration*. Oxford: Hart.

McAlinden, A.-M. (2010) 'Vetting sexual offenders: State over-extension, the punishment deficit and the failure to manage risk.' *Social and Legal Studies 19*, 1, 25–48.

McCrone, D. (2002) 'Who do you say you are? Making sense of national identities in modern Britain.' *Ethnicities 2*, 3, 301–320.

McEwen, N. (2001) 'The Nation-Building Role of State Welfare in the United Kingdom and Canada.' In M. Keating and T. Salmon (eds) *The Dynamics of Decentralization: Canadian Federalism and British Devolution*. Montreal and Kingston: McGill-Queens University.

McEwen, N. and Moreno, L. (eds) (2005) *The Territorial Politics of Welfare*. London: Routledge.

McEwen, N. and Parry, R. (2005) 'Devolution and the Preservation of the United Kingdom Welfare State.' In N. McEwen and L. Moreno (eds) *The Territorial Politics of Welfare*. London: Routledge.

McGarvey, N. and Cairney, P. (2008) *Scottish Politics: An Introduction*. Basingstoke: Palgrave.

McGhee, J. and Francis, J. (2003) 'Protecting children in Scotland: Examining the impact of the Children (Scotland) Act 1995.' *Child and Family Social Work 8*, 2, 132–4.

Melton, G. (2005) 'Mandated reporting: A policy without reason.' *Child Abuse and Neglect 25*, 1, 9–18.

Miller, J. and Warman, A. (1996) *Family Obligations in Europe*. London: Family Policy Studies Centre.

Milner, J. and O'Byrne, P. (2002) *Assessment in Social Work*. Second edition. Basingstoke: Palgrave.

Mooney, G., Scott, G. and Williams, C. (2006) 'Introduction: Rethinking social policy through devolution.' *Critical Social Policy 26*, 3, 483–497.

Mooney, G. and Williams, C. (2006) 'Forging new 'ways of life'? Social policy and nation building in devolved Scotland and Wales.' *Critical Social Policy 26*, 3, 608–629.

Mooney, G. and Wright, S. (2009) 'Introduction: Social policy in the devolved Scotland: Towards a Scottish welfare state?' *Social Policy and Society 8*, 3, 361–365.

Morris, L., Williams, L. and Beak, K. (2007) *A Study of Case Reviews Submitted to the Welsh Assembly Government Under Chapter 8 of 'Working Together to Safeguard Children: A Guide to Inter-Agency Working to Safeguard and Promote the Welfare of Children'*. Cardiff: University of Wales, Newport/ National Assembly for Wales.

Munro, E. (2011) *The Munro Review of Child Protection, Interim Report: The Child's Journey*. London: Department for Education.

Murray, K. and Hill, M. (1991) 'The recent history of Scottish child welfare.' *Children and Society 15*, 3, 2666–81.

National Assembly for Wales (2006) *Keeping Us Safe: Report of the Safeguarding Vulnerable Children Review*. Cardiff: National Assembly for Wales.

National Assembly for Wales (2007) *A Guide to the Legislative Process in the National Assembly for Wales*. Cardiff: National Assembly for Wales.

National Assembly for Wales Members' Research Service (2011) *Legislative Powers of the National Assembly for Wales*. Cardiff: National Assembly for Wales Members' Research Service.

National MAPPA Team (2009) *MAPPA Guidance 2009*. London: National Offender Management Service Public Protection Unit.

Nelson, B. (1984) *Making an Issue of Child Abuse and Neglect: Political Agenda Setting for Social Problems*. Chicago: University of Chicago Press.

Newman, J. (2001) *Modernising Governance: New Labour, Policy and Society*. London: Sage.

Northern Ireland Office (undated) *Guidance to Agencies: Public Protection Arrangements*. Belfast: Northern Ireland Office.

Office of the First Minister and Deputy First Minister (2006) *Our Children – Our Pledge: A Ten Year Strategy for Children and Young People in Northern Ireland 2006–2016.* Belfast: OFMDFM.

Office of National Statistics (ONS) (1998) *Living in Britain: Results from the 1996 General Household Survey.* London: The Stationery Office.

Office for Standards in Education, Children's Services and Skills (Ofsted) (2008a) *Safeguarding Children: The Third Joint Chief Inspectors' Report on Arrangements to Safeguard Children.* London: Ofsted.

Office for Standards in Education, Children's Services and Skills (Ofsted) (2008b) *Learning Lessons, Taking Action: Ofsted's Evaluation of Serious Case Reviews 1 April 2007 to 31 March 2008.* London: Ofsted.

Office for Standards in Education, Children's Services and Skills (Ofsted) (2009a) *Inspections of Safeguarding and Looked After Children Services.* London: Ofsted.

Office for Standards in Education, Children's Services and Skills (Ofsted) (2009b) *Comprehensive Area Assessment: Annual Rating of Council Children's Services for 2009.* London: Ofsted.

Office for Standards in Education, Children's Services and Skills (Ofsted) (2010) *Framework for Unannounced Inspections of CRA from 1 Sep 2010.* London: Ofsted.

Onwuachi-Saunders, C., Forjuoh, S.N., West, P. and Brooks, C. (1999) 'Child death reviews: A gold mine for injury prevention and control.' *Injury Prevention 5,* 5, 278.

Owen, H. (2009a) 'Doing Serious Case Reviews Well: Politics, Academia, Risk Management and Staff Care.' In L. Hughes and H. Owen (eds) *Good Practice in Safeguarding Children.* London: Jessica Kingsley Publishers.

Owen, H. (2009b) 'From Protection to Safeguarding: Bringing You Up to Date on Statutory Responsibilities.' In L. Hughes and H. Owen (eds) *Good Practice in Safeguarding Children.* London: Jessica Kingsley Publishers.

Owers, M., Brandon, M. and Black, J. (1999) *Learning How to Make Children Safer: An Analysis of Serious Child Abuse Cases in Wales.* Norwich: University of East Anglia/Welsh Office.

Parry-Jones, B. and Soulsby, J. (2001) 'Needs-led assessment: The challenges and the reality.' *Health and Social Care in the Community 9,* 6, 414–428.

Parton, N. (1985) *The Politics of Child Abuse.* Basingstoke: Macmillan.

Parton, N. (1991) *Governing the Family: Child Care, Child Protection and the State.* Basingstoke: Macmillan.

Parton, N. (ed.) (1997) *Child Protection and Family Support: Tensions, Contradictions and Possibilities.* London: Routledge.

Parton, N. (2006) *Safeguarding Childhood: Early Intervention and Surveillance in a Late Modern Society.* Basingstoke: Palgrave Macmillan.

Parton, N. (2011) *The Increasing Length and Complexity of Central Government Guidance About Child Abuse in England: 1974–2010.* Unpublished discussion paper, Huddersfield: University of Huddersfield.

Parton, N., Noyes, P. and Rose, W. (2010) '*Every Child Matters: Change for Children* programme in England.' In A. Stafford, S. Vincent and N. Parton (eds) *Child Protection Reform across the UK.* Edinburgh: Dunedin.

Parton, N., Thorpe, D. and Wattam, C. (1997) *Child Protection: Risk and the Moral Order.* Basingstoke: Palgrave/Macmillan.

Pearson, G.A. (ed.) (2008) *Why Children Die: A Pilot Study 2006, England (South West, North East and West Midlands), Wales and Northern Ireland.* London: CEMACH.

Peckover, S., White, S. and Hall, C. (2009) 'From policy to practice: The implementation and negotiation of technologies in everyday child welfare.' *Children and Society 11,* 3, 357–394.

Pierson, P. (1994) *Dismantling the Welfare State? Reagan, Thatcher and the Politics of Retrenchment.* Cambridge: Cambridge University Press.

Pithouse, A. (2006) 'A Common Assessment for Children in Need? Mixed Messages from a Pilot Study in Wales.' *Child Care in Practice 12,* 3, 199–217.

Pithouse, A. (forthcoming) 'Devolution and change since the Children Act 1989: New directions in Wales.' *Journal of Children's Services.*

Pithouse, A., Hall, C., Peckover, S. and White S. (2009) 'A tale of two CAFs: The impact of the electronic Common Assessment Framework.' *British Journal of Social Work 39,* 4, 599–612.

Power, M. (1997) *The Audit of Society: Rituals of Verification.* Oxford: Oxford University Press.

Pringle, K. (1998) *Children and Social Welfare in Europe.* Buckingham: Open University Press.

Pringle, K. (2005) 'Neglected Issues in Swedish Child Protection Policy and Practice: Age, Ethnicity and Gender.' In M. Eriksson, M. Hester, S. Keskinen and K. Pringle (eds) *Tackling Men's Violence in Families: Nordic Issues and Dilemmas*. Bristol: Policy Press.

Pringle, K. (2010) 'Epilogue: On Developing Empowering Child Welfare Systems and the Welfare Research Needed to Create Them.' In H. Forsberg and T. Kröger (eds) *Social Work and Child Welfare Politics: Through Nordic Lenses*. Bristol: Policy Press.

Pringle, K. and Harder, M. (1999) *Through Two Pairs of Eyes: A Comparative Study of Danish Social Policy and Child Welfare Practice*. Aalborg: Aalborg University Press.

Prud'homme, R. (1995) 'On the dangers of decentralization.' *World Bank Research Observer 10*, 2, 201–220.

Quan, L., Pilkey, D., Gomez, A. and Bennett, E. (2011) *Analysis of Paediatric Drowning Deaths in Washington State Using the Child Death Review (CDR) for Surveillance: What CDR Does and Does Not Tell Us About Lethal Drowning Injury*. Seattle: University of Washington School of Medicine.

Raffe, D. and Byrne, D. (2005): 'Policy learning from 'home international' comparisons.' *Centre for Educational Sociology Briefing 34*.

Reder, P. and Duncan, S. (1999) *Lost Innocents: A Follow-Up Study of Fatal Child Abuse*. London: Routledge.

Reder, P. and Duncan, S. (2004) 'From Colwell to Climbié: Inquiring Into Fatal Child Abuse.' In Stanley, N. and Manthorpe, J. (eds) *The Age of the Inquiry: Learning and Blaming in Health and Social Care*. London: Routledge.

Reder, P., Duncan, S. and Gray, M. (1993) *Child Abuse Tragedies Revisited*. Hove: Brunner-Routledge.

Rhodes, R.A.W. (1988) *Beyond Westminster and Whitehall: The Sub-Central Governments of Britain*. London: Unwin Hyman.

Rhodes, R.A.W. (1990) 'Policy networks: A British perspective.' *Journal of Theoretical Politics 2*, 3, 296–316.

Rhodes, R.A.W. (1996) 'The new governance: Governing without government.' *Political Studies 44*, 4, 652–67.

Rhodes, R.A.W. (1997) *Understanding Governance: Policy Networks, Governance, Reflexivity and Accountability*. Buckingham: Open University Press.

Rimsza, M.E., Schackner, R.A., Bowen, K.A. and Marshall, W. (2002) 'Can child deaths be prevented? The Arizona Child Fatality Review Program experience.' *Pediatrics 110*, e11.

Risk Management Authority (2007) *Review of Current Arrangements for Risk Assessment and Management of Restricted Patients*. Paisley: RMA.

Rodriguez-Pose, A. and Gill, N. (2003) 'The global trend towards devolution and its implications.' *Environment and Planning: Government and Policy 21*, 333–351.

Rose, W. (2009) 'The Assessment Framework.' In J. Horwath (ed.) *The Child's World*. Second edition. London: Jessica Kingsley Publishers.

Rose, W. (2010) *Improving Practice to Protect Children in Wales: Developing a New National Framework for Learning and Reviewing – Next Steps. A Progress Report*. Cardiff: Welsh Assembly Government.

Rose, W. and Barnes, J. (2008) *Improving Safeguarding Practice: Study of Serious Case Reviews 2001–2003*. London: Department for Children, Schools and Families.

Royal College of Pathologists and Royal College of Paediatrics and Child Health (2004) *Sudden Unexpected Death in Infancy: A Multi-Agency Protocol for Care and Investigation*. London: Royal College of Pathologists/Royal College of Paediatrics and Child Health.

Schofield, G. (1998) 'Inner and outer worlds: A psychological framework for child and family social work.' *Child and Family Social Work 3*, 1, 57–63.

Scott, D. and Swain, S. (2002) *Confronting Cruelty: Historical Perspectives on Child Protection in Australia*. Melbourne: Melbourne University Press.

Scottish Executive (2002) *'It's Everyone's Job to Make Sure I'm Alright': Report of the Child Protection Audit and Review*. Edinburgh: Scottish Executive.

Scottish Executive (2005) *Protecting Children and Young People: Child Protection Committees*. Edinburgh: Scottish Executive.

Scottish Executive (2007a) *Protecting Children and Young People: Interim Guidance for Child Protection Committees for Conducting a Significant Case Review*. Edinburgh: Scottish Executive.

Scottish Executive (2007b) *Sharing Information When a Child is in Need of Protection: A Draft Code of Practice*. Edinburgh: Scottish Executive.

Scottish Government (2007c) *The Protection of Vulnerable Groups (Scotland) Bill: Scottish Vetting and Barring Scheme: Consultation on Policy Proposals for Secondary Legislation.* Edinburgh: Scottish Government.

Scottish Government (2008a) *A Guide to Getting it Right for Every Child.* Edinburgh: Scottish Government.

Scottish Government (2008b) *Getting it Right for Children and Young People who Present a Risk of Serious Harm: Meeting Need, Managing Risk and Achieving Outcomes.* Edinburgh: Scottish Government.

Scottish Government (2008c) *MAPPA Guidance.* Edinburgh: Scottish Government.

Scottish Government (2010a) *National Guidance for Child Protection in Scotland.* Edinburgh: Scottish Government.

Scottish Government (2010b) *Children's Social Work Statistics 2009/10.* Edinburgh: Scottish Government.

Scottish Government (2010c) *Protecting Vulnerable Groups Scheme: Guidance for Individuals, Organisations and Personal Employers.* Edinburgh: Scottish Government.

Scottish Government (2010d) *FAQ – Regulated Work.* Edinburgh: Scottish Government. Available at www.scotland.gov.uk/Topics/People/Young-People/children-families/pvglegislation/FAQs/RegulatedWork, accessed on 10 November 2010.

Scottish Government (2010e) *Draft National Guidance for Child Protection in Scotland.* Edinburgh: Scottish Government.

Scottish Office (1998) *Protecting Children – A Shared Responsibility: Guidance on Inter-Agency Co-operation.* Edinburgh: The Stationery Office.

Secretary of State for Social Services (1974) *Report of the Inquiry into the Care and Supervision Provided in Relation to Maria Colwell.* London: HMSO.

Secretary of State for Social Services (1988) *Report of the Inquiry into Child Abuse in Cleveland (Cm412).* London: HMSO.

Seden, J. (2007) 'Assessing the needs of children and their families.' *Research and Practice Briefing: Children and Families 15.* London: Department for Education and Skills, Research in Practice, Making Research Count.

Sidebotham, P., Brandon, M., Powell, C. *et al.* (2010) *Learning from Serious Case Reviews: Report of a Research Study on the Methods of Learning Lessons Nationally from Serious Case Reviews.* London: Department for Education.

Sidebotham, P., Fox, J., Horwath, J., Powell, C. and Perwez, S. (2008) *Preventing Childhood Deaths: An Observational Study of Child Death Overview Panels in England.* London: Department for Children, Schools and Families.

Sinclair, R. and Bullock, R. (2002) *Learning from Past Experience: A Review of Serious Case Reviews.* London: Department of Health.

Smith, A. (1995) *Nations and Nationalism in a Global Era.* Cambridge: Polity Press.

Smith, C. (2009) *Working with Children: Vetting and Barring – Legislation and Policy in Scotland.* Edinburgh: University of Edinburgh/NSPCC Centre for Learning in Child Protection.

Smith, C. (2010) *Vetting and Barring: Policy and Legislation in England and Wales.* Edinburgh: University of Edinburgh/NSPCC Centre for Learning in Child Protection.

Stafford, A. and Vincent, S. (2008) *Safeguarding and Protecting Children and Young People.* Edinburgh: Dunedin Academic Press.

Stafford, A., Vincent, S. and Parton, N. (eds) (2010) *Child Protection Reform Across the UK.* Edinburgh: Dunedin Academic Press.

Stanley, N. and Manthorpe, J. (eds) (2004) *The Age of the Inquiry: Learning and Blaming in Health and Social Care.* London: Routledge.

Stone, D. (1999) 'Learning lessons and transferring policy across time, space and disciplines.' *Politics 19*, 1, 51–9.

Stradling, B., MacNeil, M. and Berry, H. (2009) *Changing Professional Practice and Culture to Get it Right for Every Child. An Evaluation of the Early Development Phases of Getting it Right for Every Child in Highland: 2006–2009.* Edinburgh: Scottish Government.

Strong, P. (2001) *The Ceremonial Order of the Clinic: Parents, Doctors and Medical Bureaucracies.* London: Routledge and Kegan Paul.

Sully, D. (1885) 'Comparison.' *Mind 10*, 40, 489–511.

Swift, K.J. (1997) 'Canada: Trends and Issues in Child Welfare.' In N. Gilbert (ed.) *Combating Child Abuse: International Perspectives and Trends.* Oxford: Oxford University Press.

Thelan, K. and Steinmo, S. (1992) 'Historical Institutionalism in Comparative Politics.' In S. Steinmo, K. Thelan and F. Longstreth (eds) *Structuring Politics: Historical Institutionalism in Comparative Perspective.* Cambridge: Cambridge University Press.

Thoburn, J. (2007) 'Globalisation and child welfare: Some lessons from a cross-national study of children in out-of-home care.' *Social Work Monographs,* 70. Norwich: University of East Anglia.

Thompson, J.B. (1990) *Ideology and Modern Culture.* Cambridge: Polity Press.

Thompson, J.B. (1996) *The Media and Modernity: A Social Theory of the Media.* Cambridge: Polity Press.

Thorpe, D. (1994) *Evaluating Child Protection.* Buckingham: Open University Press.

Tierney, M., Knight, C. and Stafford, S. (2010) 'Getting it Right for Every Child in Scotland.' In A. Stafford, S. Vincent and N. Parton (eds) *Child Protection Reform Across the UK.* Edinburgh: Dunedin University Press.

Tilbury, C. (2004) 'The influence of performance management on child welfare.' *British Journal of Social Work 34,* 2, 225–241.

Trench, A. (2007) 'The Framework of Devolution: The Formal Structure of Devolved Power.' In A. Trench (ed.) *Devolution and Power in the United Kingdom.* Manchester: Manchester University Press.

Trocme, N., Tam, K.K. and McPhee, D. (1995) 'Correlates of Substantiation of Maltreatment in Child Welfare Investigations.' In J. Hudson and B. Galaway (eds) *Child Welfare in Canada: Research and Policy Implications.* Toronto: Thomson Educational Publishing.

UNICEF (2003) *A League Table of Child Maltreatment Deaths in Rich Countries. Report Card 5.* Florence: UNICEF Innocenti Research Centre.

UNICEF (2007) *Child Poverty in Perspective: An Overview of Child Well-Being in Rich Countries – A Comprehensive Assessment of the Lives and Well-Being of Children and Adolescents in the Economically Advanced Nations. Report Card 7.* Florence: UNICEF Innocenti Research Centre.

US Advisory Board on Child Abuse and Neglect (1990) *Child Abuse and Neglect: Critical First Steps in Response to a National Emergency.* Washington, DC: US Government Printing Office.

US Advisory Board on Child Abuse and Neglect (1993) *Neighbors Helping Neighbors: A New National Strategy for the Protection of Children.* Washington, DC: US Government Printing Office.

Utting, S.W., Baines, C., Stuart, M., Rowlands, J. and Vialva, R. (1997) *People Like Us: The Report of the Review of the Safeguards for Children Living Away from Home.* London: Department of Health, Welsh Office.

Vincent, S. (2008a) *Mechanisms for the Strategic Implementation, Development and Monitoring of Inter-Agency Child Protection Policy and Practice in the UK: The Role of Local Safeguarding Children Boards (LSCBs) and (Area) Child Protection Committees ((A)CPCs), Briefing No. 4, November 2008.* Edinburgh: University of Edinburgh/NSPCC Centre for UK-wide Learning in Child Protection (CLiCP).

Vincent, S. (2008b) *Inter-Agency Guidance in Relation to Child Protection: A UK Comparison, Briefing No. 2, June 2008.* Edinburgh: The University of Edinburgh/NSPCC Centre for UK-wide Learning in Child Protection (CLiCP).

Vincent, S. (2008c) *Child Protection Statistics: A UK Comparison, Briefing No. 3, June 2008.* Edinburgh: University of Edinburgh/NSPCC Centre for UK-wide Learning in Child Protection (CLiCP).

Vincent, S. (2010a) *Learning from Child Deaths and Serious Abuse.* Edinburgh: Dunedin University Press.

Vincent, S. (2010b) 'An Overview of Safeguarding and Protecting Children Across the UK.' In A. Stafford, S. Vincent, and N. Parton (eds) *Child Protection Reform Across the UK.* Edinburgh: Dunedin University Press.

Vincent, S. and Daniel, B. (2010) 'Where now for child protection in Scotland?' *Child Abuse Review 19,* 6, 438–456.

Waldfogel, J. (1998) *The Future of Child Protection: How to Break the Cycle of Abuse and Neglect.* Cambridge, MA: Harvard University Press.

Waldfogel, J. (2008) 'The Future of Child Protection Revisited.' In D. Lindsey and A. Schlonsky (eds) *Child Welfare Research.* New York: Oxford University Press.

Ward Platt, M.P. (2007, Summer) 'Child death reviews: Progress in the North of England.' *Exchange 4.*

Wardle, C. (2006) 'It could happen to you.' The move towards 'personal' and 'societal' narratives in newspaper coverage of child murder, 1930–2000.' *Journalism Studies 7,* 4, 515–33.

Warner, N. (1992) *Choosing with Care.* London: HMSO.

Waterhouse, R. (2000) *Lost in Care: Report of the Tribunal of Inquiry into the Abuse of Children in Care in the Former County Council Areas of Gwynedd and Clwyd Since 1974.* London: The Stationery Office.

Weaver, B. (2009) *Sex Offender Community Notification in Scotland.* Edinburgh: Scottish Centre for Crime and Justice Research.

Weaver, B. (2010) 'Multi-Agency Public Protection Arrangements (MAPPA) in Scotland: What do the numbers tell us?' *The Scottish Centre for Crime & Justice Research Briefing 01/2010.* Glasgow: Strathclyde University.

Webster, R., Schnitzer, P., Jenny, C., Ewigman, B. and Alario, A. (2003) 'Child death review: The state of the nation.' *American Journal of Preventative Medicine 25,* 1, 58–64.

Welsh Assembly Government (2004) *Children and Young People: Rights to Action.* Cardiff: Welsh Assembly Government.

Welsh Assembly Government (2006) *Safeguarding Children: Working Together Under the Children Act 2004.* Cardiff: Welsh Assembly Government.

Welsh Assembly Government (2007a) *Safeguarding Children: Working Together Under the Children Act 2004: Children and Young People: Rights to Action.* Cardiff: Welsh Assembly Government.

Welsh Assembly Government (2007b) *Fulfilled Lives, Supportive Communities.* Cardiff: Welsh Assembly Government.

Welsh Assembly Government (2009) *Statutory Guidance on the Role and Accountabilities of the Director of Social Services.* Cardiff: Welsh Assembly Government.

Welsh Assembly Government (2010a) *Local Authority Child Protection Registers, 2010.* Cardiff: Welsh Assembly Government.

Welsh Assembly Government (2010b) *Referrals, Assessments and Social Services for Children, 2009–10.* Cardiff: Welsh Assembly Government.

White, S., Hall, C. and Peckover, S. (2009) 'The descriptive tyranny of the Common Assessment Framework: Technologies of categorization and professional practice in child welfare.' *British Journal of Social Work 39,* 7, 1197–1217.

Williams, C. and Mooney, G. (2008) 'Decentring Social Policy? Devolution and the discipline of Social Policy: A commentary.' *Journal of Social Policy 37,* 3, 489–507.

Williams, F. (1989) *Social Policy: A Critical Introduction.* Cambridge: Polity Press.

Wirtz, S.J., Foster, V. and Lenart, G.A. (2011) 'Assessing and improving child death review team recommendations.' *Injury Supplement 17,* 1, 1.

Wolman, H. and Page, E. (2002) 'Policy transfer among local governments: An information approach.' *Governance 15,* 4, 477–502.

Yeates, N. (2008) *Understanding Global Social Policy.* Bristol: Policy Press.

Subject Index

Author Index